Forgotten Aviator

The Adventures of Royal Leonard

Mail Pilot, Racer, China Aviator

by

Barry S. Martin

Permissions

Permission to use unpublished documents granted by Airline Pilots Association, China National Aviation Corporation Association, Delta Air Lines, Gerrie Dubé, Frank Evans, Harvard University Archives, Hoover Institution Archives, John Korompilas, Elizabeth Leonard, Royal S. Leonard, Pan Am Historical Foundation, Princeton University Library, and University of Miami Libraries.

Copyright permissions granted by Langhorne Bond, Anna C. Chennault, China National Aviation Corporation Association, Gerrie Dubé, Col. John Doolittle, Ret., Frank Evans, Elizabeth Leonard, Royal S. Leonard, Lydia Rossi, Elizabeth Young Roulee, Stanford University, and Whiting Willauer, Jr.

Interview quote permissions granted by Moon Chin, Rudy Eskra, Peter Goutiere, Angela Shrawder, Felix Smith, and Louis Stannard.

Website use permissions granted by Tom Moore (cnac.org) and Samuel Williamson (measuringworth.com).

Photograph credits: John Amendola, Gerrie Dubé, Frank Evans, John Korompilas, Elizabeth Leonard, Royal S. Leonard, and Museum of Flight, Seattle, WA.

First published by Dog Ear Publishing
4010 W. 86th Street, Ste H
Indianapolis, IN 46268
www.dogearpublishing.net

ISBN: 978-160844-929-3

This book is printed on acid-free paper.

Printed in the United States of America

Dedication

For my wife, Carolyn

To Art and Jane Crognale
from Geraldine (Gessie) Leonard
Dubé
Nov. 2011

TABLE OF CONTENTS

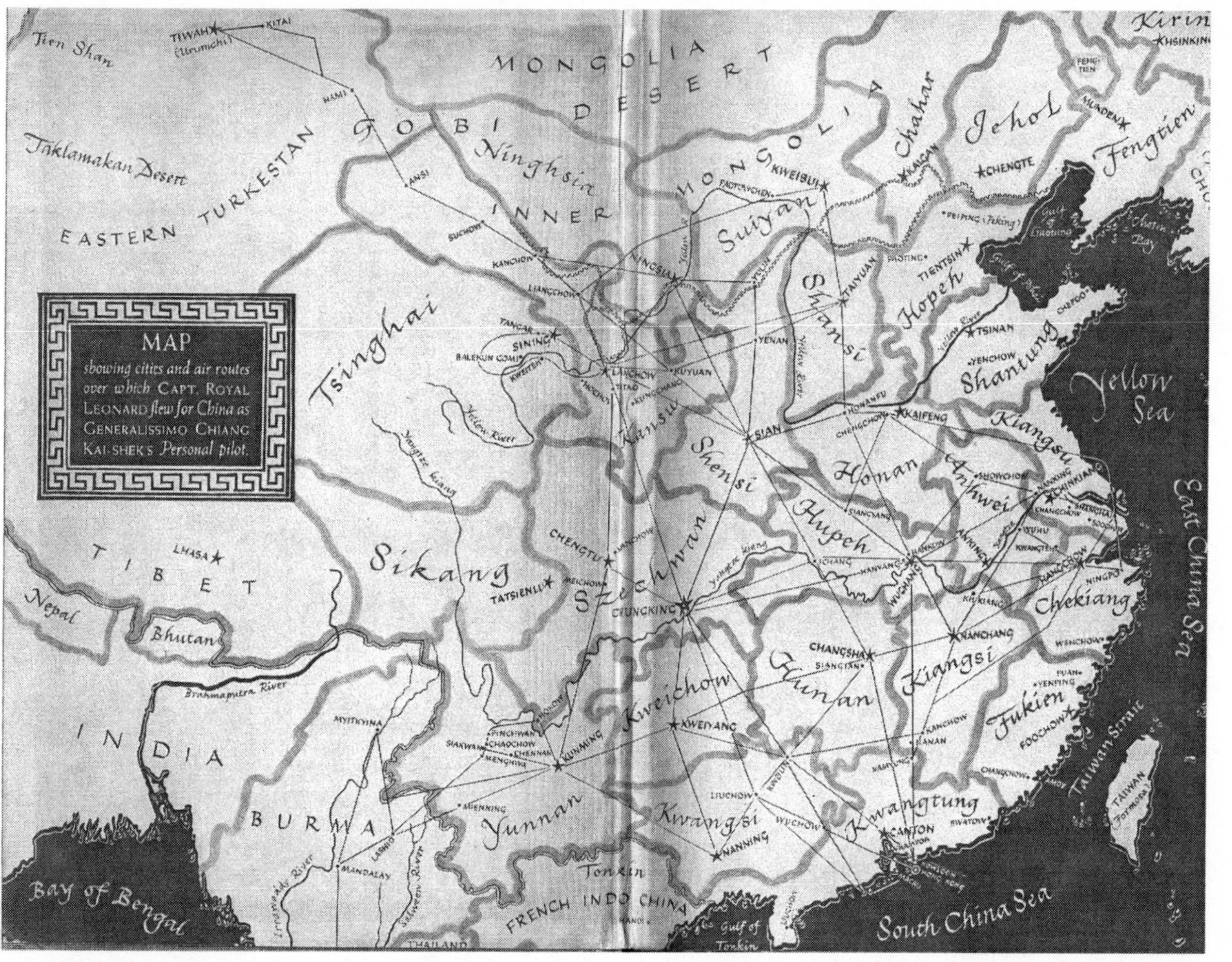
MAP
showing cities and air routes over which CAPT. ROYAL LEONARD flew for China as GENERALISSIMO CHIANG KAI-SHEK'S Personal pilot.
Tien Shan
Taklamakan Desert
EASTERN TURKESTAN
GOBI
MONGOLIA
DESERT
INNER MONGOLIA
Ninghsia
Suiyan
Chahar
Jehol
Fengtien
Kirin
Tsinghai
Kansu
Shensi
Shansi
Hopeh
Shantung
Honan
Kiangsu
Anhwei
Hupeh
Szechwan
Sikang
Chekiang
Kiangsi
Hunan
Kweichow
Fukien
Kwangsi
Kwangtung
Yunnan
TIBET
Nepal
Bhutan
INDIA
BURMA
THAILAND
FRENCH INDO CHINA
Tonkin
Gulf of Tonkin
Bay of Bengal
South China Sea
East China Sea
Yellow Sea
Taiwan Strait
TAIWAN (Formosa)
Gulf of Pohai
Gulf of Liaotung
Yellow River
Yangtze Kiang
Brahmaputra River
TIWAH (Urumchi)
KITAI
HAMI
ANSI
SUCHOW
KANCHOW
LIANGCHOW
NINGSIA
PAOTOWCHEN
KWEIBUI
KALGAN
CHENGTE
MUKDEN
HSINKING
PEIPING (Peking)
TIENTSIN
PAOTING
TAIYUAN
TSINAN
YENCHOW
KAIFENG
CHENGCHOW
HONANFU
SIAN
YENAN
KUYUAN
LANCHOW
SINING
TANGAR
HOCHOW
SIANGYANG
HANKOW
HANYANG
WUCHANG
ICHANG
NANKING
CHINKIANG
SHANGHAI
CHANGCHOW
SOOCHOW
WUHU
ANKING
KIUKIANG
HANGCHOW
NINGPO
WENCHOW
NANCHANG
CHANGSHA
SIANGTAN
CHENGTU
MEICHOW
TATSIENLU
CHUNGKING
KWEIYANG
KUNMING
CHENNAN
CHAOCHOW
SIAKWAN
MENGHWA
MIENNING
MYITKYINA
LASHIO
MANDALAY
LIUCHOW
WUCHOW
NANNING
CANTON
KANCHOW
KIANAN
FOOCHOW
YENPING
CHANGCHOW
SWATOW
LHASA

Chapter 1

ROCKY MOUNTAIN MAIL PILOT

(April 3, 1905 – March 1929)

Early on the frigid evening of December 4, 1928, Western Air Express ace mail pilot Royal Leonard circled like a "lost eagle" in dense fog blanketing Denver, Colorado. Flying an open-cockpit, single-engine Stearman C-3B biplane, Royal was not enjoying a Rocky Mountain high. He could not see the ground or the rotating beacon light at Lowry Field. His plane was not equipped with a radio. Because his altimeter only measured to the nearest fifty or one hundred feet he was unsure of his altitude. His compass was untrustworthy due to magnetic influences inside and outside the cockpit. Glimpsing a flare from Colorado Airways Airport, he tried to find Alexander Airport four miles southeast of the city limits and then the airfield in suburban Littleton southwest of the city. He could only estimate the distance he had flown from Colorado Airways Airport because his air speed indicator did not show ground speed.

As Royal circled and circled for an hour and a quarter, concerned citizens, hearing his engine drone, telephoned the airline hangar and inquired about his plight. A sweet lady offered to leave her porch light burning to help the "dear brave boy" land on her lawn. By dead reckoning, estimating his ground speed since leaving Colorado Airways Airport, taking into account any tail or head wind, as well as crosswind drift, the lost eagle arrived over what was, in his judgment, Alexander Airport, dropped a parachute flare in the center of the eighty-acre L-shaped sod-and-gravel field and finally landed safely.[1]

Only the best mail pilots survived their skirmishes with fog. In the late 1920s, an estimated one percent of U.S. pilots could fly five miles into dense fog, turn around, and fly out safely. Without a visible horizon, pilots lost their sense of balance, became disoriented, and put their planes into stalls, spins, or dives, often resulting in fatal accidents. Four months before Royal joined Western Air Express, another pilot had taken off from Denver in foggy conditions, crashed, and died. Royal's replacement arrived over Cheyenne, Wyoming, in dense fog, tried to find an emergency field, apparently mistook a beacon light for his destination, and smashed into a rocky hillside and was killed.[2]

Royal, the survivor, was born April 3, 1905, in Madison, Wisconsin. When he was four, his father and mother, Louis and Bertha, moved to a farm outside Waco, Texas. Royal soon proved he could take care of himself in his new environment. He and his younger brother Morris were walking barefoot to a three-room school. Local boys taunted them as Yankees. Morris started a fight, and Royal finished it. The altercation was more successful than farming in a drought period. "There were cracks in the ground two inches wide from the heat," remembered Morris.

After the family moved into Waco in 1913, Mr. Leonard had a hard time earning a living. Royal's mother instilled in him ambition and determination. She emphasized taking the initiative, self-reliance, and not fearing failure. Royal picked cotton, delivered newspapers, mowed lawns, chipped mortar from used bricks, and helped put up and take down the big-top tent when the circus came to town. He won second prize in a contest to sell the most *Saturday Evening Post* subscriptions in northern Texas. The family operated a laundry, and the boys earned five cents from delivering and picking up packages and additional money from selling candy to soldiers restricted to Camp MacArthur Army Base.

One weekend in 1916, Royal and Morris heard a loud noise above their house. Running outside, they saw an immense object in the sky. When the mysterious object landed, the boys jumped on their bikes and pedaled to a nearby farm for a closer look. They gawked at a strange man-made contraption with double wings mounted on a large tricycle-like chassis, a Curtiss Pusher biplane. The seventy-five horsepower rotary engine installed on the lower wing behind the pilot and passenger seats with the propeller facing rearward was capable of sixty miles per hour top speed. Barnstormer Cap Theodore, wearing goggles and with his flying cap turned backward, offered rides for fifteen dollars.

"I'll go up with you," said proud but poor Royal, "if you give *me* fifteen dollars."

Left to his own devices, teenager Royal methodically taught himself to walk a slack wire. He experimented with stepping along a one-and-a-half–inch diameter pipe about three feet above the ground in a schoolyard. Next, in his backyard, he traversed a seventy-five–foot-long wire strung three feet high between vertical posts held erect by cables. Gaining confidence, he raised the wire to six feet above the ground. Just walking the wire, however, soon bored him. In a "thrilling and hair-raising" PTA carnival performance, he sat and balanced ten feet above the ground in a chair with its two rear legs on the wire. Royal did not realize it then, but he was honing his aptitude for flying. According to U.S. Army Air Corps expert Major William C. Ocker, a pilot positioning his plane imitated "the acrobat who walk[ed] a 'slack rope.'"

On May 31, 1923, Royal graduated from Waco High School. His picture does not appear in the school yearbook senior section, and he did not purchase a copy of the book. He had a more important use for his money, a university education. He rode his bicycle, mostly on gravel and dirt roads, to Madison, Wisconsin, working along the way in harvest fields and on a construction project, and enrolled in the University of Wisconsin as an agriculture major. Self-disciplined, he recorded his mileage daily and calculated he had pedaled 1400 miles.

At the University of Wisconsin, Royal carried a full academic load. An enterprising young man, he invested in a bee farm in Cassville, 110 miles from Madison, and shipped honey in fifty-gallon cans to Waco for resale by his parents. Upon completing his freshman year, however, Royal was broke, so he dropped out of school and worked on an automotive plant assembly line. When the factory closed for a model changeover, Royal drove his Harley-Davidson motorcycle to Waco in four days, "a record-breaking trip," according to a Waco newspaper reporter. Returning to Madison, Royal, despite stopping twice for flat tires and coping with Chicago, Illinois rush-hour traffic delays, completed the trip in even less time—three days.

While a student at the University of Wisconsin, Royal was promoted to sergeant in the U.S. Army Reserve Officers Training Corp (ROTC) and qualified as a rifle and pistol marksman. He participated on the university wrestling squad and, on weekends, competed in slow-speed bicycle races in which the winner balanced and pedaled as slowly as possible to cross the finish line last. Inventive by nature, he replaced his motorcycle front wheel with a short ski, enabling him to travel faster and more safely on snowy streets.[3]

During the 1920s, many adventurous young American men, including Charles Lindbergh, shifted from riding motorcycles to flying airplanes. Royal read a *Popular Mechanics* magazine aviation school advertisement promising flyer pay of $125 to $225 a week ($1520 to $2730 in 2009 dollar purchasing power) after ten hours or less of training "under skilled men." Intrigued by aviation's possibilities, Royal rode his Harley in May 1926 to Great Lakes Naval Station in Chicago and took an aviator physical examination. He achieved the maximum score for distance judgment, needed for evaluating terrain, and depth perception, critical for landing aircraft. He also enjoyed his first airplane ride in a Navy seaplane.

Hooked on flying, Royal completed his sophomore year at the University of Wisconsin in good academic standing and left to pursue his dream of becoming a pilot. He decided to enroll in the Sweeney School of Aviation in Kansas City, Missouri, but injured his knee in a motorcycle accident.[4]

There was another way to learn to fly. Congress had authorized the Army to train a military pilot cadre so the U.S. would be prepared in the event of another major war. On September 18, 1926, Royal enlisted in the Air Service 60th Squadron stationed at Fort Crockett near Galveston, Texas. He disliked military life and asked his mother to get him discharged. She was unsuccessful.

The U.S. Army Air Corps "West Point of the Air" in San Antonio, Texas, where Charles Lindbergh had trained three years earlier, offered the best pilot preparation in the world. In March 1927, Royal, two other enlisted men, and 158 military officers and college graduates matriculated in the Brooks Field four-month primary flying program. Despite outstanding instructors like 1st Lieutenant Nathan F. Twining, future Chairman of the U.S. Armed Forces Joint Chiefs of Staff; 2nd Lieutenant Lawrence C. Craigie, first U.S. military officer to pilot a jet aircraft; and senior check pilot 1st Lieutenant Claire L. Chennault, later of World War II Flying Tigers fame, less than twenty percent of the cadets earned their wings. Royal was the third member of his class to solo in a Consolidated Aircraft Corporation PT-1 training biplane (top speed ninety-two miles per hour), noting in his journal: "Never Hesitate!"

The flying cadets, nicknamed "Dodos," were guinea pigs in a Brooks Field School of Aviation Medicine experiment designed to identify likely pilots. Many aviators crashed because they flew by the seat of their pants, relying on their instincts and sense of balance rather than on their aircraft instrument readings. The "embryo flyers" were subjected to the Ruggles Orientator, which theoretically tested their inherent flying ability. They sat in a miniature cockpit suspended from a rectangular frame. Mr. Ruggles used his controls to put the flyers in contorted positions, as they checked their instruments and tried to use their controls to right themselves. Their reactions to his efforts supposedly showed their ability to coordinate mind and muscle. They were graded on their performance during three ten-minute "hops" in the diabolical contraption. Lieutenant Chennault disdainfully said he could determine whether his plane was right side up by lighting a cigarette and watching which way the smoke blew. More critical to Royal's future survival in the air than outfoxing Mr. Ruggles was familiarization training with the Martin NBS-1 bomber and observation aircraft, as well as fifty hours training in aircraft engine maintenance and twenty-five hours each in navigation, meteorology, and topography.

Even with state of the art training, Royal made two forced landings due to engine failure. Both times he only slightly damaged his plane. In contrast, Cadet Charles Lindbergh had totaled a plane. Engaged in a mock dogfight, Lindbergh had collided with his opponent, climbed from the cockpit, jumped backward, pulled his parachute ripcord, and landed unhurt. Lindbergh almost washed out of America's best flying program because of this incident.

Royal witnessed perhaps the first two-plane-and-automobile accident. An instructor's plane and car were parked side by side. A Dodo taxiing in a crosswind inexplicably sped up his motor. Sensing the Dodo was headed toward him, the instructor ran for his life. Hearing a crash, he rushed back to find out what had happened and saw the trembling Dodo leaning from the cockpit of his plane, which was perched on top of a wrecked aircraft and automobile. Clutching his hair, the instructor screamed, "My plane! My car! My God!"

Only fifty-five of Royal's 162 classmates graduated from Brooks Field Primary School and entered the Kelly Field six-month advanced flying program. Royal ranked in the top ten percent of his class and was selected for pursuit (fighter) training. He flew a Curtiss Hawk AT-4 capable of reaching 150 miles per hour and mastered combat formation, dog fighting, ground-strafing, light-bombing, and observation techniques. He led the elite 43rd Pursuit Squadron on a training flight from San Antonio to Fort Clark at Brackettville, Texas (near the Mexican border) and back. In February 1928, he graduated with twenty-eight other cadets.

Royal was an enigma to his classmates. As one of three enlisted men and from an economically deprived background, he was reserved in the company of officers and college graduates, many of whom were from wealthy families. The Kelly Field yearbook editors characterized him as "Our Sphinx" and editorialized: "Here we have a strange combination [of] contrasts. Airplanes and books; Tightrope walking and Volleyball; Always at home and a moto[r]cycle. What to do? Figure it out for yourself. He'l[l] probably be in the cockpit when many others are history."[5]

Although he was one of only nineteen graduates offered an active duty assignment, Royal declined a commission because the Army Air Corps had trained more pilots than it needed and prospects for a long-term military career were not good. But there was a promising opportunity open to him. "Lucky" Lindbergh's solo nonstop trans-Atlantic crossing in May 1927 had stimulated investor interest in aviation. Boeing Air Transport and National Air Transport were providing transcontinental mail service between New York City and San Francisco, and smaller airlines on feeder routes were connecting with the transcontinental lines. Pilots with night flying experience were needed, and Kelly Field graduates were among an exclusive group with this training.

In April 1928, Western Air Express hired Royal as a reserve pilot on its Commercial Air Mail Route 12 (CAM-12) between Cheyenne, Wyoming, and Pueblo, Colorado. To supplement his income Royal enlisted in the Colorado National Guard in Colorado Springs and also worked as an assistant barnstormer, flying "an ancient spit-and-pray" Hess Bluebird around eastern Colorado. His barnstorming boss, Mr. Smith, had lost his front teeth in a crash that had killed the pilot. With Royal at the controls, Smith walked on the wings and performed stunts on a rope ladder to attract customers. The plane carried two passengers at three dollars a head. Royal averaged thirty dollars a day around Colorado Springs and cleared $250 on one especially profitable weekend at Canyon City.

During the late 1920s, Western Air Express (predecessor to Western Airlines and Delta Air Lines) was the most successful U.S. airline. In October 1927, the Guggenheim Fund for the Promotion of Aeronautics had advanced Western Air Express money for developing a model commercial passenger service between Los Angeles and San Francisco. In 1929, Western Air Express became the first U.S. airline to pay a stock dividend.

In his third week on the job with Western Express, "eagle of the air" Royal Leonard gave "Air Mail Week" a "brilliant send-off." Under a minimal cloud ceiling, he skimmed barely above telephone poles between Denver and Pueblo, Colorado. Battling extremely strong headwinds in his Stearman (126 miles per hour top speed and 108 miles per hour cruising speed), he completed the 100-mile trip in two and a half hours flying time, rather than the scheduled hour. "I flew so long over this hill and then another and would look down and see the same hill," exaggerated the young avigator, "that the thing was no longer funny." A *Pueblo Chieftain* reporter noted Royal was "stamped with the courage and the 'will to win' against the elements which air mail pilots have so eminently exercised to make mountain flying practical."

In mid-September 1928, another Western Air Express pilot disabled his plane in windy conditions at Cheyenne. Royal flew to the Wyoming capitol to pick up the Colorado mail left by a Boeing Air Transport plane. When Royal cut his motor to glide down, the wind pushed his plane backward; he had to restart the motor in order to land. As he taxied slowly and carefully on the gravel surface, a tremendous gust of wind picked up the plane and it came to rest upside-down. Royal was not hurt.

"I can believe that happened," says Rudy Eskra, who has flown a Stearman along the Rocky Mountains. "I've been caught trying to land my Stearman in gusty forty to fifty-mile-per-hour winds. The plane goes all over the map coming down. You wonder whether you can keep it in one piece. After you hit the runway, you have to keep the power on, fly it to the hangar, and hope that somebody grabs the wing handles to keep it down."

Returning from Cheyenne in mid-October through fog-bound hills, Royal found his way by flying a few feet above a road. Spotting Royal's oncoming plane, a bus driver almost drove into a ditch, and a pedestrian dived on his belly. "Of course I could see objects far enough ahead of me to zoom up enough to miss them," said Royal. "That is not like having a big cliff loom up in front where I could not turn quick enough to miss.... There was only one thing that worried me on that trip, I wanted to be sure that I kept that road in under me and I was only hoping that I could turn enough to follow the turns...."

After a terrifying experience in January 1929 when his primitive instruments failed and he circled, hopelessly lost, for an hour in fog and landed almost out of gas, Royal decided to learn how to fly blind when fog or clouds prevented him from seeing the ground along CAM-12. He used a methodical approach, ensuring the highest probability of success. In deference to his imprecise altimeter, he flew blind on his every-other-day mail flights whenever there were 2,000 feet snow-bottomed ceilings. At first, his plane quickly dropped from the clouds upside down, but eventually, relying on his turn and bank indicator, he succeeded in flying level for ten minutes. When he descended, Royal could usually identify his location because rotating beacon lights on fifty-foot-high steel towers visible forty miles away were spaced about every ten minutes between the airports at Cheyenne (6200 feet), Denver (5280 feet), Colorado Springs (5980 feet), and Pueblo (4690 feet), as well as ten emergency fields. Where the route changed direction, a fifty-four–foot-long concrete arrow pointed to the next beacon to the north and the butt aimed at the closest beacon to the south. Intermittent gas blinkers confirmed whether his plane was on course, and four warning flashers marked elevated hazards along the United States' "highest air mail line."

During winter months, the temperature when Royal crossed the Palmer Lake Divide between Denver and Colorado Springs dipped below zero. He wore a leather cap with ear flaps, a heavy fleece-lined flying suit, and extra-large, loose, wool-lined mukluks. "He sprinkled red pepper in his socks and wrapped each foot in a paper sack to keep them warm," recalled his younger sister Alice, who flew a chilly trip with him. Royal persisted, twice almost freezing his face, until he had flown blind in segments the entire 199-mile-long CAM-12 route.

Unlike Jimmy Doolittle's historic first round-trip blind flight under controlled conditions eight months later, lone eagle Royal's blind-flying accomplishment under operating conditions attracted no attention. Doolittle, who held a Massachusetts Institute of Technology PhD in Aeronautics, took off seated in a covered rear cockpit with an observation pilot in the unobstructed front cockpit. In his fifteen-minute flight, Doolittle relied on state-of-the-art instruments—an artificial horizon accurately showing his lateral and longitudinal positions, a directional gyroscope showing any veering, a visual radio beam indicator for keeping on course when approaching the runway, and an altimeter accurate within a dozen feet.[6]

During his year flying on CAM-12, Royal and his fellow pilots completed ninety-eight percent of their scheduled flights. An attempted mail flight had to last at least ten minutes for an airline to receive payment from the U.S. Post Office Department. Most pilots, trying to meet scheduled transcontinental connections, did not waste time on the ground waiting for an improvement in the weather. They took off and coped with whatever conditions confronted them. For risking his neck making a 100-mile flight from Denver to Cheyenne at night in perilous weather, Royal added to his paycheck, at ten cents a mile, the magnificent sum of ten dollars ($125 in 2009 purchasing power).

"I don't know how those early pilots could fly almost every day," comments Rudy Eskra. "It's a very risky business flying a light biplane in all kinds of weather along the front range of the Rockies. Winds come from both the east and the west. If you're just holding your heading and can't see the ground, you can be blown off course. There are tremendous downdrafts that last a long time. The seventy-three-hundred-foot elevation Black Forest can rise up and get you. And that's not even taking into consideration dealing with fog without modern navigational instruments."

On off days, Royal served in the Colorado National Guard based at Lowry Field and, on weekends, barnstormed around eastern Colorado. Promoted to second lieutenant in the 120th Observation Squadron, 45th Division Air Service, he flew the Douglas G-2C observation plane. In September 1928, Royal and friend Fred Jacob purchased a Lincoln Page LP-3 two-place biplane. Operating as the Denver Aircraft Sales Company, they advertised three-dollar rides with the "best of pilots and plane."

"Royal was a precision pilot," recalled Jacob. "He was very careful. Nobody hurried him when he made his walk around inspection before a flight. He always checked the gas tank."

As a night mail pilot on CAM-12 along the backbone of the continent, Royal's performance surpassed that of Lindbergh's a couple years earlier on CAM-2 between St. Louis, Missouri, and Chicago, Illinois. Lost in fog near the Windy City and believing he was out of fuel, Lindbergh, in his words, "neglected to cut the switches" and bailed out. While Lucky Lindy dangled in his parachute, the engine started and the plane circled him five times, once within 300 yards, before he alighted safely in a cornfield. Lindbergh bailed out two other times from mail planes. Making four successful parachute jumps, Lindbergh earned the dubious distinction as the world's only four-time member of the "Caterpillar Club" named for the insect that spun the silk used in parachutes.[7]

Unlike Charles Lindbergh, Royal never used a parachute or destroyed a plane, either as a flying cadet or a mail pilot.

Chapter 2

DANGEROUS ENCOUNTERS

(April 1929 – May 1934)

In recognition of Royal's outstanding performance (and perhaps knack for survival), Western Air Express in April 1929 transferred him to its transcontinental passenger and mail service. He needed every ounce of his skill on his new assignment. The Fokker passenger aircraft he flew had a fatal structural defect. The mail planes were not any safer. Gas fumes seeped into Northrop Alpha cockpits and almost asphyxiated pilots and Lockheed Orion engines mysteriously shut off in flight.

On June 1, 1929, Royal piloted a ten-passenger, three-engine Fokker F-10, which cruised at 120 miles per hour, on the inaugural "Dawn-to-Dusk" Kansas City, Missouri, to Los Angeles, California, flight. The early-morning takeoff was delayed because several passengers, including former heavyweight boxing champion Jack Dempsey, were late making connections from a westbound train. As a newsreel man filmed this notable occasion, youthful-looking Royal walked toward the plane. "Get that kid out of here!" yelled the irritated cameraman. Royal chewed out his tormentor with a few earthy phrases.

The "Boy Pilot's" pet cinnamon bear, Jess, became the Western Air Express mascot and the airline newsletter *The Dashboard Record* reported Jess's carnivorous antics. One night, Royal's roommate found Jess sleeping in his bed and insisted that Royal move him to a hangar at the Kansas City Airport. "Jess is a bear of a mechanic," quipped Royal. But Jess showed a profound dislike for everyone except Royal unless fed a lump of sugar. When Royal was transferred to Los Angeles, Jess was flown to Albuquerque, New Mexico, and housed near the terminal. Waiting passengers fed him chewing gum. Jess searched passenger compartments for lunch boxes and earned the nickname "Nose Dive."

Always alert to publicity opportunities, Western Air Express management decided that a Tin Pan Alley song might improve the airline's name recognition. Newspapers in nine cities (New York, Boston, Buffalo, Cincinnati, Cleveland, Indianapolis, Kansas City, San Francisco, and Oakland) sponsored a contest to pick the song title. A New York City businessman submitted *Big Boy Jess of the Western Air Express.* The airline paid $5,000 to well-known songwriter George Whiting, whose work included *My Blue Heaven, Who Told You I Cared?, Strolling Through the Park One Day*, and other hits, for writing the memorable lyrics:

Steamboat Bill! Casey Jones! And others I could mention.

I used to think that they were fast,

Back in the dim and distant past!

There's a new someone who has won the world's attention.

He's of the modern school, and he's a flying fool!

(Chorus)

"There he is!" you'll hear somebody cry.

And then out from the Sky, drops BIG BOY JESS

Of the Western Air Express!

How those air-cooled mammas gather around,

Yes sir, they certainly hound that BIG BOY JESS

Of the Western Air Express.

Jess really did win worldwide attention. Royal liked to walk him on a leash around the San Francisco Bay Area Aerodrome terminal to say hello. As Jess ambled down hallways, he turned doorknobs, opened doors, and peered into rooms. One day Jess checked out a usually vacant office and surprised a distinguished-looking gentleman. Royal jerked the cub back and pulled him down the corridor. Jess had met Crown Prince Leopold of Belgium. A newspaper reporter asked the prince if the bear had frightened him. "No," replied Prince Leopold, "It was precisely what I expected to see in the wilds of America."

Jess thrived on airport leftovers and grew to weigh 350 pounds. In their last impromptu wrestling match, Jess pinned Royal and Royal had to brace a foot against a fence post to push off the bear. Royal finally gave Jess to a private zoo.

In addition to promotion, Western Air Express was an industry leader in utilizing radio communication and navigation. In June 1930, Royal's picture appeared in a *Los Angeles Times* article about a two-way radio training program. Pilots could now report their positions and obtain weather information from airport radio operators. This procedure was so novel that a newspaper published an article headlined "Flying Fireman" about Royal spotting an early-stage southern California fire, radioing information to a nearby airport, and enabling firefighters to suppress the conflagration before it spread. Pilots also could listen through headphones for radio beam signals along the transcontinental and California coastal routes and determine whether they were on course ("on the beam").[8]

Western Air Express' leadership role in U.S. aviation, however, was short-lived. Forty-four airlines, many underfinanced and unreliable, were competing for U.S. airmail and passenger business. Postmaster General Walter Folger Brown wanted to establish financially strong passenger airlines not dependent on airmail revenues. The McNary-Watres Act, effective in April 1930, empowered him to attain this objective. The Act changed the basis for airmail compensation from pounds flown per mile to amount of space available for mail and provided bonuses for use of multi-engine aircraft equipped with modern instruments. The Act further authorized the postmaster general to award airmail contracts to the lowest responsible bidder and to consolidate existing routes in the public interest.

In May 1930, Brown summoned major airline officials to Washington, DC, for a meeting later called the Spoils Conference. Brown informed Western Air Express president Harris Hanshue that only one company would be awarded the airmail contract for the central transcontinental route through Kansas City. Brown offered Hanshue the opportunity to merge his company with Transcontinental Air Transport, which operated a competing New York City–Los Angeles passenger service, and Pittsburgh Aviation Industries Corporation, which operated over the Allegheny Mountains. Hanshue agreed to a partial merger because Western Air Express could not operate profitably on the transcontinental route without airmail revenue. In early October 1930, Brown awarded the central transcontinental and Los

Angeles–San Francisco airmail contracts to Transcontinental and Western Air, Inc. (T&WA), the northern San Francisco–New York City route to United Air Lines, and the southern Los Angeles–Atlanta, Georgia route to American Airways.

Because T&WA took over the aircraft and routes he had been flying, Royal transferred to this new airline, which commenced operations on October 25, 1930, The next year T&WA lost $1,011,338 due to declining passenger revenue. Pilot pay was a major expense. As a cost-cutting measure, T&WA changed pilot compensation from a base-pay-plus-mileage system with upward adjustments for hazardous terrain and night flying to a trip-pay system based on average route times. T&WA pilots feared this modification would lead to lower pay in the future when faster aircraft were introduced.

To gain bargaining leverage, a small group of pilots from several airlines in May 1931 founded the Air Line Pilots Association (ALPA). Royal joined this professional union and served on the national board of directors, as well as the Master Executive Council that negotiated with T&WA management. He was also chairman of the T&WA Pacific Division Pilots Council, which was composed of pilots and copilots domiciled in the San Francisco and Los Angeles metropolitan areas.

Fanatically anti-union, twenty-seven–year-old T&WA vice president Jack Frye launched a concerted effort to decimate his airline's ALPA membership. At age eighteen, Frye had traveled to Los Angeles, worked as a soda jerk to earn money for flying lessons, and soloed after seven hours of instruction. Using profits from operating a flying school and performing motion picture aerial stunts, Frye and partners Paul Richter and Walter Hamilton in 1927 had founded Standard Airline, which primarily served Los Angeles and Phoenix, Arizona. Standard's pilots occasionally made unscheduled stops for lady passengers' comfort in the Mojave Desert near a gas station with outhouse facilities. In April 1930, Frye and his partners had sold Standard to Western Air Express, and when that airline had partially merged into T&WA, Frye had become vice president of operations.

Frye pressured several pilots, who feared losing their jobs, into leaving ALPA and joining the management-controlled company union called the T&WA Pilots Association. He infiltrated pilot Jack Thornburg as a company spy into the ALPA Master Executive Council to try to destroy it as a bargaining unit. Thornburg urged Royal to "sell out" and said he might be chosen T&WA chief pilot if he resigned from ALPA.

"To do his bidding," said Royal, "I would have to renounce all the principles that I had been upholding. I had been one of the charter members of the association, and had I not believed that we were right from the beginning, I would not have joined in with the other fellows. We needed an association and needed it badly, and I could not see myself doing anything that would jeopardize its early existence. The bait was very attractive, and it would have been very much to my personal gain to have swallowed it. Being one of the senior pilots, I realized that my resigning would have quite an influence toward getting some of the other pilots to resign, and I knew that Mr. Frye was thinking about that also. Every time that Mr. Thornburg came to me with a new proposition, my answer was always the same: 'If it is necessary to sell out my fellow pilots as well as myself, than I am not interested. If my own merits are not enough to speak for themselves, then I shall be too busy trying to improve on my merits to be interested in what you have to offer.'"[9]

Despite Royal's ALPA activities, T&WA management recognized his ability and continued assigning him flights on the four-engine Fokker F-32, "the biggest, most costly and least successful land-based airliner of its time." When still with Western Air Express, Royal had been copilot on a highly publicized F-32 coast-to-coast flight terminating at Alhambra Field in Los Angeles, where chorus girls had danced on its ninety-nine–foot long wing in front of 25,000 spectators. Royal's selection as an F-32 pilot, stated a Denver newspaper reporter, "is an expression by Western Air Express officials of their confidence in him as a flyer with whom the safety of large loads of passengers can be intrusted."

Only ten F-32s were manufactured; four of them were purchased for $110,000 each by Western Air Express and transferred to T&WA; and two of these were flown between Los Angeles and San Francisco. The sixty-nine–foot, ten-inch–long aircraft attained 140 and 123 miles per hour maximum and cruising speeds. Apart from size, the F-32's most notable feature was air-cooled, twin-tandem engines, which made it unwieldy to fly. The forward engines had two-blade tractor propellers, which rotated counterclockwise, and the rear engines had three-blade tractor propellers, which turned clockwise. In the luxurious compartment, passengers sat in reclining seats under reading lights and pushed call buttons for stewards to bring refreshments.

In a publicity stunt to help demonstrate the worldwide capability of International Telephone and Telegraph Company, Royal flew an F-32 over San Francisco Bay in December 1930, in the first combined airplane radio-phone, telegraph land-line, and submarine-cable transmission experiment. Christmas messages were sent to and received from London, Paris, Manila, Shanghai, and Buenos Aires. The *Oakland Post-Enquirer* called the event "a novel and at the same time practical demonstration of the powers of man."

After a highly publicized crash on March 31, 1931, however, in which an F-10 wooden wing fell off and Notre Dame football coach Knute Rockne and all others aboard were killed, T&WA discontinued flying Fokker aircraft because of the uneconomical amounts of time and money involved in periodically disassembling and inspecting the wings for internal wood rot.

In his year behind F-32 controls, Royal believed he had accumulated more four-engine flying time than any other U.S. pilot. One F-32, which had carried 50,000 passengers and flown 2500 hours and 250,000 miles, was sold for $1,000, moved to the corner of Wilshire Boulevard and Cochran Street in Los Angeles, and converted into a gasoline service station. The *Los Angeles Times* called it the world's largest and costliest freak filling station. [10]

Royal was domiciled at Grand Central Air Terminal, the "Airport to the Stars," in Glendale, northeast of downtown Los Angeles. He purchased a home near the airport, worked in his garage on designing a flying wing, and practiced wire walking in the backyard. He was supporting his mother and putting his sister Alice through junior college and UCLA.

"Airplane watchers" waiting near the colorfully lit, neoclassical California mission-style Grand Central Air Terminal commented on the peculiarities of airline pilots as they approached and touched down on the 2,744-foot concrete runway. Royal always swung north and flew over his residence to alert Alice to drive to the airport and bring him home. "He flies so low over the house, he parts the trees in the cemetery!" commented a neighbor.

During the spring of 1931, T&WA provided its pilots instrument training to qualify them for the U.S. Department of Commerce Scheduled Air Transport Rating (SATR) required for flying on scheduled interstate passenger routes. In an effort to prove that commercial flying was possible using only instruments and the radio beam, Royal had been flying the 360-mile corridor between Los Angeles and San Francisco with cardboard blocking his cockpit windows and his copilot's view unobstructed. Jack "Shorty" Lynch, one of Lindbergh's first flying instructors, was the T&WA instrument training and check pilot.

He sat in the Stearman C-3B training plane front cockpit. "I did acrobatics never looking out," said Royal, "just looking at the instruments. He put me in all sorts of positions—upside down, spins, rolls, and every way possible—and g[a]ve it to me to straighten out. He told me I did better than some of the T&WA pilots back east who flew blind for long periods of time because they had to."[11]

In April 1931, Royal started flying smooth-skin, metal Northrop Alpha mail planes resplendent with trousered wheel covers. During their first six months in service, T&WA's eleven Alphas were involved in eleven accidents, primarily due to ground looping. When the tail wheel touched down, a wing would hit the ground and the Alpha would spin and tip on its side. After a year in use, six T&WA Alphas were seriously damaged and out of service. Royal ground-looped twice in Alphas, resulting in minor damage. He was not disciplined because of his excellent record, his lack of experience with the aircraft, and the Alphas' propensity for ground looping. Eventually, T&WA mechanics widened the Alphas' landing gears and eliminated the problem.

A few T&WA pilots were almost asphyxiated flying Alphas. Carbon monoxide fumes rose up the shaft above the tail wheel well and seeped into the cockpit. T&WA pilot Ted Hereford landed an Alpha, walked into the airport operations office, and started disrobing. Witnesses thought he was drunk. When another pilot collapsed after flying an Alpha, a doctor diagnosed his condition as carbon monoxide poisoning. Resourceful T&WA mechanics remedied this hazard to pilot health by stuffing leather socks in the wheel wells.

Flying idiosyncratic aircraft, Royal coped successfully with adverse weather along the T&WA transcontinental mail route. In zero-zero (no ceiling and no ground visibility) fog, he approached the Wichita (Kansas) Airport, which was rimmed by forty-foot–high power poles and lines. Standard procedure was to drop down to the minimum allowable altitude of 200 feet and pull up within thirty seconds if the field was not visible. For more than an hour Royal descended, flew about three minutes looking for a hole in the fog, climbed, and circled back for another try. When he finally saw the ground, Royal landed, walked to a farmhouse, and telephoned the airport manager to send a gas truck. After his plane was refueled, Royal took off for Kansas City.

"I wondered at the time, and still do, whether any other pilot could do this and get away with it," said Ted Hereford (retired from TWA in 1970), who witnessed the drama. "Royal was an exceptional pilot, always ahead of his time."[12]

In May 1933, Royal started flying T&WA's three Lockheed Model 9E Orions. On the positive side, the Orion was the fastest U.S. mail plane, cruising at 200 miles per hour and cutting ninety minutes from the westbound and sixty minutes from the eastbound transcontinental mail times. On the negative side, the thirty-five Orions manufactured by Lockheed Aircraft Corporation were involved in nineteen civil accidents, killing twenty-five people.

The tiny Orion cockpit was behind the engine and above and in front of the wing. "I was one of the smallest pilots flying them, and I was so cramped in the cockpit that I hardly had room to work the controls," said five-feet, eight-inch, 150-pound Royal. "It will always be a mystery to me how the larger pilots could get in those cockpits and still have room to fly."

"It was the worst cockpit design I ever saw," concurred six-foot–tall, 185-pound Ted Hereford. "I could just wedge myself in. My toes went practically between the cylinders."

"All the controls and instruments," said Royal, "were jumbled together any old way. The man that designed the famous carnival Bug House where everything is backwards could not have done a better job of disarranging the cockpit."

The stick for operating the elevators on the horizontal stabilizer in the tail that controlled moving the nose up and down was between the pilot's knees. The hydraulic pump lever to raise and lower the retractable landing gear pressed against his right side. Two engine switches intruded on his right elbow space.

When testing an Orion's engine switches that turned on and off and retarded or advanced two spark plug sets, Royal discovered that he had been flying with one switch off. He wondered if he had become absentminded and forgotten to turn both engine switches back on after testing them before taking off. One night, he discovered what was happening. As he worked the landing gear lever, he would strike an engine switch with his elbow. "It really was a mere trifle," said Royal, "but it scared me to think how serious it could have been... had I accidentally hit the switch[es] and turned off both sets of plugs just after taking off. At first I would not have known what had happened. A pilot's first thought, if his motor fails him on takeoff, is, 'Did I forget to turn on my gas?' I would never have thought of the switch. Even had I felt myself hit the switch, I would not have been able to turn it back on again before I would have crashed."

Royal reported the Orion cockpit configuration problems to T&WA maintenance superintendent Walter Hamilton, Frye's former Standard Airline partner. "I might just as well have pulled a lion's tail," said Royal.

"If you fellows don't want to fly the airplanes that we give you to fly," bellowed Hamilton, "we will just get some other pilots. There are plenty of pilots who would be tickled to death to fly anything we have." Hamilton was not making an idle threat. Seven thousand licensed transport pilots were competing for an estimated 680 commercial pilot jobs.

After a month of unsatisfactory experiences with the Orions, the T&WA–ALPA Master Executive Council members took their complaints to the next level—Jack Frye. They emphasized their main concern was that a pilot in a crash would be crushed to death by the engine pushed back into the cockpit. They also pointed out it was almost impossible to move a switch with the right hand when trying to shut off the engine to prevent a fire and it was difficult to reach a switch with the left hand when wearing winter clothing.

Frye turned down the Council request that T&WA order new Orions with the cockpit behind the wing. He claimed that Lockheed engineers preferred the cockpit behind the engine to simplify installation of controls, a change would increase production costs, and pilot visibility was better from a cockpit behind the engine than in back of the wing. Anticipating these arguments, Royal had contacted Lockheed factory personnel and evaluated the visibility issue. He told Frye that Lockheed engineers actually preferred placement of the cockpit behind the wing and this change could be implemented at no extra cost with only a two-week delay in delivery time. Royal challenged Frye with a chart he had prepared demonstrating that pilot visibility angles were better from a cockpit behind the wing. Flummoxed, Frye heatedly stated that no pilot would be forced to fly an Orion against his will.

Following their meeting with Frye, the Master Executive Council members summarized their Orion criticisms in a telegram addressed from Wayne Williams' hotel room to the president of the General Motors Corporation subsidiary that controlled T&WA. When Frye learned about the pilots going over his head, he immediately fired Williams. Word leaked out that Royal would be next. Rather than terminate him, Frye met with Royal, explained that T&WA had decided to replace the Orions with Northrop Gammas, and asked him to sign a statement retracting the telegram.

"Under the circumstances," explained Royal, "I was quite eager to make peace in the family. Thus, I signed the statement.... The way things were going, I was tired of it all. I wanted to have nothing more to do with our peculiar politics." He resigned from the Master Executive Council but maintained his ALPA membership.[13]

Until replacement Gammas were available, however, T&WA continued using Orions. On July 28, 1933, Earl Noe took off from the Kansas City Airport in an Orion, banked to the right, crashed into the Missouri River, and broke his neck and died. Management maintained that his propeller tore loose from the motor, but the propeller and motor were found intact.

Suspicious about the accident's cause, Royal conducted his own investigation. He needed to know why Noe had crashed, for his, as well other pilots', sake. He learned that the salvaged plane's engine switches were in the off position and the landing gear was down. Royal surmised that Noe, banking to the right and working the lever to raise the landing gear, had accidentally hit the switches with his elbow, cutting off both spark plug sets and turning off the engine.

Royal could not understand, however, why Noe could not have maneuvered the stick to keep up the nose and glide to a safe landing.

Nascent test pilot Royal reconstructed Noe's accident. At a safe altitude, he lowered an Orion's wheels, placed the stabilizer in the takeoff position, cut the engine switches, and discovered with the stick all the way back that he could not hold up the nose. Despite his best efforts, the plane dove. Because the cockpit was so cramped he had very little room to maneuver the stick, which had to be wound back several turns before there was enough control to hold the plane in a normal glide. A good share of the fore and aft control had to be accomplished through the stabilizer, which was clumsy and slow.

T&WA mechanics installed metal shields over the Orion engine switches so a pilot could only operate them with his fingers and not accidentally turn them off with a bump of the elbow.

Two years later, on August 15, 1935, Wiley Post and his famous passenger, Will Rogers, took off near Barrow, Alaska, in a modified former T&WA Lockheed Orion. Post had replaced the Orion's Pratt & Whitney Wasp S1D1 engine with a Wasp S3H1-G, which was 145-pounds heavier, removed the retractable landing gear and operating lever, replaced the Orion wing with a Lockheed Sirius wing, and attached pontoons. Post banked sharply to the right, the engine stopped, and the plane crashed. Both men were killed. The impact with the engine mangled Post's body. The cause of the crash has never been definitely determined. Most experts maintain that the engine stopped because of insufficient carburetor heat. Another theory holds that fuel failed to reach the carburetor from a banked, almost empty tank, but there is no post-accident record of which tank Post was using and whether it was almost drained.

Post, who had purchased the plane from a broker, probably had not known about the engine-switches problem or the T&WA mechanics' solution of a metal shield. The switches in Post's cockpit may have been near his right elbow as in the three T&WA Orions and in the only Orion now in existence which is in the Swiss Transport Museum in Lucerne, Switzerland. Post's modification work list item number fourteen specifies "controls to be used as installed by Lockheed factory," which did not include a metal shield over the engine switches.

Royal had flown Post's Orion when T&WA had owned it, but probably did not know about Post's modifications, which made the plane even more nose heavy. Royal suspected that when Wiley banked sharply to the right, his heavily clothed right elbow had hit the engine switches and cut off the engine. No record, however, exists of the engine switches' positions in Post's salvaged plane.

In Royal's opinion, the cockpit was too cramped for Post effectively to use the stick and the stabilizer too clumsy and slow to keep up the nose. "No matter what made the motor sputter enough after that fateful take off," Royal opined, "Post should have been able to have made a normal landing again had it not been for these peculiarities of his plane."[14]

Ever innovative and safety conscious, Royal helped T&WA pioneer the use of celestial navigation by U.S. commercial airlines. He took a celestial navigation course offered at Grand Central Air Terminal by U.S. Navy Lieutenant Commander P.V.H. Weems, who had developed condensed tables, which eliminated the need for extensive mathematical computations. Royal's classmates included Douglas "Wrong Way" Corrigan, who later took off from Brooklyn, NY, supposedly headed for California, and landed in Ireland; Wiley Post, who made two round-the-world flights; and Howard Hughes, millionaire manufacturer and movie producer. "Howard looked like a bum," said Royal's barnstorming friend Fred Jacob, who had moved to Glendale and also took the class. "He had on dirty tennis shoes and dirty light-colored pants."

"I sure have to laugh at our officials," Royal said. "When they first saw me carrying my sextant around practicing from the air, they laughed at me, then accused me of getting ready for an ocean hop and all sorts of those things." Royal routinely took night shots with his sextant from Northrop Alpha open cockpits and revised T&WA maps to conform to his determinations. He convinced Frye to provide celestial navigation expert Peter Redpath a free pass to travel the T&WA system and train pilots at their personal expense.

In May 1933, *Western Flying* magazine published Royal's article about the usefulness of celestial navigation on commercial flights when not flying on the radio beam or when radios malfunctioned. His article explained that a pilot skilled in celestial navigation could work out a line of position in five minutes, check his drift estimate, and avoid lost time and excessive fuel consumption. "In summing up the possibilities of celestial navigation," Royal concluded, "I will have to admit it does not constitute the final solution to our problems of navigating. I like to look at it this way. It is only one method of checking our dead reckoning, but very often it will be the most important."

After T&WA in December 1933 took delivery of the experimental DC-1 prototype for the revolutionary DC-2 passenger transport, Royal test flew the DC-1 and helped design a cockpit folding hatch for making celestial navigation observations. When the DC-2, which cruised at 195 miles per hour, was put in service the New York City–Los Angeles passenger flight time was cut to twelve hours eastbound and sixteen hours westbound, as compared with forty-eight hours by train at night and plane in daylight five years earlier when Royal had made the inaugural "Dawn to Dusk" flight.

Despite tremendous technological progress during the early years of the Golden Age of American Aviation, U.S. airlines almost ground to a halt when government airmail contracts, their primary revenue source, were cancelled as a result of suspected fraud in the Spoils Conference award process. Between February 19 and May 2, 1934, the Army Air Corps, at a cost of twelve pilot lives, transported mail until reorganized airlines (T&WA became TWA) were awarded mail contracts. During this period, Royal, who ranked seventh in seniority, took a short vacation, flew his allotted western division passenger flights, and transferred to the eastern division for familiarization with its routes. He also worked with inventor Roy Franklin on a cargo dropper—a parachute with a timing device—for delivering mail and packages to small towns without airfields. Experiments with the device failed because it was impossible to consistently predict drift.

As U.S. airlines struggled to survive, a challenging opportunity beckoned Royal in international aviation.[15]

Chapter 3

RACE OF THE CENTURY

(June 1934 – January 1935)

Australia represented the frontier for international air racing and passenger service. There was no trans-Pacific or trans-Atlantic race and no airline linked the United States or Europe with the continent down under. Hoping to stimulate investment in an air line service to Australia, Sir Macpherson Robertson sponsored an 11,323-mile race from London to Melbourne described by a leading aviation historian as "the most significant air race of all time," by *Time* magazine as the "greatest race in aviation history," and by *Aviation* magazine as the "race of the century." Lloyds of London predicted that one in twelve participants would perish.

Jackie Cochran, a twenty-eight–year-old former beautician with two years' flying experience, wanted to win the MacRobertson Race $15,000 first prize and achieve international recognition as an aviatrix. Her sugar daddy, forty-two–year-old close friend (and married) multimillionaire Floyd Odlum, had held fourteen million dollars in cash and other liquid assets before the 1929 stock market crash. He used his monetary hoard to acquire bankrupt companies for less than book value and sold their assets for huge profits. He controlled, managed, and reorganized Greyhound Bus Lines, RKO Motion Pictures, Bonwit Teller Department Stores, and Goldman Sachs. *Fortune* magazine dubbed him "Depression Phenomenon Class A."

Jackie needed experienced copilots for the race. She hired T&WA pilot Wesley Smith, known for his instrument flying ability, to accompany her from London to Allahabad, India. And she hired Royal because of his celestial navigation expertise and knowledge of Australian aviation to accompany her from Allahabad to Melbourne. Under Jack Frye's direction, Royal had studied the possibility of T&WA making United States–Australia passenger flights. In December 1933, Royal had consulted with Donald Douglas and his engineers about designing a transport plane capable of carrying passengers across the Pacific Ocean. Royal had worked with Australian Harold Gatty, navigator on Wiley Post's first round-the-world flight, plotting route survey maps and had prepared a confidential report on the trans-Pacific project. But the new TWA board of directors had not been interested and had left the trans-Pacific opportunity to Pan American Airways and its Clippers.

After Jackie met the June 1 race registration deadline, Odlum cabled his London agent that he was "not financing this or any other pilot or ship," that he was "terribly anxious [to] avoid any publicity whatsoever," and to "keep my name out of it altogether." Odlum assigned code names for use in trans-Atlantic cables: "Florida" for Jackie, "Stars" for Wesley, "Sky" for Royal, "Sand" for the plane, and "Wind" for the U.S. State Department.[16]

On June 28, 1934, TWA granted "Sky" a leave of absence (he flew for the reconstituted air line only about two months), and "Sky" devoted all his time to race preparations. He hired two men to work in his home making route maps. He coordinated with Northrop factory personnel in readying Jackie's Gamma Model 2D for the race and supervised installation of removable plate glass sections in the cockpit windshield for making celestial navigation observations. He visited March Field near Riverside, California, to learn more about an experimental Curtiss-Wright liquid-cooled Conqueror SGV-1570 F-4 engine with a General Electric supercharger. He also mediated between Jack Northrop, who preferred a Wasp engine, distrusted the experimental engine, and worried about the effect of its failure on his company's reputation, and Jackie, who believed Curtiss-Wright officials' representations that the engine was developing nicely.

Jack Frye, who had entered a TWA DC-2 in the race, proposed that Royal and Wesley reconnoiter the race route as passengers in the TWA plane. The air fare he wanted, however, was too high. Even when Frye cut it in half, Jackie regarded his demand as outrageous. She realized that Frye was trying to get Odlum indirectly to finance his race entry and turned him down.

Using TWA pilot Harlan Hull as his intermediary, Frye exerted pressure on Royal to persuade Jackie to change her mind. Hull had been a delegate to the first ALPA convention. Like Royal, he had served on the T&WA Master Executive Council. Unlike Royal, he had deserted ALPA and joined the T&WA Pilots Association company union, becoming its president.

Hull urged Royal to tell Jackie he would quit if she did not accept Frye's proposal, but Royal believed she would fire him if he tried to intimidate her. Frye assured reluctant Royal that she would not terminate him because he could threaten to publicize Jackie and Floyd's personal relationship and they would quickly pay Frye's price. Frye warned Royal that he had better think carefully about his decision because his future with the air line might depend on the kind of judgment he used. Royal weighed his boss's admonition but could not betray Jackie and Odlum, and defied Frye. Stymied in finding a financial backer, Frye angrily withdrew from the race.[17]

Participation in the MacRobertson Race was not the only point of contention between Royal and his boss. Frye's executive secretary, Florence Suddarth, was pregnant. Frye was married and Royal was single. Frye and Florence maintained Royal was the father and Royal contended Frye was the responsible party.

Florence ardently admired both her boss and Royal. She described Jack as "quiet, calm, like a seasoned sailor guiding his ship safely through a storm. He worked with us and for us, so that the distinction of 'employer' and 'employee' was never particularly stressed." But Frye despised one type of employee—the union man. And Florence was vigorously pursuing Royal, whispering in his ear that she could help him become chief pilot. Privy to airline schedules and ticket sales information, Florence often occupied unsold seats on Royal's passenger flights. "Royal was a rather private person," recalled Ted Hereford, "and I seldom saw him, as he seemed to have numerous local people that he visited rather than staying at the hotels." Rather than rooming with other pilots during layovers, Royal sought refuge from Florence in his friends' homes.

At Frye's behest, Harlan Hull cornered Royal and threatened through legal process to prevent him from leaving the United States on a race-reconnoitering trip unless he financially accommodated Florence during her pregnancy. Desperate to fly in the race, Royal, without consulting an attorney, signed a note authorizing Hull to pay Florence hush money. "I thought you would be the last person in this outfit that would ever get in trouble," said Hull once he had the note in his hand.

Leaving New York City on July 25, Royal traveled to England on a passenger ship and to Singapore on commercial planes. In Rangoon, Bangkok, and Singapore, he collected weather information and evaluated landing fields. Between Singapore and Derby, Australia, he made celestial navigation observations from the deck of a ship. On September 21, he returned to Los Angeles and submitted to Odlum and Jackie a thirty-three–page report including detailed information about emergency landing fields.

During Royal's round-the-world tour, the experimental engine had blown up on a factory test block and Jackie and Wesley Smith had not been able to fly the Northrop Gamma 2D. The plane, which cost an estimated $40,000 ($641,000 in 2009 purchasing power), impressed Royal. "Such a beautiful thing!" he exclaimed. "This looks like a flying shark!" Savvy Harold Gatty also regarded the plane favorably and predicted it would win the race, if the engine did not fail, because it was the fastest entry.[18]

Seeking an optimum altitude for speed and fuel consumption, Royal in the rear cockpit and Wesley in the front cockpit on September 24 finally test flew the Gamma, now powered by a Conqueror engine with a Curtiss-Wright supercharger. At altitudes up to 20,000 feet, the engine emitted smoke and flames. Royal and Wesley inhaled gas fumes and worried about a fire. An engine change was essential. Jackie's attorney, Mabel Willebrandt, former U.S. Assistant Attorney General in charge of nationwide enforcement of Federal Prohibition laws, persuaded the London race committee to approve the substitution of a standard Conqueror engine for the Conqueror with the Curtiss-Wright supercharger. On September 29, a U.S. Department of Commerce inspector cleared the aircraft for racing.

Four days before their passenger ship was scheduled to depart New York City for England, Jackie, at the Gamma rear cockpit controls, and Royal, in the front cockpit, took off from Los Angeles Municipal Airport. They planned to make a practice run along the TWA mail route to Kansas City, where Wesley would replace Royal and continue to the east coast.

"My better judgment told me not to take off with that motor," Royal remembered. "It still was not running right when we were ready to take off.... The motor was still throwing too much flame from the exhaust stacks. I guess everyone thought we must have been on fire because the flames were shooting way back and playing over the tail, and the occasional shower of sparks gave us the resemblance of a giant rocket. However, the motor sounded very nicely, so I headed east. Under any other circumstances, I think that I should have landed again, but I was not too keen on landing during the dark. I was practically a stranger to that plane, and I had never flown it from the front cockpit before."

Over Kingman, Arizona, Royal told Jackie they were averaging over 250 miles per hour ground speed. "We'll win the race, all right!" she shouted. "No one can stop us now!"

Royal also felt optimistic and forgot his doubts about the motor. "There was just a little thrill to think that I was flying over my old mail route in this charging monster," he recalled. Royal imagined averaging 250 miles per hour and shattering the England-to-Australia six days, seventeen hours, and fifty-six minutes flight record.

A screeching noise interrupted Royal's reverie. The motor kept running but lost power and showered sparks. He tried switching the ignition but could not diagnose the problem, so he considered his options. The plane could not reach the Winslow (Arizona) Airport. They were flying over rugged, pine-tree–covered high terrain, so an emergency landing was impossible. Royal asked Jackie if she could jump, and she replied that she could not get on her parachute. Taking into account her predicament, the engine performance, the difficult terrain, and the distance to Winslow, Royal decided to try to land at the Ash Fork (Arizona) emergency field. "Wonder if I can land this thing?" Royal asked himself. "Gee, wish I had some landings in the daytime with this crate; gee, if I had only one landing, I would have an idea of how this thing lands. Nothing now but to do my best!"

As Royal descended, the motor slowed ominously. He worried about maintaining enough power to compensate for any error in his glide and practiced placing his hands on the landing flap and light switches. Unlike with the mail planes he had flown, Royal did not have enough experience flying the Gamma to operate its controls without looking at them. Even though the engine died, he made a successful landing.

The Ash Fork field attendant drove Royal and Jackie into town. She telephoned a Curtiss-Wright official, vehemently expressed her opinion about the engine, and arranged for factory mechanics and spare motor parts to be flown to Ash Fork. The mechanics replaced a disintegrated impeller and gearing and assured Royal that the Gamma would fly to at least New York City.[19]

Accompanied by mechanic D. C. Sneed, Royal flew to Albuquerque, New Mexico. When he tried to resume the flight, however, the starter gear stuck. Sneed quickly remedied this malfunction, and they headed east.

Shortly after midnight on October 2, Royal heard a loud "rock crusher" sound and ducked as a motor fragment zinged past his ear. Ahead, a glow loomed above Tucumcari, New Mexico. Although Royal could see the emergency field boundary lights, the Gamma could not fly that far. He did not want to bail out and abandon special race equipment. With the engine stalled, Royal decided to glide to a place he remembered from his mail flights east of Tucumcari and try to land. He dropped a flare and recognized the terrain.

"I was quite pleased with my good fortune," he recalled. "It was going to turn out all right after all. Maybe we could still be in the race."

Royal descended at minimum speed, clearing wire fences and ditches. As he started to touch down, more fences loomed in his left landing gear light. He pulled up the nose, slid the plane to the right, shoved down the nose, and hauled back on the stick just before the wheels touched down. He smashed into one ditch and then another.

"Gee," said Royal, "it seemed as though I could never stop it. Then we hit a fence. The wires stretched, and we seemed to stop all of a sudden. I can still hear that 'tszing!' as a fence post broke off and went sailing just over my head. I just had a fleeting glimpse of it as it passed through the gleam of the landing light. When we finally stopped, I was glad that helpless feeling was over. It gives a pilot such a helpless feeling to have to come down with the motor completely dead."

A sheriff, believing the plane's occupants had been killed, arrived on the scene. When he saw Royal and Sneed, he thought they were ghosts. The lawman extinguished a small ground fire and drove the lucky pilot and mechanic into town. Royal telephoned Jackie, who was in Chicago, and reported the latest setback, describing the damage as a bent left landing gear shock unit and a few fuselage dents.

"Why, you crazy fool," shouted Jackie, "you rode it down! Why didn't you jump out? You landed in country like that, and it isn't cracked up! If you had jumped, it would have been all smashed, and I would have been glad." Calming down, Jackie instructed Royal to call Jack Northrop and order replacement parts flown to Tucumcari.

Neither Royal or Sneed "would talk any at all," reported the *Tucumcari Daily News*, "saying they had orders not to discuss their landing, but the *Daily News* has learned that Leonard was given an honest-to-goodness bawling out from his superior in Chicago for not leaving the plane via the parachute route, they being 12,000 feet up when the engine went dead."

In better light the next morning, Royal discovered a sprung fuselage center section, which could not be repaired quickly. He telephoned Jackie, told her the bad news, and recommended she drop out of the race.

Jackie ignored his advice. She was the only American woman entry, and she owned another fast airplane. When Jackie had registered her Gamma in the race, she had allowed Clyde Pangborn, who, with Hugh Herndon, had made the first trans-Pacific nonstop flight, to enter her $23,065 ($370,000 in 2009 purchasing power) Granville Brothers Gee Bee, nicknamed *Q.E.D.*, with the understanding that he would relinquish the aircraft upon her request. Pangborn had not been able to obtain financial backing. Race officials quickly approved his nomination of Jackie as the *Q.E.D.* pilot and Royal and Wesley as copilots.

During the trans-Atlantic voyage, seasick mechanics were unable to complete the modification of the *Q.E.D.* for the long-distance race and had to finish their work in England. Hampered by mechanical difficulties, Wesley and Jackie were unable to make any extended practice flights. The day before the race started, Wesley landed with a thud and wobbled to a stop. Journalists nicknamed the plane HeebeeGeebee.

Royal, meanwhile, had traveled to Allahabad, 465 miles northwest of Calcutta, in north-central India. Maharajahs and other dignitaries had set up a small tent city on the airport edge and were awaiting the arrival of the world's best planes and pilots. Less-fortunate natives camped on any available space within a few miles of the airfield.

"As I looked out over this sea of humanity that had gathered so many days ahead of time," recalled Royal, "I wondered if it would not be a good thing for the aviation industry to have a race like this periodically. It could turn into a classic. Such an event every two years would be far reaching politically, as well as technically. The local airport had some wonderful improvements that never would have been completed had it not been for the race. Certain countries had let down their rigid bars to aviators for this race. After several of these events, they would find it to their advantage not to be so strict in their flying regulations. Everyone the world over becomes geography conscious. It certainly would do a lot to lessen international friction."

But there was a very real potential downside to flying Royal's part of the race. What would happen to a heavily loaded plane speeding at 250 miles per hour between Allahabad and Australia into heavy rain and pitch-black clouds 20,000 feet or higher? "Would the airscrew or the wings come off first?" wondered a British aviation writer. A year later, noted Australian aviator Charles Kingsford-Smith disappeared over the Bay of Bengal trying to set a world speed record.[20]

Shortly before the race starting time, Royal cabled the Cochran team in England and asked what type of radio had been installed in the *Q.E.D.*, as well as its call letters and frequencies. The response: "NO RADIO."

On October 20, Jackie and Wesley took off from the Royal Air Force Base at Mildenhall, fifty-five miles northeast of London. Trying to switch from an empty fuel tank to a full one, Jackie endured several terrifying moments before she realized that the "on" switches were incorrectly labeled "off," and vice versa. Approaching Bucharest, Romania, Wesley attempted to lower the wing flaps to decrease the plane's speed. The corroded stabilizer stuck. One flap went down, and the other stayed in place. With the plane wing-heavy and unbalanced, Wesley made two unsuccessful landing attempts. On the third try, both flaps went down. The *Q.E.D.* approached too fast, hit hard, and stopped just short of the runway end. Recognizing that they could not land the *Q.E.D.* on shorter fields and that the three days necessary for repairs eliminated any hope of winning a prize, Jackie reluctantly withdrew from the race. She would not need the services of a masseuse and cook waiting at a marquee tent in Darwin to freshen her for the dash to the Melbourne finish line.[21]

Englishmen C.W.A. Scott and Tom Campbell-Black won the MacRobertson race with a time of seventy hours, fifty-nine minutes, and fifty seconds. They reached Darwin in two days, four hours, and thirty-eight minutes, smashing the England–Australia record by four and a half days. When they refueled at Allahabad, Royal had closely inspected their specially designed de Havilland Comet. He did not know whether he would be brave enough to fly it because he thought the workmanship shoddy and wings too flexible. "Of course when comparing it with the Gee Bee, I could not have much to say," Royal commented, "but as I examined it I could not refrain from comparing it with our lamented Northrop. I thought, 'If only we could have had good luck with the Northrop, we could show these folks how real airplanes are built'.... A losing racer always likes to have just a little satisfaction about what he could have done if—!"

A *Western Flying* reporter empathized with Royal, stating that Miss Cochran had hired as copilots "two of the best airmail pilots in the United States," was "the most thorough" in race preparations, and "met with a good deal of tough luck." His future wife's day in the race of the century cost Floyd Odlum a couple million dollars in 2009 purchasing power.

Feeling betrayed by Lady Luck, Royal returned to England on a Dutch KLM airline passenger plane and met with Floyd Odlum. Jackie cabled Odlum's London business agent: "Satisfactory Leonard Wait Over But I Plan Sail Secretly... And Probably Better We Not On Same Boat."

But Odlum had a job for Royal. Pan American Airways was attempting to obtain the U.S. rights to a trans-Atlantic passenger service through the Azores Islands, a Portuguese archipelago about 930 miles west of Lisbon and 2400 miles east of the North American coast. Odlum wanted to beat Pan Am to the punch. On his behalf, Royal visited the Azores and investigated potential landing sites. Eventually, the Portuguese government granted exclusive Azores landing rights to a French airline and Odlum abandoned his idea of starting a trans-Atlantic airline.

By the time Royal set foot on U.S. soil in late January 1935, Florence Suddarth had given birth, named the child Royale Regina Leonard, and listed Royal as father on the birth certificate. Ignoring the assurance of an extension given to Royal by western division superintendent Paul Richter, TWA president Jack Frye ordered recently named chief pilot Harlan Hull to obtain Royal's resignation on the ground that he had overstayed his leave of absence. The underlying reasons for Royal's termination, however, were resisting executive secretary Suddarth's pleas and Frye's pressure to marry her, rebuffing Frye's demand to help arrange financial backing from Floyd Odlum for Frye's MacRobertson Race entry, and fighting as an ALPA officer for safer mail planes.

Royal was too principled to win in the company politics game, but another racing opportunity awaited him.[22]

Chapter 4

DEATH RACE

(February – November 1935)

Royal Leonard and eight other "nationally known airplane pilots" vied for the $12,500 prize in the August 1935 Bendix Trophy Air Race between Burbank, California, and Cleveland, Ohio. This 2,046-mile competition was the Kentucky Derby of American aviation distance racing; there was no comparable event like the Preakness or Belmont Stakes in horse racing. The *Los Angeles Times* described the Bendix Race as "America's testing laboratory for advanced ideas in airplane designs and speed." Cutting-edge aircraft testing, which today is conducted by manufacturer and military pilots, was performed in the mid-1930s by race and airline pilots shaking out bugs and hoping for the best along race courses and mail routes. The Bendix Race demanded the utmost from competitors in flight planning and meteorology and from aircraft in design, durability, and speed.

In exchange for tutoring her in flying the Gamma 2D, Jackie Cochran permitted Royal to enter the *Q.E.D.* in the Bendix Race. Royal thought the *Q.E.D.* looked "like a big green elephant with big ears." Aviation historian Charles A. Mendenhall states that "*Q.E.D.*" is an abbreviation of the Latin term *Quad Erat Demonstrandum*, meaning "It is proven." The plane's designers defined *Q.E.D.* as "quite easily done."

Originally painted Lucky Strike green because glamorous Jackie Cochran graced American Tobacco Company advertisements, the teardrop–shaped plane was powered by a 675-horsepower Pratt and Whitney R-1690 Hornet radial engine capable of reaching 295 miles per hour. Two guy wires helped attach each half-wing to the fuselage. A small door in the sixty-one–inch diameter flying bomb provided an escape hatch from its enclosed tandem cockpit. The *Q.E.D.* was designed for speed, not safety.

The Granville Brothers Gee Bees were nicknamed "Widow Makers." Acknowledging their reputation, Don Dwiggins entitled a book chapter "The Gee Bees—Born to Kill." By 1935, three pilots had already died in the six Gee Bee racers. Lowell R. Bayles, attempting a world speed record, had perished in Gee Bee Model Z when its right wing folded off; Russell Boardman, taking off in the 1933 Bendix Race, had expired in the R-1 when it rolled into the ground; and Florence Klingsmith had lost her life during the 1933 Phillips Trophy Race when part of the Model Y wing fabric tore off.

After world speed record holder Jimmy Doolittle won the 1932 Thompson Race in the R-1, another pilot inquired how the plane handled. "Don't ask me," Doolittle replied, "I never did fly that wild son of a bitch." Calling the R-l the most unforgiving airplane he had flown in his highly successful career and believing he had exhausted his share of luck, Doolittle retired from racing.[23]

Before risking his life in the *Q.E.D.*, Royal dealt with a personal problem. Florence Suddarth had filed a paternity suit for $150 monthly in child support, a potential $37,800 total liability ($591,000 in 2009 dollar purchasing power). Described by the *Los Angeles Times* as the "romantic airport affair between Mrs. Florence Suddarth, blonde secretary to the president of an airline, and Royal Leonard, crack pilot of the line and entry in the recent London-Melbourne air dash," the trial commenced on August 2, 1935, before Judge Fletcher Bowron. Unfortunately, Royal waived a jury trial. A panel of peers may have been more sympathetic to a boyish-looking pilot and less enamored of a scheming older woman than the judge.

It is my conclusion that Mrs. Suddarth, who was married to an elderly retired army officer, did not meet the burden of proof in establishing paternity because the evidence clearly showed she and Royal did not have intercourse during the conception period. Florence testified that she and Royal had slept together in Kansas City on March 21 and March 26, 1934. Royal's logbook, which was admitted into evidence, showed that he was in Kansas City on March 21, but not March 26. An impressive witness, TWA chief engineer Herbert Hoover, Jr., the former president's son, vouched that he had accompanied Royal all day and night on March 21 and never left him alone with Florence. A letter was introduced into evidence from Florence to Royal indicating no contact between them during his February vacation or his March 12 through April 17 furlough. Royal thought that the child was "a perfect image" of Jack Frye, but the boss cagily stayed away from the courtroom.

Ending a four-and-a-half-day trial thoroughly covered by Los Angeles newspapers and the Associated Press, Judge Bowron, swayed by Mrs. Suddarth's testimony, decided against Royal and ordered him to pay fifty dollars ($781 in 2009 purchasing power) in monthly child support.[24]

After the trial concluded, Royal traveled to New York City and prepared to fly the *Q.E.D.* to Burbank—not a "quite easily done" task. Since Jackie and Wesley Smith's MacRobertson Race mishap, the Granville Bothers factory pilot, taking Chilean Air Force officers for a demonstration ride, had made a crash landing in the *Q.E.D.* When Royal climbed into the cockpit, nobody was available to instruct him on the plane's idiosyncrasies. There was not even a logbook that might indicate potential mechanical problems. His predicament was more precarious than that of a test pilot, who at least could review engineering data before making his first flight in an aircraft. Royal would have to fly by his wits.

"The fact that I had not even flown the Gee Bee did not seem to matter," commented Royal. "I still did not know whether or not I could fly the Gee Bee. And to think that I refused to fly it in the [MacRobertson] race when I first signed the contract because I thought it would be too dangerous to fly! Its smaller brothers had a bad reputation of killing pilots for no reason at all. They landed fast and were tricky to handle. Could I expect this one to be so much different from the others?"

Feeling like he was walking behind a vicious mule, Royal started the *Q.E.D* down the runway, intending to throttle back when he reached forty miles an hour. He eased on the throttle, but the plane leapt, felt like it hit a bump, and jumped airborne, so he practiced stalls, vertical banks, and dives for an hour. Realizing that the *Q.E.D.* would land fast, Royal decided to err on the side of caution and make several passes at the field, touching the wheels on the ground each time. The plane handled well on the first approach, so he decided to land. Much to his consternation, however, at the end of its roll, the wheels and tailskid bounced like a bucking elephant.

Striving to master the HeebeeGeebee's peculiarities, Royal practiced takeoffs and landings. He had flown many planes with extremely sensitive controls, but none as touchy as this one. He could not remove his feet from the rudder pedals more than a second without the tail whipping like a flag in a strong wind.

Feeling none too confident, Royal headed for the west coast. Two hours after taking off, he dropped a map on the cockpit floor. He could not retrieve it without taking his foot off the left rudder pedal. As his hand touched the map, he kicked the pedal and heard an explosive ripping sound. An object hit him in the head.

Blinded by dust, Royal had no idea what had happened. He feared that the *Q.E.D.*, which was flying on its side, was breaking apart. After he righted the plane and got it under control, he noticed that the cockpit hatch cover had ripped off and surmised that a corner had struck him.

Seated in an open cockpit, Royal landed at Kansas City. A mechanic found several broken exhaust pipe pieces in the oil-soaked engine cowling through which gas fumes blew. Royal thanked his lucky stars that the plane had not caught fire in the air.

The next morning, Royal continued west. He flew blind through torrential rains in eastern Colorado and New Mexico. Lightning struck the plane, and he felt shocks through his left hand resting on the throttle. He thought he heard a clap of thunder and felt a violent bump.

Approaching Burbank Airport, Royal realized his landing speed would be too fast. He decided to roll his wheels on the ground before going around for another try. When he crossed the edge of the field, however, the motor sputtered and stopped. He checked the gas pressure indicator, which "was dead," worked the wobble pump supplying fuel to the carburetor, and started the motor. Every time he stopped pumping, however, the motor sputtered and died. His landing speed was too fast, and he did not cherish riding out a forced landing, but he was too close to the ground to do anything else if the motor stopped. The plane acted like it was out of fuel, but he was sure that the tank held at least forty gallons. Then the motor quit.

As he started to land cross wind, Royal spotted another plane taking off, and his heart jumped into his mouth. He was afraid that the aircraft would collide in the middle of the field, but he was helpless to avoid a crash. He had to make believe he had the field all to himself and concentrate on making a good landing because he could not go around if he miscalculated. A fraction of a second before the *Q.E.D.* crossed the runway intersection, the other plane passed a few feet above him.

After he landed, Royal climbed from the cockpit and looked at his plane. What he saw left him speechless. Most of the lower cowling had blown away. A wire holding a half wing to the fuselage had broken. If the other wire had snapped, the half wing would have torn off in the air. He realized that what he had thought was a clap of thunder had been the sound of the wire breaking. "Lady Luck was still sitting on my shoulder!" Royal exclaimed. Mechanics told him the motor had sputtered because the fuel line was choked with whitish sediment. They worked around the clock to get the *Q.E.D.* race ready. "They found so many things wrong," said Royal, "that I began to marvel at the fact that I was able to get it to the west coast at all."[25]

Unlike Royal, the other Bendix Race Gee Bee entrant, thirty-year-old appliance salesman Cecil Allen, was not an exceptional pilot. Backed by the mysterious "Mrs. C.L.D." and her "Youth Division of the Religious Policy Association," Allen had purchased the Gee Bee designated R-1/R-2 and named it *Spirit of Right.* His plane was a composite of the R-1 in which Jimmy Doolittle had won the 1932 Thompson Race and in which Russell Boardman had crashed and died, and the R-2, in which Russell Thaw had cracked up during the 1934 Bendix Race. Factory mechanics had repaired the R-1 fuselage, attached the R-2 wings, added a conventional tail, and substituted a tailskid for the tail wheel. Allen foolishly modified his hybrid aircraft, compounding its aerodynamic shortcomings. He enlarged the cockpit canopy and increased the fuel capacity, which adversely affected the center of gravity. Observers called the *Spirit* "a murder ship." In the days preceding the race, mechanical problems prevented Allen from testing his plane's mettle. When he finally was able to fly it, Allen overshot the Burbank field three times before landing.

"None of us were ready," said Royal, "and I doubt if there will ever be a similar race where everyone will be ready." He preferred finishing the fine-tuning of his plane a week before the race and going fishing rather than struggling with last-minute adjustments. But he wanted to win the race more than anything else in life.

Howard Hughes, however, knew that his mysterious sardine-shaped, $120,000 ($1,880,000 in 2009 purchasing power) H-1 Racer was not ready. His plane had gear problems. "It's too expensive a ship to take a chance with until we get further along with tests," Howard told reporters, explaining his withdrawal from the race.

Ready or not, Royal, Cecil Allen, Jackie Cochran, and six other competitors attended the midnight race weather conference on August 29, 1935, in Union Air Terminal. Although thick fog blanketed the Los Angeles area, the U.S. Weather Bureau forecasted clearing skies along the race route.[26]

"The drama of the scene was intense" as "nine bullet-nosed" planes looking "ghostly across the fog covered field" waited "for a break in the ceiling." At 12:54 a.m., Amelia Earhart, first woman to fly solo across the Atlantic, took off in a Lockheed Vega. Her copilot, Paul Mantz, wrote his race predictions on a piece of paper and handed it to her. Roscoe Turner, two-time Thompson Race winner and MacRobertson Race third-place finisher, growled that somebody was going to get killed if everybody took off in foggy conditions.

Fog did not intimidate blind-flying expert Royal Leonard. "Gee," said one of the ground crew as Royal climbed into the *Q.E.D.* cockpit, "I hope some of these other fellows don't get excited and want to take off too when they see you have gone. Some of them don't know a thing about weather or blind flying. If they try what you are going to do, someone will get killed, if I don't miss my guess."

Although Royal could see halfway across the field, there was almost no ceiling. He requested a red flare placed at the end of the runway as a direction guide, taxied to the starting line, stopped, gunned his engine, throttled back, and indicated he was ready. The starter swung down his flashlight at 3:42 a.m., and Royal carefully proceeded down the runway, lifted off, flew blind, and started battling the *Q.E.D.*'s chronic instability. If he momentarily removed his hand from the stick, the plane leaned into a vertical bank because the replacement half wing wire had not been rigged properly.

As Royal sped eastward, Cecil Allen careened down the runway in the *Spirit of Right*. A leaky fuel tank had delayed his takeoff. His mother, sensing a premonition of death, begged him not to fly. His sister, who had not seen him in twenty-six years, was waiting at Wichita, Kansas, in case he refueled there. The *Spirit* was extremely difficult to handle, especially with a heavy fuel load. Less than two minutes after taking off, Allen's plane crashed in a potato field, blasting a hole six feet deep. Allen was decapitated.

Royal, not Allen, refueled at Wichita before 10,000 spectators. A quarter hour after he left the Municipal Airport, oil splattered on his windshield and smoke billowed from the motor. Worried about a fire,

Royal stuck his head out the cockpit for a closer look, and oil splashed over his face. "You crazy nut," he muttered, "you should have known better than that!" He wiped his goggles, but smoke still obstructed his view. He turned back to Wichita. He considered dumping fuel and making an emergency landing but then remembered that the 275-gallon main fuel tank dump valve had been sealed to prevent leaking. If he crash landed with a full fuel load, Royal realized, he would probably burn to death.

Feeling extremely tired, hungry, and not eager for a long hike, Royal pondered making his first parachute jump. He played with the controls and, at minimum power, kept the engine from stalling or smoking excessively. He decided not to bail out.

Approaching the Wichita airport, motor smoke and his oil-smeared goggles impaired Royal's vision. If he held his head back against the headrest, however, he could see the runway. When close to the ground, he could only guess how high he was above it. Oil spurted from under the engine cowling. He gunned his sputtering engine a couple of times and made a pretty three-point landing.

Climbing from his oil-splattered ship, Royal showed mechanics a broken oil line. He said the plane had lost oil pressure and a couple of rods. The twenty-eight–gallon oil tank was less than half full, and the broken main bearing lay like wheat chaff in the oil sump that collected crankcase drainage.

As Royal thanked the fire gods for sparing him, Benny Howard, a United Air Lines pilot, crossed the Cleveland finish line in his self-designed *Mr. Mulligan* in eight hours, thirty-three minutes, and 16.3 seconds, only 23.5 seconds faster than second-place finisher Roscoe Turner in a Wedell-Williams racer—the closest finish in Bendix Race history.

Finishing fifth, Amelia Earhart taxied to a stop and looked at Paul Mantz's handicap card. He had correctly predicted Howard as the winner, followed by Turner, Russell Thaw in a Northrop Gamma, and Roy Hunt in a Lockheed Orion. Jackie Cochran had dropped out early in the race with an overheated and excessively vibrating engine. After Cecil Allen's name, Mantz had doodled a black wreath. Flying a bastardized Gee Bee had demanded too much of an appliance salesman.

In an editorial titled "Tragedy and Rain," the *Cleveland Plain Dealer* commented: "Allen's tragic death adds his name to the many others who risked their lives in this most exciting of sports, and lost. It does not, however, dampen enthusiasm for flying or discourage others from engaging in it. Others take up the work he was doing, and the development of the industry will not be checked."

Returning to Los Angeles, Royal gazed from a train window and mused about Old Man Jinx and Lady Luck. "Was it 'Old Man Jinx' that was causing me all this grief and trouble," he wondered, "or was it 'Lady Luck' that always saved me when disaster struck?"

Barely two weeks later, on Friday, September 13, Howard Hughes set a 352.58-mile per hour world speed record in the H-1 but crashed in an attempt to improve the mark when his auxiliary fuel tank would not activate.

Four years later, Mexican pilot Francisco Sarabia would crash and die in the *Q.E.D.* Final score: six Gee Bees and five dead pilots.[27]

Convinced that Judge Bowron's paternity judgment was wrong, Royal decided to appeal. Herbert Hoover, Jr., found Royal another attorney, who filed a motion to reopen the case and submitted two affidavits as newly discovered evidence. L.T. Riley averred that Suddarth had tried to blackmail him into marrying her by claiming Riley got her pregnant; she denied the allegation. A medical expert opined that only a twenty-five percent probability of conclusively proving non-paternity was possible using available test methodology. On November 15, 1935, Judge Bowron denied the motion and affirmed the paternity decision.

This miscarriage of justice paid unexpected dividends. Enclosing the final support check four years later following the child's premature death from congenital heart disease, Royal asked his attorney to tell Suddarth that he extended his "thanks for all the things she has done for me.... Were it not for her I would never have gone to the places I did in China, done the things which I did, saw the things I did nor would I have had the experiences I have had. I would not care to do them again, but I wouldn't take a million dollars for the experiences I have had in China. Yes, tell her that thanks to her, as far as experiences are concerned, I am a millionaire."[28]

Louis and Bertha Leonard with baby Alice and Royal behind Morris in Waco, Texas, about 1913. *(Frank Evans)*

Teenager Royal Leonard, a cautious daredevil, taught himself to walk a wire. *(John Korompilas)*

Inventive Royal replaced his front motorcycle wheel with a ski for Wisconsin winter. *(John Korompilas)*

The Brooks Field School of Aviation Medicine subjected cadets to the diabolical Ruggles Orientator to evaluate flying aptitude. *(John Korompilas)*

Possibly the first two-plane–car accident occurred at the "West Point of the Air" in San Antonio, Texas. *(John Korompilas)*

Army Air Corps Cadet Leonard was third in his class to solo in a PT-1 biplane at Brooks Field. *(John Korompilas)*

Royal (lower right) was leader of the elite 43rd Pursuit (fighter) Squadron, Kelly Field, Texas, 1928. *(John Korompilas)*

Royal flew a Stearman C3-B for Western Air Express on CAM-12 along the Rocky Mountains. *(John Korompilas)*

Royal pioneered celestial navigation on U.S. commercial passenger flights. *(John Korompilas)*

Royal believed the Lockheed Orion cockpit configuration with the engine switches near the pilot's elbow may have caused the Wiley Post–Will Rogers crash. *(Author's Collection).*

Royal in "77" and Cecil Allen in R1/R2 flew Gee Bee's in the 1935 Bendix Trophy Race. *(Painting by John Amendola)*

Chapter 5

CHINA: HE COVERED THE WHOLE LAND

(December 1935 – November 1936)

In late 1935, Royal was not yet a millionaire in experiences. Old Man Jinx still haunted his life. His aircraft factory job paid only a few dollars more per month than his court-ordered child support payment. But then Lady Luck intervened. His Brooks and Kelly Field classmate Julius Barr cabled: "WOULD YOU LIKE TO FLY FOR CHINA?"

Royal suspected the offer might be a hoax because Julius had a reputation as a practical joker. A Kelly Field yearbook editor had noted, "Don't anyone tell Julie a new stunt—he'll probably try to do it." In China, passenger Chiang Kai-shek asked Barr why their flight was so rough. Julius explained that turbulence affected the regular airways "because the air has holes poked in it from aero planes." Chiang responded that Julius was "full of seaweed."

After cabling Julius several times, Royal learned that his friend was overworked as a warlord's personal pilot and a flying school operator, could not do both jobs adequately, and needed help. Royal accepted a position as assistant pilot and flight instructor for $1,000 monthly ($15,600 in 2009 purchasing power); U.S. airline pilots were averaging $541 monthly.

In early November 1935, Royal sailed from San Francisco on a Dollar Steamship Lines passenger vessel. "Had a pearl diver just extricated himself from the tentacles of an octopus," Royal ruminated, "he would have shared my feelings as I watched the coast of America fade into the horizon. I didn't know what kind of flying I would do in China nor did I know where I would live. Foolish as it may sound … I even reflected on the possibilities of having a beautiful Chinese princess for my wife…."

When the ship docked at Yokohama, Japanese customs officials noticed that Royal's passport identified his occupation as "Flyer." They questioned him politely, but thoroughly, about whether he was a civil or military aviator. He concealed the mercenary nature of his work. "I told them 'Civil,'" said Royal. "This was not exactly true, but it got me through."[29]

Royal arrived in a China writhing in the tentacles of Japanese invaders and torn by civil war between the Nationalists and the Communists. Military dictator Chiang Kai-shek's Nationalist government with its capital in Nanking controlled most of the fragmented country. The Japanese occupied Manchuria and manipulated puppet governments in five northern Chinese provinces, and the Soviet Union dominated Sinkiang province in western China. In the Northwest and Southwest, warlords ruled three provinces. In Shanghai, gangster Tu Yueh-sen controlled the municipal government and the United States, Great Britain, Japan, and France governed International Settlement sections and the French Concession. Despite university student demonstrations demanding expulsion of the Japanese invaders, Chiang Kai-shek was determined to destroy 30,000 Chinese Communist Party (CCP) troops who had recently completed their "Long March" to northwestern Shensi province and were setting up a base area for receiving materiel assistance from the Soviet Union.

China's Nationalist leadership desperately needed skilled pilots for air transportation because the immense country lacked modern railways and highways. A 585-mile Shanghai–Hankow trip took three days in a Yangtze River boat or three hours in a plane. After completion of the Burma Road in 1938, the 720-mile trip from Kunming to Lashio, Burma, took three hours by air or seven days, if all went well, by motor vehicle. Air travel enabled Chiang Kai-shek and his subordinates to journey to remote parts of China, establish personal contact with local officials, and resolve problems difficult to solve through slow correspondence, "so it is safe to say," explained coauthors Chiang and Madame Kai-shek, "that the airplane has been one of the greatest factors in facilitating the unity that China now enjoys."[30]

For the next six years, Royal's primary role would be to transport Nationalist leaders and foreign dignitaries between transitory Chinese capitals, interior China hot spots, and the British Crown Colony of Hong Kong. Royal would not only become personal pilot for Chiang Kai-shek but would also fly and befriend members of the Soong Dynasty—the U.S.-educated children of Shanghai financier Charlie Soong, who had backed Chiang Kai-shek's rise to power. The youngest Soong daughter, May-ling, married Chiang, and the middle daughter, Ching-ling, wed Sun Yat-sen, the founder of modern China. Chiang appointed their brother T.V. Soong, as well as H.H. Kung, husband of the oldest Soong daughter, Ailing, to important ministerial and diplomatic posts. Royal called the Soong Dynasty members "the big bugs of China."

Royal's employer, the thirty-seven–year-old "Young Marshal," Chang Hseuh-liang, was the most powerful warlord in northern China. His father, Chang Tso Lin, the "Old Marshal," had been dictator of Manchuria. The Young Marshal had graduated from a Manchurian military academy, observed army maneuvers in Japan, and implemented reforms in the Manchurian Army. As Director of Aviation, the Young Marshal planned a commercial airline network and oversaw the construction of modern airfields. In June 1928, Japanese operatives had assassinated the Old Marshal. Inheriting power from his father, the Young Marshal had ordered the execution of two Chinese generals he believed were implicated in the assassination.

After the Young Marshal allied with the Nationalist Government, Chiang Kai-shek appointed him commander in chief of the 400,000-man Northeastern Border Defense Army opposing Russian and Japanese forces. When the Japanese invaded Manchuria in 1931, the Young Marshal swallowed his desire to resist, grudgingly obeyed an order from Chiang Kai-shek, who naively believed that the League of Nations would force Japan to evacuate Manchuria, and led his 130,000-man army west into Shensi province. Addicted to opium, the Young Marshal underwent a cure in a Shanghai hospital and recuperated for several months in Europe. Upon the Young Marshal's return to China in early 1934, Chiang appointed him Nationalist Northwest Bandit (Communist) Suppression Headquarters commander.

"My first impression of the Young Marshal," said Royal, "was that here was the president of a Rotary Club: rotund, prosperous, with an easy, affable manner. His twinkling black eyes were the most prominent feature of his round, open countenance. We were friends in five minutes."

American journalist Helen Snow concurred in this evaluation, describing the Young Marshal as boyish, husky, and athletic with an easygoing manner and a man that westerners liked immediately because he seemed intelligent, competent, honest, generous, modern-minded, and democratic in outlook. Realizing that Manchuria, rich in industrial and natural resources, could not stand alone between the Soviet Union and Japan, the Young Marshal was a strong Chinese patriot but was also ambitious for personal power.[31]

In their first meeting at Sian, the capital of Shensi province and the eastern terminus of the ancient Central Asian Silk Road, the Young Marshal warned Royal in fairly good English that the Communists might torture him if he were captured. The Young Marshal explained that the Communists seated prisoners on sharp-edged crosspieces of sawhorses and tied weights on their feet, slitting their groins and causing excruciatingly painful deaths. He also said that they tied victims in chairs with hands behind them, sliced open the backs of their necks, and poured in mercury, slowly separating skin and flesh.

Duly warned about his job risks, Royal visited the Sian airport and inspected the Young Marshal's prize plane—a Boeing 247D. Unable to pronounce the manufacturer's name, Chinese peasants called the plane *Bai Ying*, meaning White Eagle, though the plane's anodized aluminum skin was grayish. Powered by supercharged 550-horsepower Pratt and Whitney Wasp twin engines, the Boeing could reach a maximum speed of 200 miles per hour, stay aloft six and a half hours, and carry two crewmembers, six passengers, and a 2,582-pound payload.

As Royal's first assignment, the Young Marshal ordered him to assist Julius Barr in airlifting supplies to Kanchuan, a strategically important walled village under Communist siege about 150 miles north of Sian. After a few flights, Royal replaced Barr in the B-247D cockpit and daily dropped bread bags, ammunition, clothing, and money to the garrison. When the plane dove to 500 feet above ground level, Communist soldiers shot at it. A bullet nicked a control cable, cutting two strands, another bullet passed through an engine, barely missing the carburetor, and others almost hit the fuel tanks. "No more bullet holes in the plane," ordered the Young Marshal. "Go very high. If the bags all fall out, no matter. Come back and get another load, but no more bullet holes." Unable to tolerate more damage to his precious Boeing 247D, the Young Marshal ordered Royal to stop flying to Kanchuan and assigned Chinese pilots in other planes to the mission. They, however, failed miserably, and the Young Marshal then directed Royal to resume the supply flights.

Beginning in mid-February 1936, Royal flew almost every day to Kanchuan. The Communists had been driven back several miles from the village, eliminating the danger from rifle fire. To Royal, who referred to his job as "aerial truck man," the flights were "as monotonous as living on a farm and hauling potatoes to market." To relieve the boredom, he buzzed Communist communities. "Sometimes," he said, "we would sneak up on Communist villages with motors throttled back and then dive under full power, putting the propellers in low pitch to make a penetrating noise. The Communists would run frantically, forgetting to shoot. They would bump into one another, knock one another down, get up again, and run into one another again."

In a four-day period, Royal delivered twenty tons of supplies to Kanchuan and nearby villages. The recipients of this largesse were very appreciative. Manchurian Army officers marched unexpectedly into his Sian residence and presented Royal a silver cup engraved with his name. The interpreter explained that "Leonard" was synonymous with "forest" in Chinese and he deserved this name because he "*covered the whole land*" [emphasis added].[32]

After completing the Kanchuan assignment in early March 1936, Royal flew a variety of missions. Flying conditions were not up to American standards. Weather reports were unavailable and maps inadequate. To determine wind direction, Royal buzzed sheep and watched which way the dust blew. Based on his celestial navigation calculations, Royal located Sian ten miles east of its placement on his best map. City names varied with dynastic changes, and English and German maps designated cities differently.

Before taking off, Royal and his passengers compared maps and pronounced the destination name every possible way until reaching a compromise. Even if they agreed on a city name, they might not know the direction or distance to it. In this situation, Royal telephoned Mr. Li, the Young Marshal's highly efficient transportation secretary:

Royal: Where Kujuan?

Li: No know.

Royal: North, south, east, west?

Li: You find.

Royal: Ask somebody.

Li: Nobody here.

Royal: Ask Young Marshal.

Li: Not here. Nobody here.

Li would hang up, and Royal "would be left to guess [his] way through the wild, unfathomed air of central China."

"It was almost like hunting for a raft out on the ocean someplace," Royal said. "I would pore over the maps, trying to find a name that sounded like the place the Young Marshal had mentioned. Sometimes the missionaries helped me, but on many occasions I hopped off, just hoping I had guessed right and with no more assurance than that hope."

Sandstorms on Gobi Desert flights often obscured Royal's vision. Unable to fly above a maelstrom at fifteen thousand feet, he flew blind at one thousand feet through thick dust sticking to the cockpit windshield like brown sandpaper. His experience as a Kelly Field cadet relying on a compass flying across uniform Southwest Texas terrain stood him in good stead. "It was impossible to fly by landmarks," he said, "and without a drift indicator in the Boeing I could only dead-reckon where I was heading. Though I never carried a lucky charm, I always felt the good right hand of Providence on my shoulder when I finally arrived home safely."

In rough flying conditions, Royal could not take his hands off the controls and write down course changes. "Over and over to myself," he said, "I sang my compass courses and the number of minutes I traveled on each and committed these to memory in the same manner that I would have memorized an epic poem. Ninety-five degrees, five minutes—fifty-three degrees, two and one half minutes—one hundred and seventy degrees, four minutes. That was the litany I said to myself during most of these flights."

Flying over Mongolia presented a special problem. "It looks just like the waves on the ocean," Royal said, "the same shape and so forth, and in their troughs would be an occasional pool of water." Maps did not accurately show the few small rivers that continually changed courses with shifts in the sand. To land on sand dunes, Royal perfected the "Leonard special seesaw landing," following the dune contours down with the tail on an upgrade and the nose on a downgrade.

Leery of torture if he made an emergency landing in Communist territory, Royal carried two Thompson submachine guns. In friendly regions, curious guards liked to probe the *Bai Ying* fuselage with their bayonets. They also blew up the nose opening for the metal tube connected to the air speed indicator. Fearing they would damage the instrument, Royal kept the heating element hot. "After a few Chinese had burned their lips they learned to keep away from it," remembered Royal. "But the air-speed indicator—what made it hot and kept it hot—was ever after a great source of philosophical discussion among the Chinese peasants."

In March 1936, Royal, using inaccurate Chinese and sketchy British maps and relying on instinct and dead reckoning, made the most adventurous flight of his career—the first military aerial reconnaissance over northeastern Tibet. "It was a world of steel-blue sky above and a black, desolate land underneath," he wrote. If the *Bai Ying* engines had conked out, he would not have been able to make an emergency landing because he never saw a level place where he could set down.[33]

During April and early May, the Young Marshal loaned Royal and the Boeing 247D to forty-eight–year-old Chiang Kai-shek, the "number one man of China." While attending a military school in Tokyo, Chiang had met Sun Yat-sen. Chiang had participated in the 1911 revolt against the Manchu Dynasty and in 1924 was appointed commandant of the Whampoa Military Academy. After Sun Yat-sen's death in 1925, Chiang had been named National Revolutionary Army commander in chief. In 1929, Chiang had become head of the Nationalist government. Notwithstanding Kuomintang (KMT) political party and Nationalist government organization charts, Chiang Kai-shek embodied the party and government, and, in his mind, the nation. During World War II, he held eighty-two official positions, most importantly Supreme National Military Council chairman, but also government president; party chief executive; and army, navy, and air forces commander.

Often referred to as the "Generalissimo" (meaning commander in chief and sometimes shortened to "Gimo"), Chiang Kai-shek possessed several planes, including American Ford "Flying Washboard" Tri-Motors and Italian Capronis but disliked their aerobatically inclined Chinese pilots and preferred riding in the comparatively quiet Boeing 247D. "He was a small, ascetic-faced man," noted Royal, "with a shaven head and diffident manners, who might have passed for an Episcopalian minister or a Y.M.C.A. secretary. The Generalissimo rarely talked, his orders being transmitted through his staff. Even to them he was monosyllabic, with his conversation consisting largely of 'Yes' and 'No.'"[34]

After resuming reconnaissance flights for the Young Marshal, Royal in mid-October 1936 flew to a mysterious city. The Young Marshal pointed on his map to a spot in Mongolia north of Yulin.

Royal's chart "showed a large blank space between longitude and latitude." When Royal looked down where the Young Marshal's map indicated a camel trail, he saw several tracks headed in different directions. The Young Marshal confessed that he had been lost for a long time. As Royal decided to turn back, the Young Marshal jumped up and down and pointed ahead. "I looked," said Royal, "and on the horizon was a city which seemed weirdly out of place in these barren, wind-swept wastes of sand. It was composed of great buildings covered with beautiful green tile, shimmering like the fabulous Emerald City of Oz in the afternoon sun. It still seems like a dream." They circled the city towers several times, but the Young Marshal did not want to land nor reveal the city name. Royal never saw this magical place again.[35]

In early November, the Young Marshal decided to find a Chinese Communist army trying to reach the Outer Mongolia border and pick up war materiel sent from the Soviet Union. The weather was poor, and Royal almost said they could not fly. Nevertheless, he took off in the Boeing 247D with the Young Marshal, four generals, and staff officers.

When they spotted a Manchurian Army detachment, the Young Marshal dropped a message, asking the Communists' location. Flinging themselves on the snow to form Chinese characters, the soldiers spelled "follow the road to the east." Heading that direction, Royal flew over Manchurian troops moving along the Yellow River east bank, hoping to encounter Red soldiers about seventy-five miles south of Ningsa. "The road for miles and miles was alive with men on the march," Royal recalled, "and from the air it resembled a long serpent come to life—crawling and worming its way along the road."

A heavy snowstorm forced Royal to turn back briefly, but the Young Marshal insisted on following another river. "It was a winding, playful path," stated Royal, "which, without warning, made reverse turns, hairpinned back and forth, then abandoned one valley to follow another, so that I soon lost it." He dodged several peaks and ridges. They flew over a walled village, and the Young Marshal asked its name. Royal circled, recounted his memorized headings, and suggested Tingyuanhsien. The Young Marshal disagreed and dropped a message. When the townspeople failed to respond, the Young Marshal realized that the plane was over enemy-controlled territory.

Despite rapidly approaching bad weather, the Young Marshal still wanted to hunt for the Communist army. Royal, however, convinced him to head for the closest airfield. He tried to follow the road to

Kuyuan, but the storm worsened, and visibility diminished. The road vanished, and a mountain loomed ahead. Royal swerved and missed it. He turned back, looked at his map, and noticed a river fork that might lead to Kuyuan. If he followed the river, he would not fly into a box canyon where he could not turn around nor vanish over a mountain ridge and disappear into clouds. He followed the river a few miles and suddenly came upon a Communist army column. The surprised troops, trying to run away, bumped into each other, lay down and tripped their comrades, fell prostrate in a little stream, and dived into caves. "It reminded me of a row of dominoes," stated Royal, "stretching out to the horizon, that the Boeing had pushed over."

The Boeing 247D flew over the Communist column, which Royal estimated as twenty thousand troops, until the Young Marshal ordered him to climb. "We no can do," Royal protested in Pidgin English.

"Must go more high," reiterated the excited Young Marshal. "Catch plenty bullets here."

"No matter if everybody shoot," replied Royal. "We go more high, we get in clouds." He pointed to snowflakes and cloud wisps obscuring their vision.

"No matter," insisted the Young Marshal. "Must go more high."

"Go more high more dangerous than bullets," argued Royal. "Get in clouds, no enough gasoline get down again. Maybe hit mountain."

"Stay low, they shoot us," pointed out the boss.

"Let them shoot us," said Royal sternly. "We no more go high."

The Young Marshal said nothing further but looked like he had received a death sentence.

The Boeing 247D flew mile after mile over the Communist column. The enemy troops stumbled and tripped in panic and tried to hide from the menacing war bird. Not one shot was fired.

As Royal flew beyond the column, he worried about losing sight of the winding river in the heavy snowfall. He dared not make a forced landing and risk his important passengers' capture and torture nor turn back and hazard drawing enemy fire. He could not safely fly into the clouds without a directional radio or beyond the storm without running out of fuel.

Where the river forked four ways, Royal circled, looked at his compass, and recalled his headings. Trusting instinct, he followed the branch he thought flowed south until, through swirling snowflakes, he saw the Kuyuan walls. He landed the plane on the airfield covered with six inches of fresh snow. "The Young Marshal was delighted with my aeronavigation," recalled Royal, "though at the time I hoped that my expression of blank surprise did not give me away."

The next day, Royal and the Young Marshal retraced their route and searched for the Red Army. They circled the maximum distance that the Communists could have marched in any direction but found no trace of them. Swooping close to mountainside caves, Royal saw "every entrance filled with peering, soil-stained faces." The Young Marshal dropped messages to his troops about the Communists' location. Later, Royal heard that the Manchurian Army fought the Communists in an inconclusive battle. "However, when I heard that news I knew that they were not annihilated," Royal commented. "I knew that many of them had suddenly turned into peaceful looking farmers, and others had simply scattered to be reunited again at a more opportune time. Such were the problems of fighting these wild communists."[36]

Less than a year had passed since Royal had arrived in the Orient. He had not found his Chinese princess and he yearned for sunny and clean California. He and Julius Barr were not getting along. Royal had received three job offers and believed he could earn almost as much money without dodging bullets. He was one of forty foreigners residing among half a million Chinese in Sian. Staying in an abandoned mission school building, he felt unsafe; a dining room wall tablet was dedicated to two workers and six students massacred by an infuriated mob. He knew from reading tombstones that most missionaries buried in Sian had died from typhus. At Lochwan, "a vermin-filled hole," he lived in a mud hut with a public latrine on an outside wall. He awoke with rats, half as large as house cats, crawling across his face and endured lizards, fleas, bed bugs, and lice. If he continued living like a hermit, Royal worried he would not know how to act among civilized people. He felt like "a political prisoner might have when cast into a Siberian dungeon. It was a feeling of despair, as if I had no other choice, as if I were doomed to live in those mud walls and mingle with the rats and bed bugs."[37]

But, in his own words, "one of the most sensational upheavals" in modern Chinese history changed Royal's attitude toward China and thrust him into a dizzy chain of historical events. Communist leader Chang Kuo-t'ao called it "the most dramatic event in modern Chinese history." John Gunther, best-selling American author of international affairs books, described it as "one of the most unusual dramas in history" and analogized it to "the sensation that would have been aroused" if the British prime minister had been kidnapped in a remote part of Ireland and held captive almost two weeks by opposition, third party, and Communist leaders and then rescued by his wife, foreign secretary, and an adviser "while the bigwigs of Westminster sent bombing planes to blow up everybody."[38]

Chapter 6

A KIDNAPPER'S PILOT

(December 1936)

Recalling his reconnaissance flights with the Young Marshal, Royal identified one event that portended a significant Chinese political upheaval. In the early fall of 1936, the Young Marshal fell seriously ill and his doctors urged him to enter a Shanghai hospital. His generals, however, refused to let him leave Shensi. "I wondered at the time just why they were so anxious to keep him there," Royal wrote. "They were certainly afraid of serious consequences if he left them and I have wondered since, whether that incident had [any] connection with the mutiny that took place a few months later."

Unknown to Royal, the Young Marshal had made a decision that would change the course of Chinese history and elevate him to the status of a national hero. Chiang Kai-shek was following a policy of internal pacification before resistance against external aggression. The Young Marshal advocated the opposite policy. He wanted Chiang to defeat the Japanese and then deal with the Communists. The Young Marshal hated the Japanese for assassinating his father and driving the Manchurian Army from its homeland. His soldiers disliked fighting other Chinese and wanted to take back Manchuria. And the Young Marshal realized that Chiang Kai-shek wanted the Manchurian and Communist Armies to weaken each other in battle and pave the way for a Nationalist Army occupation of Northwest China.

Royal did not know that the Young Marshal had been busy on two diplomatic fronts. During Royal's early spring assignment with the

Generalissimo, the Young Marshal and Chou En-lai, the Chinese Communist chief political strategist, met and secretly discussed an alliance against the Japanese. After Royal resumed flying for him, the Young Marshal surreptitiously met in Nanking and Shanghai with Soviet (Russian) agents and proposed that Stalin back him as the leader of China in a war against the Japanese. In an attempt to disguise these trips as playboy fun, the Young Marshal ordered Royal to fly in a vertical bank with one wing almost touching the street past Shanghai's Park Hotel where one of the Young Marshal's girlfriends was staying. "We passed within ten feet of the façade," said Royal, "the noise of the motor rattling the panes like castanets."

In late June 1936, the Young Marshal publicly advocated uniting the Manchurian, Communist, and Nationalist armies under Chiang Kai-shek's command. Late in July, Stalin, concerned about the Japanese military threat from Manchuria to his Far Eastern frontier, directed Mao Tse-tung and the Chinese Communists to stop fighting the Nationalists and, under Chiang Kai-shek's leadership, start resisting the Japanese.

Chiang Kai-shek, however, was determined to annihilate the Chinese Communists. On October 21, 1936, he arrived in Sian. His Blue Shirts, who were a blindly obedient, disciplined secret police and military force often compared to Hitler's Brown Shirt and Mussolini's Black Shirt thugs, were spying on the Young Marshal and Shensi warlord and Northwest Army commander Yang Hucheng, arresting their pro-Communist officers, and disrupting the Communist underground network in Sian. Chiang denounced the anti-Japanese united front concept and ordered the Young Marshal and Yang to attack the Communists. In reply, they urged him to end the civil war and resist the Japanese. Infuriated, Chiang flew to Loyang, 200 miles east of Sian, and began organizing an all-out attack on the Communists. He replaced the Young Marshal as Northwest Bandit Suppression Headquarters commander and deployed about thirty army divisions, one hundred airplanes, and a tank unit.

Confident that he would destroy the Red Army by the end of the year, Chiang Kai-shek returned to Sian on December 4. He again ordered the Young Marshal and Yang Hucheng to attack the Communists. If they disobeyed, Chiang threatened to transfer their armies elsewhere in China where his superior forces could easily destroy them. Having agreed on forming a united front and realizing that the larger Nationalist Army would crush their troops outside Shensi, the

Young Marshal and Yang decided to persuade Chiang, preferably through reasoning, but, if necessary, through force, to accept their point of view.

Convincing the Generalissimo to change his mind, however, was an almost impossible task. "Chiang Kai-shek was," observed Royal in his book, *I Flew for China*, "a formidably stubborn character. He wields the strongest power in China because he has the strongest face. And his face is strong simply because he is phenomenally strong-willed. The Generalissimo's ability to stick to what he believes right amounts almost to a mania, but it has been his salvation and that of his country."

Royal had firsthand experience with face. The Young Marshal had ordered him to fly to Taiyuan and pick up Shansi warlord Yen His-shan. His passenger made him wait three days. "Guess he thinks he was making face to have the chariot wait so long for him," commented Royal.[39]

On December 7, the Young Marshal visited Chiang Kai-shek at Lintun, a resort about twenty miles north of Sian, and urged him to abandon his Communist-extermination policy. "Even if you should level your gun at me to demand my life," exploded Chiang, "I would never change my plan for the suppression of the Communists.... [E]xcept in the Northwest and except for you, Chang Hseuh-liang, no one dares talk with me in the manner as you did and none dare criticize me. I am the Generalissimo; I do not err; I am China; and China cannot do well without me!"

Two days later, 15,000 students, incited by Communist agitators, demonstrated in Sian against Japanese imperialism and Chiang Kai-shek's Japanese-appeasement policy. Blue Shirts fired on the demonstrators, wounding two. Enraged, the students marched toward Lintun, intending to confront Chiang. When the Generalissimo heard about their approach, he ordered the Young Marshal to stop them and, if necessary, use force. The Young Marshal, who had provided financial support to many colleges, intercepted the marchers, promised to present their petitions to Chiang, and persuaded them to return to Sian. When the Young Marshal met with Chiang, however, he was again rebuked.

Seeing no alternative, the Young Marshal and Yang Hucheng boldly decided to kidnap Chiang and force him to change his policy. About 5:30 a.m. on December 12—the Double Twelve—the Young Marshal's men broke into the Gimo's Lintun compound and killed several of his bodyguards. In the confusion, Chiang escaped in his pajamas and slippers, climbed over a high wall, and fell, wrenching his back. His captors found him hiding partway up a hill. By noon, Chiang Kai-shek was under house arrest in Sian.[40]

That morning, Royal awoke in his abandoned mission residence to the sound of gunfire. Believing soldiers were conducting training maneuvers, he resumed sleeping. Unknown to Royal, Yang Hucheng's poorly disciplined troops were shooting at Blue Shirts and starting a three-day looting rampage. Royal's roommate, Jimmy Elder, Jr., the Young Marshal's financial adviser, returned from a walk and reported that the city gates were closed. Royal tried to make a phone call, but the operator, indicating that some sort of revolution was in process, refused to place it. "From that moment on," recalled Royal, "we were prepared for the worst. Sianfu was noted for its violent anti-foreign feeling.... A ray of hope lay in the fact that our wire was still uncut, and there was the chance that whoever won the revolution would want my services as a pilot. The welfare of the other foreigners in Sian, Jimmy Elder told me, might rest upon my gaining the winner's good will."

Royal was unsure about forty-three–year-old Yang Hucheng's role in the upheaval. Yang had fought against the Manchu Dynasty during the 1911 Chinese Revolution, organized a peasant resistance movement against oppressive debt collectors, and been appointed Nationalist Army commander in northern Shensi. In 1926, Yang and his outnumbered troops had defended Sian in an eight-month siege. Responding to a capitulation demand, Yang had roared: "Not until every cow, every horse, every cat, and every dog has been eaten will I surrender." Fifty thousand Sian residents died. As a reward for Yang's steadfastness, Chiang Kai-shek had appointed him governor of Shensi and commander in chief of the provincial Nationalist Army. In 1933, Chiang had replaced Yang as governor but left him in command of the Northwest Army.

Royal was dumbfounded by the unfolding events. He believed the conflict was probably between the Young Marshal and Yang Hucheng because Yang resented the Young Marshal's presence in Shensi. Royal had heard rumors that Yang had induced the Generalissimo to come to Sian and eject the Young Marshal and also that Yang had double-crossed Chiang Kai-shek and the Young Marshal, captured the Gimo, and was trying to take over all China. The rumor that the Young Marshal and Yang were cooperating made the least sense to Royal.[41]

The Young Marshal had ordered Yang's army to occupy Sian. Yang's soldiers disarmed Chiang's army units; arrested his officers, pilots, and Blue Shirts; and seized the airport, radio transmitters, and war planes. After securing the city, the Young Marshal and Yang cabled their eight-point demands to Nationalist authorities in Nanking, seeking resistance to Japan, cessation of the civil war, reorganization of the government, release of political prisoners, and adoption of Sun Yat-sen's democratic principles. The Young Marshal also cabled Madame Chiang Kai-shek that her husband was safe and invited Communist leaders to Sian to participate in negotiations.

Armed with two Thompson submachine guns, a .45-caliber revolver, a .22-caliber rifle and hollow bullets, and a shotgun, Royal and Jimmy Elder prepared to fight for their lives. Royal did not expect to see civilization again for a long time. He was imprisoned inside Sian's massive walls. Although he was the rebels' only trustworthy and dependable pilot, he was walking a tight wire and could not make a false move. He felt that Yang Hucheng was giving him "the special care and attention usually accorded a Thanksgiving turkey who does not know Thanksgiving is near."

Coping with uncertainty, Royal started making fantastic plans. He knew he would be valuable to the winning side and believed he would probably be offered the job of flying the Boeing 247D. If that happened, he planned to deliberately fly into rough air, loop the loop several times until his passengers were airsick, tie them up, and escape to the International Settlement.

Although the gunfire ceased by midafternoon, Royal and Elder still feared for their lives. Nationalist war planes droned overhead. Mr. Li, the Young Marshal's transportation secretary, reconnoitered the airport and told Royal that Yang's troops had occupied it but had not disturbed the Boeing 247D.

The tension finally broke when Royal's phone rang at 11 p.m. The Young Marshal asked Elder to come to his headquarters immediately. Royal went to bed. When Elder returned, he told Royal that the Young Marshal and Yang were cooperating and holding Chiang Kai-shek prisoner. Meanwhile, the Young Marshal's soldiers took over the airport from Yang's troops.[42]

Two days after the kidnapping, Madame Chiang Kai-shek sent William H. Donald, the Generalissimo's political adviser, to investigate her husband's predicament and ascertain his captors' intentions. John Gunther rated the "chic" Madame the second most important person in China. Madame acted as Chiang's intermediary in dealing with English-speaking foreigners. Donald called Madame "Missimo" because in his opinion she thought like a man.

Missimo's emissary, known to the western press as "Donald of China," was trusted by Madame, Chiang, and the Young Marshal. Formerly an Australian newspaperman, Donald had reported for a Hong Kong newspaper on the 1911 Chinese Revolution and written several proclamations for Sun Yat-sen before establishing the Chinese Government Bureau of Economic Information. In 1926, Donald had joined the Old Marshal's staff as adviser on European affairs. After the Old Marshal's assassination, Donald had served as the Young Marshal's personal adviser and helped rehabilitate him from drug addiction. In the fall of 1934, Donald had become Chiang's key political adviser.

After meeting with Chiang Kai-shek, Donald allowed the Young Marshal to read entries in the Generalissimo's diary purportedly revealing secret preparations for resisting the Japanese. China was not ready for an all-out war. Chiang was negotiating with the Japanese and stalling for time while strengthening the Chinese Army and Air Force and modernizing the country's industrial capacity. Swayed by what he read, the Young Marshal, sure that when his motive was known, the Chinese people would approve of his action, naively promised to accompany the Generalissimo to Nanking and stand trial for his conduct. Donald telephoned Madame Chiang and assured her that the Gimo was safe.

Late that evening, the Young Marshal sent his personal car to bring Royal to headquarters and gave him orders in a private room where nobody could overhear them. Early most of the following mornings, Royal took off from the Sian airfield, returning late in the afternoon so neither Nationalist nor Japanese planes could bomb or strafe *Bai Ying*. Royal transported officers between Sian and outposts, delivered messages to Manchurian Army garrisons, and, on his own initiative, informed missionaries in Communist-held territory about evacuation plans.[43]

On December 16, Royal flew Comrade Mr. Li, the Young Marshal's personal secretary and secret Communist liaison, and the other Mr. Li, the transportation secretary, to Yenan with a three-quarter–ton load of bullets. Royal had no idea about the trip's purpose and felt a chill down his spine as he glided toward a river edge landing strip in a deep and narrow valley. It was obvious that the flight was unexpected; nobody greeted them when they landed.

As Comrade Mr. Li walked away, Royal kept the Boeing's motors running. A threatening crowd, shabbily uniformed and shouldering rifles, surrounded the plane. Some were Yang Hucheng's men, and others were twelve or thirteen-year-old boys. "Hey!" exclaimed Royal, "those are Communists, the same guys who have been shooting at us!" Royal and his American copilot, Ed Winegerter, cocked their Thompson submachine guns. When the crowd moved too close, Winegerter fired a tear gas pistol and dispersed them.

Before fighting could break out, Comrade Li returned to the plane with six dignified young men, handed them pictures of the Young Marshal, and told Royal and Winegerter to unload the cargo. Royal then realized that the bullets were the Young Marshal's peace offering to the Communists.

Hearing shouts of "*Li la*" ("Here he comes"), Royal spotted a long procession walking in traditional Manchu caste-conscious style, the most important first followed by associates in order of rank. When they reached the plane, Royal realized that he had to fly a party of Communists to Sian. "Orders are orders," he mumbled. The leader, Chou En-lai, had ridden a horse for two days on rugged mountain paths to Yenan and was ready to take his first plane ride.

After assisting Chou and eleven other Communists into the Boeing's two passenger compartments, Royal and Winegerter loaded two of their colleagues in the nose baggage space. Chou thought his pilot was an Italian, possibly sent by Mussolini. Chou was going to Sian because Stalin, concerned about the recent German–Japanese anti-Comintern mutual defense pact, had ordered the Chinese Reds to work for the release of Chiang Kai-shek as the only leader who could effectively unite the Chinese nation against the Japanese and checkmate their threat to the Soviet Union.

Disinterested in the niceties of international relations, Royal sought revenge for Communist soldiers firing at him on earlier flights and intentionally flew through rough air. He glanced into the passenger compartment and watched Chou En-lai and his compatriots hold their beards to one side and vomit into tin cans. "Well," he said to Winegerter, "so they will shoot at me, will they!"

Upon landing at the Sian airport, the Communists refused to leave the plane until enough cars were available to transport all of them. The delegation ran toward the vehicles with their coat collars turned up like criminals avoiding photographers. Although Chou En-lai may not have enjoyed his first airplane ride, he must have appreciated completing a trip in two hours that would have taken ten days on horseback.[44]

Waiting for their next assignment, Royal and Winegerter prepared the Boeing 247D for a fast getaway and a long-distance flight. Instead of draining lubricating oil each evening and refilling crankcases in the morning, they left oil in the engines. Heat from small charcoal stoves set under covers stretching from the ground to the wing engine housings prevented the oil from freezing. They soldered a funnel between the cockpit and a wing-tank overflow pipe so additional fuel could be poured into the tanks when the plane was airborne. With this modification, Royal estimated that *Bai Ying* could fly over 2500 miles nonstop.

"Night after night," Royal recalled, "I spread my maps over my desk, plotting courses and measuring distances. Many times I caught myself, eyes out of focus, staring beyond those maps, seeing mental pictures of where we might go. Mandalay, Calcutta, French Indo-China, Hong Kong, perhaps even Manila."

In Nanking, Madame Chiang Kai-shek was working feverishly to prevent a Nationalist attack on Sian that might result in the Gimo's death. Eleven Nationalist Army divisions were concentrated about eighty miles east of Sian at Tungkwan. Nationalist planes were based at the Loyang airfield 200 miles from Sian. Five days of severe snowstorms, however, grounded them. In the meantime, Missimo persuaded Minister of War Ho Yingchin, supreme military commander in her husband's absence, to arrange a truce.[45]

On December 22, Madame Chiang arrived in Sian and told the Young Marshal that she wanted to end the civil war and fight the Japanese. But the stubborn Generalissimo, having starved himself for several days to avoid loss of face from eating food provided by his captors, refused under the appearance of duress to sign an agreement. And Yang Hucheng, distrusting negotiations conducted in English without an interpreter, forbade Chiang's release without a written guarantee of his personal safety. On Christmas Day about 2 p.m., however, Yang relented and accepted Chiang's oral promise to resist the Japanese.

Once agreement was reached, the Young Marshal immediately summoned Royal to his headquarters and ordered him to prepare the Boeing 247D for a hasty flight. Royal rushed to the airport, jerked away the charcoal stoves, yanked off the covers, and started the engines. Moments later, the Young Marshal climbed into the cockpit and sat in the copilot seat. "Are you ready to go?" Royal heard a woman's voice say in an American accent.

Royal turned and recognized Madame Chiang Kai-shek seated in the front compartment. "Yes," he replied, "any time."

"Okay," she said in a loud whisper, "get out of here! Let's get going!" Royal signaled the ground crew to pull the wheel blocks and shoved the throttles forward like he was starting a race.

About five minutes after taking off, the Young Marshal called Royal's attention to another passenger. Looking over his shoulder, Royal saw the Generalissimo asleep on the front compartment lounge chair. From time to time, Royal glanced back and watched Chiang dozing, Madame gazing out a window with "a faint smile of happiness on her face," Donald chuckling, and T.V. Soong, who had arrived ahead of his sister and begun the negotiations for Chiang's release, resting with his eyes closed. "I could hardly realize," mused Royal, "that it was I who was the pilot flying the chief actors of that Sian drama out through the aerial back stage. In fact, I felt that we had sneaked out through a secret door of that stage."

As darkness fell, the Boeing reached Loyang. The Young Marshal asked Royal to circle the field and alert ground personnel that they intended to land. "Nobody send message we come?" asked Royal.

"No," replied the Young Marshal. "Not many people in Sianfu know we leave. No want anyone to know we come." When the Boeing landed, soldiers and students rushed toward it. Seeing Madame Chiang Kai-shek step from the plane, they stopped, stood at attention, and saluted.

Noticing the Young Marshal behind her, four soldiers pointed rifles at him. "Should we kill him?" one asked.

"No!" replied Madame Chiang emphatically. "Let him alone!" She and the Young Marshal intertwined arms and walked toward a car. Upon seeing disabled Chiang Kai-shek carried off the plane, the crowd cheered wildly, and some wept as the nation's leader was assisted into an automobile.

"To them," said Royal, "it was as if he had been raised from the dead."

The next day, Royal's passengers traveled to Nanking in two planes. The Generalissimo, Madame Chiang, and Donald flew in a Junkers Trimotor. Two hours later, Royal followed in the Boeing 247D, escorted by fighter planes, with the Young Marshal and T.V. Soong as passengers. When the Boeing outdistanced the fighters in a dust storm, Royal sensed an opportunity to break for freedom. The Young Marshal could order him to fly anywhere in China. "Maybe we had better not go to Nanking," proposed Royal.

"No matter," replied the Young Marshal soberly. "If someone kill me, it is all right. I don't care."[46]

Fulfilling his promise to accompany the Gimo to the nation's capital, the Young Marshal arrived at the Nanking military airport. Royal stopped the Boeing in the center of the field, and soldiers formed a path through the crowd for the Young Marshal. Royal knew from his resigned expression that the Young Marshal expected to be assassinated. "Now be careful!" Royal warned his boss. "Maybe you don't care if someone shoots you, but there are others who want you with us. Don't take any chances."

The Young Marshal turned toward Royal and, weeping, squeezed his hand. "Thank you!" he said. "Thank you very, very much! I say good-bye now. No matter about me. You take very good care of yourself. Maybe I see you no more." Walking a few steps, the Young Marshal came back and silently shook Royal's hand again.

Watching his beloved boss proceed through rows of Nationalist soldiers, Royal changed his mind about leaving China. "I knew then," he said, "that China had a place in my heart as great as any land in the world, even the United States. The sight of Chang Hseuh-liang going to his martyrdom … crystallized that feeling within me.... I was proud to know that I had had some small part in shaping this land. All the conglomerate parts of the puzzle that is China fell together for me. I saw the Communists, the Nationalists, the faction of the Young Marshal, the clique within Chiang Kai-shek's own government that would have liked to see him killed—all were of one mind in the crisis. They knew China must unite or be lost. And to the end that union should come about, they were, in the words of the founders of my own United States, ready to sacrifice 'their lives, their fortunes, and their sacred honor'.... China had become great and noble, an enduring land."

The Young Marshal's decision to surrender to his former captive and risk his vengeance is baffling to westerners. There are many opinions about why he did it. According to Dr. Wang Wen-san, a post-World War II Chinese airline board chairman, the Young Marshal's conduct expressed nobility: "It meant, 'I did what I thought best for China, and now I stand before you—do with me what you will.'" Mao Tse-tung thought the Young Marshal sought mitigation for his criminal kidnapping act and perhaps believed his only chance for survival was under Chiang's protection. In American aviation specialist Sebie Smith's opinion, the Young Marshal "was begging for punishment, which is the Chinese way of trying to ask for repentance—they beg for punishment." According to Chiang and Madame Chiang, the Young Marshal was obligated to go to Nanking because he had agreed to take full responsibility for the rebellion and it was his duty to support the Generalissimo. Having promised Chiang Kai-shek he would stand trial for disobedience, posits historian Tien-wei Wu, the Young Marshal could not expect Chiang to carry out his promise to resist the Japanese if he broke his word. Moreover, Wu states, the Young Marshal's contrition helped restore Chiang Kai-shek's stature as the national leader.

No matter what his motivation, the Young Marshal's bold action in Sian altered the course of Chinese history. "Everybody concerned," Royal pointed out, "can thank the Young Marshal that the Generalissimo is still alive. What was wanted was a fight against Japan with Chiang Kai-shek leading it. That was the reason the Young Marshal took over the airport, cooperated with the Communists, and kept the Generalissimo in his home. He had never intended any harm from the beginning. What he has done will probably save China in the long run." [47]

The Communist Army remained on Chinese soil and survived to fight another day. And the Young Marshal had become a national hero for bringing about resistance to Japan.

Chapter 7

ROYAL AND CHENNAULT

(January – November 1937)

Although a Nationalist military tribunal on December 31, 1936, sentenced the Young Marshal to ten years imprisonment, denied him civil rights for five years, and placed him under the Gimo's supervision, Royal remained loyal to his former employer. Royal tried to visit the Young Marshal at Dr. H.H. Kung's country home, halfway between the Nanking city wall and the Sun Yat-sen Mausoleum, but each time, Blue Shirt guards turned him away. Royal also was denied access to the Boeing 247D.

Disillusioned and unemployed, Royal decided to leave China. But Chiang Kai-shek needed a personal pilot. The day before Royal's scheduled departure, Jimmy Elder, Jr., now advising the Gimo, offered Royal a job paying $1200 a month and expenses ($14,900 in 2009 purchasing power); U.S. airline pilots were averaging $646 a month. Royal accepted the offer, largely from loyalty to the Young Marshal. "Certainly I could not help to get him out of prison if I left China," Royal reasoned.

Chiang Kai-shek assigned Royal to the Headquarters Transport Squadron commanded by former Nazi Brown Shirt leader Walter Stennes. After leading an unsuccessful revolt against Hitler, Stennes had been arrested, released through Hermann Goering's influence, and smuggled from Germany. Followed by an Alsatian police dog and waving a walking stick stenciled "C.G.A.T.S." (Chief of the Generalissimo's Air Transport Squadron), Stennes, who spoke fluent English, supervised pilots, mechanics, and the use of seven aircraft, including the Boeing 247D *Bai Ying*.

Distraught about his kidnapping and injured back, the Generalissimo needed time to recuperate and decide on a course of action against the Japanese. On May 24, 1937, Royal flew him to Kiukiang on the Yangtze River west of Nanking. Coolies carried the Nationalist leader in a sedan chair to his mountaintop bungalow at Kuling, the summer capital. Halfway down the mountain, Royal waited for orders at the Journey's End Inn; its bedrooms were furnished with Bibles and French pornography. Royal, a Presbyterian, worked on a manuscript about his China experiences and enjoyed walking, swimming, and occasional visits to American gunboats moored at Kiukiang. On June 2, he read in a newspaper that the Gimo had recovered his health and was ready to resume his duties.

The Japanese forced Chiang Kai-shek's hand. On July 7, 1937—the Double Seven—an incident occurred at Lukouchiao (Marco Polo Bridge) near Peking, and Japanese troops occupied the strategic Peking-Tientsin and Peking-Hankow railroad junction. Ten days later, Chiang declared war on Japan. "The Young Marshal's principles had been vindicated at last," Royal rejoiced.[48]

A few days after the Gimo made this decision, Royal flew him and Madame Chiang to Nanking. That evening, the phone rang in Royal's Metropolitan Hotel room. The desk clerk said an American gentleman wanted to visit him. Moments later, Royal heard a knock, opened the door, and was surprised to see a leather-faced man with sharp black eyes and grizzled hair dressed in a leather jacket and unpressed flannels. "For the love of Mike," said Royal, "come on in, Chennault."

The two men updated each other on their activities since parting ten years earlier at Brooks Field. They may have discussed missing each other in Cleveland two years earlier when Royal had failed to complete the Bendix Race and where Chennault had performed in his "Flying Trapeze" aerial act for spectators at the finish line.

Blocked from promotion in the Army Air Corps, disgusted with U.S. fighter tactics, partly deaf, physically and mentally exhausted, and retired as a captain at age forty-three, Claire L. Chennault, who Royal called "a boots-on officer," desperately needed a challenge and money for his children's college educations. Madame Chiang Kai-shek, whose husband had appointed her Secretary-General of the Commission on Aeronautical Affairs to prevent his enemies from using Nationalist planes against him if ever presented another opportunity like that in Sian, asked Chennault to evaluate the Chinese Air Force (CAF). Chennault accepted an assignment as aviation "adviser," responsible for training pilots, selecting military planes and equipment, and organizing an air raid warning system. He had recently inspected CAF personnel, aircraft, training facilities, and fields. A friend, a former Louisiana governor, had dubbed Chennault an honorary colonel so that Chennault could impress Chinese brass with a rank higher than captain.

Relaxing in the hotel room, Chennault and Royal discussed the pitiful condition of the CAF. Only ninety-one of five hundred planes were combat-ready. Pilots were cracking up when taking off, taxiing, and landing. Mussolini had sold China second-rate Italian planes. Italian instructors at the Chinese Central Aviation School, attuned to political reality, had graduated incompetent pilots from influential Chinese families. "Well," said Chennault optimistically, "there are a bunch of American flyers around. Maybe we can do something."

Chennault moved into Royal's hotel suite, which became known as the "G.H.Q." for American CAF advisers. During the remainder of July 1937, Royal flew messages from Chiang Kai-shek to Nationalist generals in interior China. At the end of the month, the Japanese occupied Peking and Tientsin. Early in August, Royal flew Shansi warlord Yen Hsi-shan 400 miles from Nanking to Taiyuan, mostly blind in clouds to hide from Japanese fighters. The grateful warlord rewarded Royal with $1,000 for preserving his life.[49]

Concerned that the Japanese might destroy his personal DC-2 parked at the Canton airfield in southern China, Chiang Kai-shek ordered Royal to bring the plane to Nanking. On Friday, August 13, Royal boarded a China National Aviation Corporation (CNAC) flight to Shanghai, expecting to take a connecting flight the next day to Canton. He checked into the sixteen-story Broadway Mansions Hotel behind the Whangpoo River Bund, an embanked quay lined with high-rise, western-style commercial buildings.

The City of Shanghai (not the International Settlement) was under siege. Madame Chiang asked Colonel Chennault to organize a CAF attack on the enemy. He suggested dive-bombing Japanese cruisers, including the flagship *Idzuma*, anchored near Royal's hotel.

On Bloody Saturday—August 14, 1937—Royal awoke about 10:30 a.m. thinking he was hearing thunder and seeing lightning. When the floor shook, he jumped out of bed, realized he was in a combat zone, and started packing his suitcase. No other place nearby seemed safer, however, so he watched the action from a grandstand seat—his thirteenth-floor window.

At about 4:30 p.m., a horrible incident occurred. The Italians had trained CAF pilots to drop bombs from 7,500 feet at a fixed air speed. Overcast conditions forced the bomber pilots to drop below 2,000 feet to try to hit Japanese shore batteries. Flying at a lower altitude and higher speed than at which they had been trained, the pilots failed to adjust their bombsights accordingly. One bomb landed on the Palace Hotel roof near the Broadway Mansions Hotel, and another hit 500 feet away next to the Cathay Hotel. The concussions almost knocked Royal off his feet. Amidst shattered window glass, he telephoned the CNAC office and asked for information about the next plane out of town. The operator said all flights had been cancelled.

"Chinese planes were speeding overhead," Royal recalled, "dropping bombs at intervals of a few hundred yards. The whir of motors—then WHAM! A terrific blast! BOOM—another still closer! BOOM!—then deep roar and thunder. The building tottered on its foundation. This bomb had crashed in the main section of Shanghai. There was one great puff, then clouds of debris boiled and bubbled skyward, tossing bits of buildings, boards, human bodies. It hesitated—then climbed up and up.... Still the *Idzuma* was safe." But 1,740 Chinese civilians were dead and 1,873 injured.

Chinese bombers headed toward the Broadway Mansions Hotel. Royal thought his front yard was the target for the next bomb. Japanese anti-aircraft guns popped away. When bursts exploded within 500 feet of them, the Chinese pilots turned back. "Not one of the bombs fell on Jap territory," Royal commented. "The crazy fools just got excited when the Japs started shooting at them, and dropped their bombs any old place."[50]

During a lull in shooting the next day, Royal hired twelve coolies to transport his possessions to a safer place. As the cortege of rickshaws resembling a Chinese wedding procession left the hotel and padded toward the U.S. concession, Chinese planes reappeared and dropped bombs. Japanese anti-aircraft gunners opened fire. "Like the report of the starting gun that sets off the racers," said Royal, "we were off. The momentum of the sudden start yanked me back in my seat. The coolies took the corners on one wheel. Like greased lightning we reached the American Club. Each coolie demanded one dollar extra for running under fire. They had certainly earned it!"

Better for Royal's bank account, a CNAC representative on Tuesday, August 17, offered him $1,000 ($14,900 in 2009 earning power) to fly a DC-2 to Hankow, a distance of 585 miles. "I would gladly have paid them one thousand dollars for this privilege!" said Royal.

When Royal arrived at Lungwha Field, Japanese planes were strafing and bombing the runway, which looked like a slice of Swiss cheese. Two CNAC Douglas Dolphin amphibians moored in the Whangpoo River had been sunk. The DC-2, housed in a hangar, was undamaged.

Unable to warm-up the DC-2 because any activity would attract attention from Japanese pilots, Royal started the engines and opened the throttles. The plane jumped out of the hangar like a rabbit out of a hole, skidded around two bomb craters, and climbed into the sky. Eluding a Japanese fighter, Royal nosed the plane into a cloudbank and familiarized himself with its controls. Flying blind for half an hour, he escaped his tormentor and landed safely at Hankow.

"It sure seemed funny to me to have a ticket on a CNAC plane," said Royal, "and instead of using it, to get well paid for making the same trip that I wanted to make."[51]

The next day, Royal traveled to Canton and flew Chiang Kai-shek's DC-2 to the neutral British Hong Kong Crown Colony.* This DC-2 was nicknamed *The Flying Palace* because its two lounges were embellished with black wood veneer and red carpet and furnished with upholstered chairs, an ornate writing desk, a small radio, and a food box. According to Royal, this plane was as famous throughout China as the Lone Ranger's horse, Silver, in America.

Now Royal faced a new foe—the implacable U.S. State Department. The Japanese government had demanded that all American pilots withdraw from China. Not wanting to antagonize the Japanese war machine, the U.S. Hong Kong Consulate had written American aviators and ordered them to leave China immediately. Chennault had stayed, noting in his diary, "Guess I am Chinese." Several American CNAC pilots had already departed. To avoid receiving the order, Royal and his roommate had "practiced a mild form of deceit." Each man had examined the other's mail and thrown away envelopes with a U.S. State Department return address.

*When Hong King, meaning "fragrant harbor," is mentioned as a flight point of origination or termination, the reference more accurately is to Kowloon, where Kai Tak Airport, named for two land developers, was located. The important commercial city of Hong Kong, dominated by 1805-feet high Victoria Peak, is located on seventy-nine and one half square-mile Hong Kong Island in the South China Sea. The eleven-and one-half square-mile Kowloon Peninsula juts southward from mainland China to a point about a mile north of Hong Kong Island.

Alerted to Royal's presence in the Colony, American Consul Howard Donovan summoned him and ordered him to leave China immediately. Royal refused, saying he had promised Generalissimo and Madame Chiang Kai-shek he would stay with them to the bitter end. Finishing the meeting, Donovan denied Royal permission to fly *The Flying Palace* out of Hong Kong.

The next day, Royal returned to the U.S. consulate and pressed his case. He presented an affidavit from the Kai Tak Airport manager averring that *The Flying Palace* was unarmed, a Chinese government order to fly the plane to Hankow, and blanket passes signed by Generalissimo and Madame Chiang Kai-shek. In turn, Donovan handed Royal a State Department letter requesting that British authorities temporarily stop American aviators trying to take off from Kai Tak.

Nonplused, Royal obtained Donovan's permission to test fly *The Flying Palace*, which had been undergoing repairs, in the Colony air space. After making two short flights on August 22, Royal asked the airport manager for a Hankow weather report.

"But what would you want it for?" replied the manager, who sympathized with anyone opposing the Japanese.

"It looks as though it is fogging up," said Royal, waving at the sky. "I might get lost up there. Can't tell where I might have to land."

"A very wise precaution," agreed the manager. "Just a minute." He walked to the radio shack and brought back a Hankow weather report.

"Thanks," said Royal. "Just one more flight."

"Good-bye," said the manager. "Visit us again sometime."

Encountering the thickest clouds he claimed he had ever seen, Royal somehow lost his sense of direction. He tried returning to Kai Tak but missed the field in a sudden rainsquall. Panic-stricken, apparently for the first time in his career, Royal flew a zero-compass course. Dropping below the clouds, he saw Hankow and landed. His fuel tanks were almost empty.[52]

Two and a half weeks after Bloody Saturday, on August 31, the CAF blundered again. Fighter pilots were ordered to sink Japanese ships reported in the Yangtze River mouth. The squadron leader and two other pilots dived at the American President Lines passenger ship *Hoover*, saw its American flag, and pulled up, but six aviators dropped bombs, damaged the ship, and killed a seaman. Chiang Kai-shek promptly paid APL $100,000 and set aside a $10,000 fund for the victim's family.

Dismayed by the Bloody Saturday and *Hoover* incidents, the Generalissimo decided that CAF pilots and bombardiers needed better training. Secretary-General of the Commission on Aeronautical Affairs Madame Chiang Kai-shek met with Royal and asked him to take charge of Chinese bombardment.

"I'm a pursuit pilot," replied the somewhat shaken Royal. "I don't know anything about bombardment."

"That doesn't matter," Madame countered. "You are a good flyer and you have a good head. We need your judgment. You can be trusted. This is what we want. This terrible thing, the bombing of the *Hoover*, must never be repeated."

They discussed her proposal. Royal suggested that Julius Barr, trained at Kelly Field as a bomber pilot, co-command the bombardment section, and Madame agreed.

"Well, I couldn't say 'NO,'" commented Royal, "but it certainly gave me a headache to think of the task that lay before me."[53]

But Colonel Chennault persuaded Madame Chiang to appoint Julius chief bomber instructor and Royal as assistant. Their students addressed them as Captain Barr and Captain Leonard. Unknown to U.S. State Department officials, Royal's CAF identification card classified his mercenary position as "American Adviser." Royal undertook the brunt of bombardment training duties because Julius was occupied with other assignments. Royal also continued flying for the Headquarters Transport Squadron on a reduced basis.

"It is quite a shock to be yanked out of a 'life of Riley' and be given the responsibility of a General," Royal said. "Sorta like being tossed out of a warm bed on a cold morning into a tank of ice water… All of us knew that we were in a ticklish spot, as ticklish as if a Chinese officer were given supreme authority to discipline the mistakes of the United States Army Air Corps." He started losing hair and, with several American colleagues, had his head clean shaven.

Early in September, Captain Leonard traveled to the CAF bombardment training field at Hankow, approximately 375 miles west of Nanking. He inspected a motley forty-plane squadron, including American Martin B-10, Northrop Gamma 2E, Douglas attack, German Heinkel He 111 A-0, and Italian Caproni, Bellanca, and

Savoia-Marchetti bombers. He trained the Martin and Heinkel pilots, and Captain Cigerza tutored the Savoia pilots in night landings on floodlit and marker-lit fields.

"As for blind flying," recalled Royal, "oh yes, they all knew how! I took one of them up for a test and received the dizziest spin through the clouds that I had ever had. After I had landed, having just straightened out before crashing, I climbed weakly out of the plane. The pilot seemed more chipper than I, so I said to him in Pidgin English what my instructor at Brooks Field had said to me years before on one of my first flights. 'I no know if you scare yourself ... but you scare heck out of me!'"[54]

Initially, Royal and Julius organized the bombers into two sections, mixing Martins and Heinkels. The Martin B-10, according to Royal, cruised at 200 miles per hour, but the Heinkel 111 A-O cruised at 168 miles per hour. Moving ahead of the Heinkels, Martin pilots refused to slow down, formations broke up, and Japanese fighters had a field day shooting down dispersed planes. Royal and Julius reorganized the remaining aircraft into solely Martin and Heinkel sections that held together and afforded better mutual fire support.

Flying at high altitudes, however, many bomber crews were missing their targets by as much as a mile. To find out why, Royal hid in a Martin B-10 bomb bay. When the bombardier looked through the American Mark IV bombsight, Royal scrambled from his hiding place and stared between the bombardier's feet. He discovered that the bombardier was erroneously signaling the pilot, indicating right when the pilot should turn left, and vice versa. Before resuming training, Royal flew a Martin B-10 with American engineering officer Harold Welch, who used the bombsight correctly and accurately.

As a bombing practice target, the American advisers utilized a darkened hut equipped with a camera obscura. The bomber flew over the hut, and its reflection through an aperture in the roof formed a shadow on a revolving work table from which the accuracy or inaccuracy of the simulated bomb release was calculated. The ground crew moved the base of a T-panel in the direction of any error, and the pilot rocked his wings to acknowledge receipt of the signal. "I think," Chennault wrote Royal, "that you have made remarkable progress by reducing the lateral error from 300–400 metres to 180 metres, in the short time you have had."

Upon receiving an air raid warning on October 1, Chinese and American pilots scrambled from the Hankow field. Late in the evening, Royal, assuming the attack was over because the field lights were on, made his landing approach. He noticed the silhouette of a Chinese fighter plane behind him and waved a greeting out his cockpit window. Tracer bullets zinged past him. Royal performed cartwheel maneuvers, dove to 500 feet above ground level, and pulled up. He heard an explosion, looked back, and saw a bright white light in the sky where the confused Chinese pilot's next mistaken target, a Heinkel bomber, had burst into flames.

When an accident occurred, the American instructors wanted to know what had happened so they could teach the pilot how to avoid making the same mistake. But Chiang Kai-shek's brutal disciplinary policy, which was execution for a serious mistake, discouraged candor. Chennault persuaded Chiang to approve a new policy that encouraged honest explanation and eliminated excessive discipline.

Although this change encouraged honesty, it did not solve the incompetence problem. After overshooting the field and cracking up his plane, a Chinese pilot admitted that he had ignored his angle of glide in relationship to the runway. As a reward for his forthrightness, he was assigned to a night bombing mission. Taking off in a plane heavily loaded with bombs, the pilot lost control and crashed. The explosion destroyed several Martin B-10 bombers parked nearby.[55]

In mid-October, Royal walked into their Metropolitan Hotel room and found Claire Chennault dejectedly writing a letter. The CAF had been decimated, and Nanking obviously would soon fall to the Japanese. Royal showed Chennault a newspaper headline stating that the United States government had renounced its neutrality policy and had condemned Japanese aggression. They toasted the geniuses in Washington, DC, for finally recognizing that China and Japan were engaged in a shooting war. Chennault asked Royal whether he planned to remain in China, and Royal asked Chennault whether he was thinking about returning home. Chennault equivocated. On the one hand, he yearned for his family and hunting on his Louisiana farm. On the other hand, he wanted to help the CAF defeat the Japanese. Mentioning that his contract had expired, Chennault asked Royal about his employment arrangement. Royal related his handshake promise to Madame Chiang Kai-shek to stick with China through the war without any subsequent contract extension and said he had received a pay check every month. Chennault acknowledged that he had been getting paid on time, and Royal assured him that was the way things were done in China. Making a historically significant decision, Chennault thanked

Royal and tore up the letter indicating his intention to return home. The two men had important work to do.[56]

Escalating Japanese air raids forced Chiang Kai-shek to order Nanking-based CAF personnel and planes evacuated to Hankow, which became the temporary Nationalist capital. Chennault drove to Hankow, taking his and Royal's possessions, and moved into Royal's five rooms and sleeping porch at Anlee House. According to Chennault's chief mechanic, Sebie Smith, the suite, which housed eleven Americans, was the CAF American advisers' unofficial headquarters

Unfortunately, Advisers Barr and Leonard were not getting along. Part of their problem was personal. Shortly before the Sian kidnapping incident, Royal had resigned his flying school assistant instructor position and Julius felt he had been let down. Julius resented that Madame Chiang Kai-shek initially had asked Royal to command the bomber squadron and was paying him a higher salary. On his part, Royal was mad at Julius because he had flown the Headquarters Transport Squadron Boeing 247D without Royal's permission, ground looped, and damaged the landing gear.

Part of their problem was professional difference of opinion. Royal believed that he needed to fly and familiarize himself with the Martin B-10s before starting instruction; Julius criticized him for taking what he regarded as personal pleasure rides. Royal wanted to train the best-qualified Chinese pilots first so they could enter combat sooner, but Julius preferred training and graduating the cadets as a group regardless of differences in ability.

Acknowledging Julius's superior bombardment qualifications, Royal asked Chennault for a transfer to Ichang, where he could train navigators and evacuate Headquarters Transport Squadron planes in event of a Japanese attack. As an alternative, Royal suggested an assignment training Chinese fighter pilots, who, he felt, needed "some jacking up." "In fact," Royal wrote Chennault, "rather than remain in my present position I would prefer to lead them myself provided I could fix up the ship I would fly in my own way beforehand and have it worked on by foreign mechanics." There is no record, however, that Royal ever flew combat missions against the Japanese.

In early November, Chennault ordered Royal to return to the Headquarters Transport Squadron, Julius to check out volunteer foreign pilots for an International Squadron, and the Bombardment School transferred to Nanchang under another commander. Chennault evaluated Royal and Julius's bombardment training effort as a failure, partly due to rainy and cloudy weather, an inferior landing field, and inadequate equipment, but primarily due to their lack of cooperation making them vulnerable to Chinese criticism and contributing to a loss of American prestige.[57]

By this time, China had gained an ally against Japan. In exchange for metals and other commodities, the Soviet Union provided China 400 combat planes, as well as personnel for four fighter and two bomber squadrons. In late November, Royal observed Russian trucks arriving at Lanchow in southern Kansu province; 300 Russian personnel, six bombers, and six fighters disembarking at Ichang; and Russian planes returning to Sian from a raid.[58]

As an expert on Chinese military aviation, Royal submitted a detailed report to Douglas MacArthur, private military adviser to the Philippine Commonwealth Government. Retired from the U.S. Army, "Field Marshal" MacArthur, assisted by U.S. Army Major Dwight D. Eisenhower, was building the Filipino Army to resist an expected Japanese invasion. In his report, Royal compared Japanese, American, and Russian military aircraft, as well as Japanese, Russian, and Chinese aerial combat tactics, described communications, camouflage, anti-aircraft weaponry, and ammunition and bombs, and recommended bomber and fighter design improvements. MacArthur commented:

> This is a most intriguing paper. Most of the information it contains supports the reports from our army observers and experts. The material side of aviation and the doctrine of its personnel are in such a state of flux and rapidity of change that its real potentialities, insofar as they affect basic strategy, have not as yet been demonstrated. It will probably take a world war to really give some great new military genius—one who will thereby make himself one of the notable captains of war—an opportunity to exploit the new possibilities which this weapon has placed in the hands of a commander of imagination and flexibility.[59]

Before MacArthur fulfilled his destiny, however, Royal, Chennault, and their Chinese friends endured several more years of demoralizing defeats dealt by Japanese airpower.

Chapter 8

FLIGHTS FROM DOOM

(December 1937 – December 1938)

Royal stayed a hop, skip, and a jump ahead of the Japanese war machine as it penetrated deeper and deeper into China. By the end of October, the CAF could muster less than a dozen fighter planes. In early November, the Chinese Nationalist Army retreated from Shanghai. In mid-November, they poured into Nanking and cleared a mile-wide, free-fire zone outside the city's thirty-two–mile-long walls. Royal barely escaped when this capital, and then the temporary capital, Hankow, fell, and he routinely evaded Japanese war planes pummeling the capital of last resort, Chungking. Each getaway seemed like a "flight from doom."

"The death of a city," observed Royal, "is an awesome sight from the air, great in its sadness.... But when it begins to be frightened the lights, somehow, become dull.... When the last convulsion comes there is only blackness before the burning. The whole effect is as if the city were a theater just before a grim performance. The house lights go slowly down, and then the thick dark."

Approaching Nanking on the evening of December 4, 1937, Royal saw the glow of fire on the horizon and heard the din of artillery in the distance. Houses and high trees surrounded the tiny Ming Palace field, a difficult place to land under favorable conditions and requiring luck to find at night with the airfield radio turned off. Royal searched for dim, half-turned-up lanterns marking the field edges. Hugging close to house and tree tops to hide from Japanese fighters, he flew over the field, which was two-thirds hidden in smoke. On the seventh attempt, he side-slipped the Boeing 247D into the ring of lanterns.

A sound like gunfire startled Royal. "Are they that close?" he asked a guard.

"No," replied the guard, "that comes from hot bamboo trees." Burning green bamboo in its hollow stems generates compressed steam that explodes.

Worried about approaching Japanese troops, Royal waited several hours for passengers.

Before daylight, he took off, almost clipped the top of a house with the plane's belly, and climbed through a cloud of smoke 2,000 feet thick.

"A lot of smoke back there," Royal said to Mr. Wong, a passenger. "There must be a lot of fire." Wong nodded but said nothing. "Looks like the world on fire," Royal tried again.

"That right," retorted Wong. "Plenty of fire. Nanking is torch. Torch one day help set world on fire."

Less than a week later, Japanese troops commenced the infamous Rape of Nanking. According to journalist-historian Iris Chang, they killed an estimated 260,000 to 300,000 persons and raped 20,000 to 80,000 women.[60]

Shortly before Nanking fell, Royal had lunched with officers on the *U.S. Panay* gunboat. When on standby duty at Yangtze River city airfields, Royal had visited the crews on American gunboats anchored nearby. He had brought them personal items and messages, and they had fed him, provided him medical care, and sent cable messages for him. In early December, Royal urged the *Panay's* officers to remove its American flag insignia because he feared the increasingly belligerent Japanese might deliberately attack a U.S. ship. Japanese marines had recently boarded a launch, torn down the American flag, and thrown it in a river, and Japanese planes had bombed a British gunboat and two merchant ships.

On December 12, 1937, the first anniversary of Chiang Kai-shek's kidnapping, Japanese planes dive-bombed and strafed the *Panay* for three-quarters of an hour, killing two American crewmembers and an Italian correspondent and wounding fifty persons. Captured Japanese fighter plane equipment was sequestered onboard the ship for transportation to the United States for intelligence analysis. Fortunately, the *Panay*, the first U.S. Navy vessel lost to a hostile aircraft attack in American history, sank before Japanese military personnel could search it and uncover justification for an incident. "They did it on purpose knowing it was an American boat," raged Royal. "Everyone out here is so mad we would like to start shooting Japs right now."[61]

Striking farther into China, the Japanese on January 25, 1938, bombed Ichang below the Yangtze River gorges 385 miles west of Hankow. The Chinese warning system detected the oncoming bombers, but no alarm was sounded because the airfield commander had ordered that he not be awakened. He had also refused to provide sandbag protection for *Bai Ying* because he had not been paid the exorbitant bribe he demanded. Two bombs, landing seventy-five feet away, destroyed the Boeing 247D.

Several thousand coolies, working on the airfield and believing the approaching planes were friendly, paid the ultimate price for their ignorance. An hour after the raid, Royal landed on ground soggy with human blood. "The slaughter of those thousands of coolies," he commented, "was the most horrible carnage I have ever seen.... Bits of bodies, still smoking in the cold air, lay about the field. The cries of the wounded and dying were drowned by the wails of the mourning. Hundreds of bodies were laid out beside the field, and hysterical relatives were shaking the torn corpses, shouting, slapping their faces, patting their cheeks, trying to bring the dead back to life."

Early in February, the Japanese Air Force destroyed another Headquarters Transport Squadron plane. Responding to an air raid alarm, Eric Just, a member of Baron von Richtofen's World War I German "Flying Circus" fighter group, took off from Hankow in a Junkers Trimotor. Japanese fighter pilots caught him and riddled his instrument panel and gas tanks with machine gun bullets. Just made an emergency landing and hid under his plane. When bullets hit too close, he ran into the open and was strafed but escaped injury. As he made a telephone call after the fighters departed, curious soldiers, who were smoking, walked too close to the leaking gas tanks. "[O]ne big puff—one big fire—no more airplane," wrote Royal, "only small pile of ashes." In a year, the Headquarters Transport Squadron had been reduced from seven planes to two—*The Flying Palace* and a Sikorsky amphibian.[62]

During early March, the Japanese escalated their raids on Hankow. Royal, as well as Chinese and Russian pilots, remained on alert duty by their planes from early morning until late evening. When the Chinese warning net detected enemy aircraft outside the Hankow sector, a soldier riding a bicycle told the pilots to get ready. When observers reported hostile planes entering the sector, a field attendant hoisted a black flag, signaling the pilots to start their engines. A red flag replacing the black flag indicated it was time to take off— "Enemy expected in twenty minutes." The pilots taxied into position and took off into the wind. Red and black flags raised together meant "URGENT! DANGER!" and "Enemy expected any minute!" In this situation, the pilots took off straight ahead.

"After the Russians came it was not unusual," said Royal, "to have more than a hundred airplanes parked around the edge of the field. Consequently, when our take-off was practically simultaneous, we were headed toward the center from all directions. For about thirty seconds the traffic congestion was a serious problem, and to avoid collision we often used the third dimension, wishing at the time that there was another dimension available. Just when you had about decided which of those coming toward you would go under and which go over, your crew would frantically call your attention to those coming at you from both sides. What does one do then? I don't think anyone remembers. In spite of the numerous times this happened, there was never an accident caused by that catch-as-catch-can kind of take-off."

Returning to Hankow after an alarm, Royal, who had hurriedly taken off without a radio operator, thought the raid had ended and approached the field not realizing a second wave of Japanese bombers was approaching. The Chinese spotlighted the enemy and Royal's aircraft and blasted away with anti-aircraft fire. Fortunately for Royal and the Japanese, the Chinese aim was poor that night.

Friendly fire also endangered personnel on the Hankow field. The machine guns mounted in Russian E-15 fighter wings were controlled by a cable from the cockpit. If the cable was moved a fraction of an inch, the guns fired. Chinese E-15 pilots had a nasty habit of ground looping, digging a wing into the ground, and activating the trigger cable. As the guns emptied in all directions, everyone hugged the ground.[63]

Worried about incessant Japanese raids on Hankow, Chiang Kai-shek ordered Royal to keep *The Flying Palace* at Kai Tak Airport in neutral Hong Kong Colony. In early May, Royal felt paralyzed below the waist and spent eleven days in a Hong Kong hospital. He suspected Japanese espionage agents had poisoned him during a secret mission with Madame Chiang Kai-shek. His doctors initially feared he had contracted infantile paralysis but finally diagnosed shingles, which is an inflammatory skin disease with neuralgic pains. They ordered him to take a vacation. He visited the Philippine Islands, worked on a manuscript about his China experiences, and recuperated.

When Royal returned to China in mid-July, Kasy Sutter, a beautiful young Chinese–Indian woman whose Swiss husband was helping set up the CAF radio-warning network, met him. "Royal was a terrific man—one of the two nicest Americans I ever met," recalled Kasy. "He never said much, but when he did, it meant a lot." Royal, who stood five-feet, eight-inches tall and weighed 150 pounds, impressed Kasy, who was five-feet, two-inches and 110 pounds, with his physical strength. "I was sitting on a dining room chair," said Kasy. "Royal kneeled, gripped one chair leg, and, as he rose lifted me to his shoulder level. I've never seen another man do that."[64]

Later in July, Royal learned that Chiang Kai-shek planned to discharge him, so he protested Chiang's decision to Mr. Donald. Royal believed that rumors about his recent protracted illness, including an alleged nervous breakdown, might have led to the decision, and he pointed out that U.S. Navy doctors, based on a thorough physical examination, rated his health as almost perfect. He emphasized to Donald his unblemished flying record, reliability as a teetotaler, and instrument, navigation, night flying, and test pilot skills. He mentioned nearly losing his passport for remaining in China contrary to U.S. State Department orders and volunteered to assist the CAF by flying special missions to guerilla units and by test flying Curtiss Hawk fighters. Donald replied that Chiang had reduced the Headquarters Transport Squadron personnel because its two planes were used only occasionally and that he had released Royal because of his higher salary and rumored poor health.

The discharge was friendly. Royal received a generous bonus and travel allowance. In a commendation dated August 3, 1938, Madame Chiang Kai-shek omitted any mention of mercenary activities:

> TO WHOM IT MAY CONCERN:
>
> I am glad to be able to testify to Mr. Leonard's efficiency as a pilot and as a navigator. He has had to fly great distances over difficult and indifferently mapped country, and has a record of achievement unmarred by loss of time or by accident. Mr. Leonard has always stood by his planes

> during air raids, taking off frequently in the face of great danger from Japanese raiders.
>
> It is with regret that we have to part with Mr. Leonard's services, but only do so because the great cost of the war in which we are involved constrains us to curtail expenditure and reduce the Headquarters Squadron.
>
> I can confidently recommend Mr. Leonard for his competency, his conscientiousness, his courage, and his courtesy, and wish him well wherever he may go.[65]

Briefly footloose and fancy free, Royal made good use of his rare leisure time. After reading a newspaper story reporting rumors of Royal's death, Hollywood movie studio film cutter Maxine Thayer, "a piquant brunette, with an independent spirit," had decided to accept his three-year standing marriage proposal. She cabled him: "YES IF YOU ARE STILL ALIVE MAXINE." He sent her passage money before she could change her mind.

Thirty-three–year-old Royal and twenty-seven–year-old Maxine exchanged wedding vows on September 17, 1938, in the Kowloon Union Church. The *South China Morning Post* headline proclaimed, "Mme. Chiang's Pilot Weds American from Paramount Studios." Following their honeymoon at Repulse Bay on Hong Kong Island, they moved into the luxurious Peninsula Hotel on the Kowloon waterfront.[66]

Three weeks before Royal and Maxine's wedding, Japanese fighters had attacked a China National Aviation Corporation (CNAC) DC-2, killing fourteen. Flying the plane was thirty-two–year-old Hugh Woods, who had attended Friends University in Wichita, Kansas, flown Caribbean routes for Pan American Airways, and joined CNAC as chief pilot in 1933. Woods, his radio operator, and one passenger survived the attack. According to historian William M. Leary, Jr., this CNAC plane was the first commercial airliner destroyed by an attack from the air.[67]

When the Japanese government announced that their fighters would continue shooting down civilian planes over China, CNAC—known to the Chinese as the "Middle Kingdom Space Machine Family"—canceled all flights. Japanese fighters had also attacked two Eurasia Aviation Corporation passenger planes. Needing air service to maintain contact with the outside world, the Chinese government requested that CNAC and Eurasia, in which it owned fifty-five percent majority interests, schedule night flights between Hong Kong and Chungking.

Although Eurasia agreed to provide this service, forty-four-year-old CNAC vice president and operations manager William Langhorne Bond maintained that night operations were unsafe and impractical. Bond, who held a private pilot license, had supervised the construction of a Curtiss-Wright Caproni aircraft factory in Baltimore, Maryland and in 1931 had been sent to China by Curtiss-Wright as a troubleshooter to protect its CNAC minority interest. Bond worked diplomatically with a Chinese government-chosen managing director and supervised day-to-day activities. In opposing Hong Kong night flights, Bond was mainly concerned about diplomatic complications with the U.S. State Department if CNAC, now forty-five percent owned by a Pan American Airways subsidiary, became involved in the Sino-Japanese War.

But former U.S. night mail pilots Royal Leonard, temporarily unemployed, and Ernest A. "Ernie" Allison, an adviser to the Chinese Commission on Aeronautical Affairs, who both had flown around the Rocky Mountains, were convinced that Hong Kong night flights were practicable. Allison had overridden another Kelly Field officer's decision to wash out Flying Cadet Claire Chennault and had also flown the initial and last legs of the first U.S. day and night transcontinental round-trip airmail flight.

Royal and Ernie met with T.V. Soong, acting head of the Commission, and presented a Kai Tak night flight plan. Soong had earned a B.A. in economics from Harvard University. In 1928, Chiang Kai-shek had appointed him Minister of Finance, and he had later established the Central Bank of China and the China Development Finance Corporation. Pursuant to Soong's instructions, Allison contacted Bond and offered CNAC one last chance to provide the Hong Kong-Chungking service. When Bond insisted that evening flights were impossible, Allison said that the Chinese government intended to operate the service with him and Royal as pilots.

Responsible for preserving Pan Am's investment and realizing the Chinese government majority owner easily could take over CNAC operations, Bond agreed to provide a Hong Kong–Chungking night service. Royal was the only available pilot with extensive night-flying experience over mountainous terrain. "Leonard is," Bond wrote to Pan Am vice president H.M. Bixby, "so good that I would like to see him in the Pan Am organization somewhere."

On October 1, 1938, Bond hired Royal at his former Headquarters Transport Squadron $1200 monthly salary ($18,300 in 2009 purchasing power and about double U.S. airline pilots' $678 average monthly pay) for making a weekly 1540-mile round-trip flight. A contract was not signed. The CNAC Board of Directors specifically ratified the higher salaries of Royal and thirty-year-old chief pilot Chuck Sharp for this extremely dangerous assignment. Sharp had graduated from the University of Texas and Kelly Field, failed to find a U.S. pilot job, and joined CNAC five years earlier.

Sharp lacked mountain night-flying experience, so Royal piloted the first Hong Kong–Chungking night flight, with Sharp as copilot. "He expressed his apprehension to me about this night work," said Royal, "wondering if a pilot could see enough at night to avoid the mountains."[68]

As CNAC resumed its Hong Kong–Chungking service, Japanese army and naval forces were closing in on Hankow. Chiang Kai-shek requested CNAC to evacuate key Nationalist government personnel from the temporary capital. Japanese air superiority mandated that the operation be conducted at night. Bond selected Royal and Sharp for the task. They were to fly DC-2s from Chungking 440 miles to the west, land at the lighted Hankow military field shortly after dark, airlift passengers 600 miles west to Chengtu because it was impossible to land at night on the Chungking island field, and return to Hankow before daylight for another load bound for Chungking. This grueling plan required flying about 2080 miles in fourteen hours.

On October 22, Royal left Chungking about 5:45 p.m. Upon landing at Hankow, he heard a distant rumble of artillery. In peacetime, he would have delayed taking off because heavy rain near high mountains on his route and snow and icing conditions rapidly approaching Chengtu augured a difficult flight. Under the circumstances, Royal took off as soon as passengers boarded, climbed to a safe altitude, and flew in clouds. Nearing Chengtu in a rainstorm, he could barely see the city's blurred lights. Guided by faint illumination from seventeen airport lanterns, he landed safely but had to wait for engine oil to be brought to the field for his plane.

When Royal took off, his estimated time of arrival (ETA) at Hankow was about ten minutes after daybreak. Nearing his destination, he spotted a fighter plane and turned, dove, and hovered above the flooded Yangtze River. He knew a fighter pilot at an altitude of several thousand feet would have a difficult time detecting his plane close to the water. After evading the suspicious aircraft, Royal, who had not been informed that the air field alarm signal equipment had been evacuated, called the Hankow radio operator and was told that there was no air raid alarm. He decided to land, but the sky suddenly filled with aircraft.

"Is there an air raid alarm?" inquired Royal.

"No alarm," replied the Hankow field radioman.

Royal thought the planes might be Chinese or Russian aircraft returning to Hankow, but he felt uneasy because they shifted formations in an unfamiliar manner. "Are those Chinese planes circling overhead?" he asked.

"No," responded the radioman.

"Whose planes are those overhead, anyway?" Royal pressed.

"They are Japanese, but there is no air alarm!" was the response.

"Now I saw them," said Royal, "diving, dropping bombs, strafing the ground just as I again approached the airport."

Royal decided not to land. Waiting passengers scrambled in all directions, hiding in a drainage ditch, jumping into bomb holes, and ducking into a bomb shelter.

"It was throttles open, nose down and westward," said Royal. He zigzagged through low hills. After a quarter of an hour, he relaxed and eased back on the motors. Half an hour later, specks in the sky startled him.

"Do you think I was scared?" Royal asked rhetorically. "Nope—nothing scares me any more like I once was scared by a flock of ducks.... I thought their formation was a formation of Jap fighters coming after us—certainly looked like it—anyway all I have to say for myself about that is that it certainly makes you feel like a goose to find that you have been scared by a duck."

Reaching the Ichang airfield 170 miles west of Hankow, Royal saw white ground panels warning: "DANGER! ENEMY AIRPLANES COMING! DON'T LAND!" He adopted escape and evade tactics for half an hour, flying west to mountains and circling fast enough to maintain altitude. Upon receiving an all-clear message, Royal landed. Ichang was within Japanese fighter and bomber range, so he refueled his DC-2 and headed for Chungking.

When Royal landed on the island air field at mid afternoon on October 23, Bond congratulated him on successfully completing a difficult flight and said another was scheduled in two hours. Royal looked surprised but replied that he would be ready. "Don't be foolish, Royal," said Bond. "This is no time for foolish heroics. I have already canceled your flight." Bond pointed out that Royal had been involved in the Hankow evacuation for twenty-two hours in addition to arduous flights the previous evening of October 21–22 when, with an hour's rest, he had flown 2160 miles, making a Hong Kong–Chungking roundtrip and then a Hong Kong–Chungking trip with Sharp as a passenger. Despite Royal's strong protest, Bond ordered him to get some sleep while Sharp made one Hankow flight.[69]

Somewhat rested, Royal left Chungking at 4 p.m. on October 24 for Hankow. He instructed his copilot to fly on a ninety-five–degree compass course and relaxed in the passenger compartment. He returned to the cockpit about ten minutes before the ETA, requested a Hankow bearing, and was told sixty degrees. If this reading was accurate, either a strong south wind had buffeted the plane or the copilot had flown off course. Successive bearings kept turning them north. Royal assumed the controls, took more bearings, and held steady at forty degrees. He studied the terrain below but it did not match his mental map. He verified his compass course and saw mountains northwest of Hankow. Seeing headlights from a Japanese truck convoy, Royal realized what had happened. Japanese radio operators had intercepted his bearing requests, confused the signals, and almost drawn him within anti-aircraft fire range from Japanese ships in the Yangtze River. Royal corrected his approach and found the road leading northwest from Hankow. Two minutes later, he spotted the Han River and followed it. He heard battle sounds and saw brilliant flashes in the sky to the southeast.

Guided by airport lantern lights, Royal landed. A thick black pall of smoke hung a few feet above the ground, which was shaking from battle tremors. Royal did not know how far away the Japanese troops were, but he understood the situation was desperate. More than two hundred terrified Chinese scrambled toward his plane. Royal instructed his copilot to keep the motors running and told CNAC field personnel to board only fifteen passengers. Twenty-two piled in.

At about 5:30 a.m., Royal taxied down the smoke-shrouded field, which was mined and studded with unfilled bomb holes. "We soared up through the smoke," recalled Royal, "the DC-2's motors roaring like mad. I climbed as steeply as I could with my load and looked back. Hankow was ringed with the white flash of cannon fire, the flickering of red flames. It was October twenty-fifth. The Japanese were marching into the doomed city that we had left behind us."

Twenty-four–year-old Chinese–American pilot Moon Chin made the last Hankow evacuation flight. Moon had been born in China and had graduated from a high school and the Curtiss-Wright aircraft maintenance school in Baltimore, Maryland. He had earned a limited commercial pilot license, returned to China, and been hired by CNAC as a copilot and promoted to pilot in 1936.

Waiting in a seaplane at the Hankow waterfront for remaining CNAC employees, Moon was informed that Japanese troops had entered the city. Fearing the invaders would prevent his departure if he waited for daylight, Moon, even though he had no night-flying experience, took off with fourteen passengers. At Shasi, about halfway up the Yangtze River to Ichang, he decided to touch down. His copilot pointed a flashlight out the cockpit window and yelled when the plane was about six feet above the water. Moon prayed to Buddha and dropped down for a perfect landing. He completed the trip to Chungking in daylight.

In total, Royal, Sharp, and Moon made fifteen Hankow evacuation flights, transporting 296 essential government personnel. "The men all did a fine job and I am sincerely proud of them," wrote Bond to the Pan American Airways head of Pacific operations, "but no one could keep that up long. I don't see how they accomplished as much as they did." A tradition was in the making: "CNAC men never abandon an airport until they see the whites of Jap eyes."

But lurking Japanese fighters forced CNAC to cancel most scheduled flights. After CNAC pilots were trained in using the German Telefunken radio navigation system and Sharp felt comfortable taking off from and landing at Kai Tak in the dark, Sharp took over the Hong Kong–Chungking night service. Royal's $1200 monthly salary was reduced to $450 with the explanation that he had been hired under the stress of the circumstances to help the company through an awkward period until Sharp gained night-flying experience over mountainous terrain. This negative experience marked the beginning of Royal's conflict with Sharp and, to a lesser extent, with Bond.

Temporarily without any assigned flights, Royal, accompanied by Maxine, vacationed in the Philippine Islands. A bout with typhoid fever interrupted his work on a magazine article about the Hankow evacuation. After recuperating, he performed slack wire tricks for his host. On December 14, Royal returned to Hong Kong on a Pan American flight and piloted the Martin M-130 Clipper flying boat for about an hour.

A few days later Maxine threw an early Christmas party for Royal, Chuck Sharp, and Emil Scott, who were leaving for Chungking. Alone on Christmas Day, she cried away the holiday. Two days later, despite Royal's radio warning to him about bad wind and icing conditions, CNAC pilot Jack Johnson crashed in Yunnan province and died.

"I wish Royal would give this business up and come home," Maxine wrote her mother on New Year's Day 1939. Her husband was thinking along the same line. Following the loss of Shanghai, Nanking, and Hankow in less than a year, he was losing faith in China's leadership. "I am beginning to wonder whether or not the Generalissimo is the man every one seems to think that he is," Royal said. "The crazy fool still keeps the Young Marshal as a prisoner when if he was free he could be doing a lot of good."[70]

Chapter 9

CLOSE ESCAPES

(January 1939 – February 1941)

Japanese fighters swarming around Hong Kong and bombers pounding Chungking set the parameters for the next three years of what Royal described as "nip-and-tuck" flying. Hong Kong was Nationalist China's main contact point with the outside world. The Japanese held Peking in northern, Canton in southern, Hankow in central, and Shanghai in eastern China; they controlled a puppet government in Nanking and territory along the Yellow and Yangtze Rivers. The key Nationalist-held cities in western China were Chungking, capital of Szechwan province, which was perched on a ridge at the confluence of the Yangtze and Chialing Rivers 1400 miles from the east coast, and Kunming, capital of Yunnan province, which was terminus of the railway from Haiphong 380 miles to the south in French Indo-China. CNAC flights between Hong Kong and the two western China cities were the principal means of transportation to and from Free China for Nationalist, as well as foreign, diplomats and businessmen.

Still making special flights for Chiang Kai-shek, Royal believed he was a prime target for Japanese fighter pilots whose number one prey was the Gimo. A few days after the *Panay* sinking, Japanese fighters almost caught Chiang, Madame Chiang, and an American pilot (name unknown), but the Boeing 247D outdistanced six Japanese fighters after a 175-mile chase.[71]

The Japanese maintained an excellent spy network in Hong Kong Colony. Coolies working at Kai Tak notified Japanese military personnel across the Colony border about impending CNAC flights. Unknown to his CNAC pilot customers, a barber passed information to a Japanese fighter base that was ten minutes flying time from Kai Tak. An airline mechanic also may have been an informer.

Royal knew firsthand about the effectiveness of Japanese spy work. In late March 1939, he was asked to make a secret flight from Chungking to Urumchi in Sinkiang province and was instructed not to tell his wife or anyone else about it. Before leaving, he tried to dial a British news broadcast from the Shanghai International Settlement and heard an announcer on a Japanese-sponsored English-language station report that, based on reliable sources, a Chinese diplomat and the Russian ambassador would depart the next morning on a CNAC plane for Moscow via Urumchi. Actually, Royal's passenger was a mysterious, sly-faced Russian with detailed knowledge of his background courtesy of the Soviet Secret Service. For his part, Royal was reporting on Russian military activity in China to the American Embassy in Chungking. The takeoff was delayed until afternoon. A sandstorm fortunately screened much of the flight. The Russians, who controlled Sinkiang province, drained the gas and oil from the plane engines and detained Royal and copilot Moon Chin in Urumchi for two weeks.

Contrary to standard airline practice, CNAC aircraft stayed on the ground at Kai Tak in good weather and flew mostly on dark and, preferably, stormy nights. Takeoff times were not announced in advance. Passengers checked into the terminal at midnight and waited for their plane to leave. Royal and Maxine set their alarm clock for a random predawn time, awoke, dressed, and drove to the airport. He watched the passenger check-in procedure, and she waited until he left. Whether he took off and ran another Japanese fighter gauntlet depended on the weather report. A "perfect" forecast: "ceiling three hundred feet; visibility, one mile; storms brewing." A typical report: "Dark. Mist. Gloom. Ceiling not known. Visibility not known. Stars no shine. Moon no beam." If passengers complained about waiting, Royal explained that "his neck was just as important as theirs." Although T.V. Soong told fellow passenger W.L. Bond that Japanese fighters had at best a million-in-one chance of catching a CNAC plane flying at night without lights, Bond reminded him that a million chances were sold in the Chinese National State Lottery and someone always won.[72]

Winter weather conditions and superior Japanese fighter speed complicated early morning flights from Hong Kong to Chungking. CNAC planes needed to depart Kai Tak and clear the Japanese lines before daylight. DC-2s, cruising at 160 miles per hour, normally completed the 770-mile trip in about five hours. Unfortunately, winter fog often shrouded Chungking until late morning. It was unsafe to wait at the intermediate Kweilin field because air raid warnings allowed inadequate escape time. Nakajima Type 97 "Nate" Army (292 mph) and Mitsubishi A5M "Claude" Navy (270 mph) fighters and, later, the Mitsubishi A6M "Zero" (332 mph) fighter could easily overtake a DC-2.

To avoid Japanese fighters, CNAC pilots left Kai Tak as late in the morning darkness as they dared. Upon clearing the Japanese lines, they slowed and fanned their engines to prevent overheating, hoping to reach Chungking as the morning fog cleared. Approaching the 100-foot–wide, 1900-foot–long cobblestone runway on the island field that resembled a Mississippi River mud flat, a pilot had to avoid high tension wires stretched across the Yangtze River Gorge. Leaving Chungking, pilots sometimes took off when the end of the island field was blanketed in fog. Royal used a stopwatch so he could time his take-off and turn exactly forty-five seconds after lift off to avoid smashing into a hill.

It was not advisable to keep an airplane on the Chungking island field because the Japanese were trying to bomb the Chinese capital into submission. According to American journalist Carl Crow, they intended "to kill as many civilians as possible in the belief that by terrorizing a nation, they [could] compel it to sue for peace." Bombers dropped their payloads from 16,000 feet, which was 1,000 feet beyond Chinese anti-aircraft gun range. Alarm signals for the next raid often sounded before the release from the last attack. In early January 1939, Royal arrived in the middle of a raid and took evasive action until it was safe to land. During the day, he remained on standby near his plane, ready to take off if Japanese raiders approached. Rather than risk getting caught at Chungking, Royal stayed overnight at Colonel Chennault's quarters in Kunming.

In Kowloon, Peninsula Hotel life was steadily wearing on Maxine's nerves. She enjoyed Tiffin (lunch) and American movies, welcoming and bidding bon voyage to ocean liners and Pan Am Clippers, and playing tennis and badminton. But pilots' wives coped alternately with boredom and fear. "The women sit around in the lobby and drink until they could almost float a battleship in the bay," Maxine remarked. She and her friends kept pilot Jack Johnson's widow occupied for three months until the widow could book passage home. Japanese bombing raids along the Hong Kong Colony border terrified the wives. "The boys say," reported Maxine, "that the place is afire from the sky and although it looks pretty it is enough to give them the jitters."

In March, Maxine traveled to Chungking and surprised her husband. They stayed at Dr. Chester B. and Grace Rappe's American Methodist Episcopal Mission compound. Maxine spoke to a Chinese Girls School English class about Hollywood movie stars and sat on the podium during Madame Chiang Kai-shek's "International Women's Day" speech. Maxine saw a caravan she described as small horses each loaded with four five-gallon cans of aviation fuel for CNAC making the approximately 400-mile journey from the Kunming railroad station to the Chungking island field. She endured sporadic bombing raids, sometimes dashing to cover in the compound cave dug forty feet under rock. One raid interrupted a tennis match with Colonel Chennault on the compound's bamboo pole-fenced court. "You'd better get in that shelter," warned the colonel as Japanese planes started dropping bombs.

"It stinks," replied feisty Maxine. "I'm not going in there."

"You'd better," semi-ordered Chennault. "You make a perfect target in that white dress."

"No more than you in that white shirt," she retorted.

Neither player dashed for the bomb shelter. Chennault watched the air raid until it ended. Journalist Teddy White remarked that Chennault studied Japanese bomber formations like a football coach studying films of his next opponent.[73]

In early May, Royal made the first CNAC flight into Chungking following a Japanese bombing raid that laid a one and a half miles long and five hundred yards wide swath of destruction and killed or injured an estimated 3,750 civilians. On the return trip to Hong Kong, Royal and copilot Moon Chin stayed overnight at Kweilin. When they tried to take off the next morning in a heavy downpour, the plane's front wheels sank to the hubs in mud. Several curious soldiers gathered around the mired nine-ton plane and indicated that they were willing to help tow it, but by the time Royal obtained rope, they had disappeared. Lacking manpower, Royal, who had used horses to extricate U.S. mail planes, decided to use their Oriental equivalent, water buffalo, but Moon, wiser in the ways of the Orient, tried to dissuade him. Pilots before landing passed over air fields and buzzed water buffalo to drive them off the runway, so Moon reasoned that the animals might not like airplanes and recommended hiring coolies to pull out the plane.

But Royal was positive his solution was best. He supervised the hitching of twelve water buffalo to the plane with an improvised rope harness. One farmer at a time ordered his animal to pull, and the others watched. Worried about inadequate warning time if Japanese fighters approached, Royal explained the need for speed and a team effort. The farmers tried to comply, but the wary animals charged at the plane, turned, tangled in the harness, rolled in a heap, jumped up, and romped away.

Disgusted by this turn of events, Moon obtained steel plates from the local railroad yard. Coolies dug under the DC-2 wheels and laid the plates underneath them. One hundred and fifty men pulled on a rope and moved the plane to solid ground. Later, Bond asked Moon why this approach had not been used in the first place. Moon explained that he had been wearing a new suit, had not wanted to get it dirty, and had decided to let the captain try his way first.

Poor maintenance bedeviled CNAC pilots. "These kids fly these old crates," said Maxine, "and one of these days they will fall apart in the air with them." Royal meticulously checked his aircraft before a flight but still experienced mechanical problems. In mid-June 1939, he returned to Kai Tak due to motor trouble; a week later, he experienced difficulty lowering his landing gear and taxiing across the field. Three times in early July, engine trouble delayed his take off, and in mid-July, he returned to Kai Tak for the same reason. Once, he smelled gas fumes and patched a leak with chewing gum. Another time, his DC-2 tail wheel almost fell off when he landed. "The boys have been having quite a bit of trouble lately with their planes," reported Maxine, "but seem to be lucky and get in all right."

Maxine suffered through one of her husband's closest calls. As Royal approached Hong Kong, Japanese radio operators, copying CNAC's signals, sent bearings on the Kai Tak band and tried to lure him ninety miles away to Canton. Royal turned off his radio and relied on dead reckoning. Luckily, he spotted moonlit landmarks. If Hong Kong had been fogbound, he might have been forced to land behind the Japanese lines or in the South China Sea. "Needless to say how the wives feel during this struggle," commented Maxine, who, aware of the Japanese radio interference, had been waiting for him at the airport terminal.

Comparatively safe in her hotel room, Maxine squirmed in a ringside seat as the Japanese armed forces tightened their noose around Hong Kong. Japanese warships stopped British, French, and German vessels outside Hong Kong harbor. Japanese fighters patrolled at night and twice during daylight over the harbor, and bombers struck the border area and destroyed an aviation radio tower. After Japanese ground crews spotlighted and directed anti-aircraft fire at a CNAC plane, the airline temporarily canceled Kai Tak flights. In late August, Japanese troops dug in along the thirteen-mile Kowloon border and the Japanese Navy threatened to blockade Hong Kong Harbor. The British, German, and Italian governments recommended that their women and children nationals leave the Colony. CNAC personnel prepared to evacuate planes and equipment, and Maxine registered with the U.S. Consulate for departure on an American gunboat.

It was even tenser in the hinterland. Japanese fighters attacked two CNAC planes near Chungking and wounded their Chinese pilots. Hugh Woods landed on the island field during a major raid when the radio station was shut down. "You know I have a strange feeling," Maxine wrote her mother, "that one of these boys will get it one of these days."[74]

A plane, not a pilot, got it next. Deciding that the potential need in an emergency for *The Flying Palace* outweighed the risk of its destruction, Madame Chiang Kai-shek ordered Headquarters Transport Squadron commander Walter Stennes to keep the plane at Chungking. Obsessed with *The Flying Palace's* safety, Royal, who still occasionally flew Chiang and Madame, urged his former boss to return the plane to a hiding place at Kunming. "German-like," Stennes could not disobey written orders with the Gimo's *chop*, and the plane remained at the island field. In early October, a lucky hit struck *The Flying Palace* dead center. It is noteworthy that no plane, whether *The Flying Palace*, Boeing 247D *Bai Ying*, Headquarters Transport Squadron, or CNAC, was destroyed or seriously damaged while assigned to Royal.

Constant standing by for air raids and hazardous flying, however, frayed Royal's nerves. He usually spent most of a month flying between Chungking, Kunming, Kweilin, and Chengtu, and only a few days in Kowloon because Chief Pilot Sharp had assigned himself the more remunerative Hong Kong–Chungking round-trip flights. Hugh Woods had an argument with Sharp, and Royal and Hal Sweet almost quit over the flight assignment issue. Maxine believed her husband was on the verge of a nervous breakdown. Like other pilots during brief home leaves, Royal needed a few days acculturation before he felt civil. He wanted to sleep constantly, fussed about getting to sleep and upon awakening, and threw a fit if he missed any sleep. Passenger Clair

Booth Luce, journalist wife of *Time* and *Life* publisher Henry Luce, expressed concern about Royal's exhaustion.

"It seems like the only place that he could get a quiet place [would] be to get in the middle of the desert," said Maxine. When in Kowloon, Royal retired to an airfield workshop and tried to relax by fine-tuning his sextant and revising maps. Drawing on his "parenting" experience with Big Boy Jess, Royal in August found some respite helping care for a delightful six-month-old fifty-pound baby panda named Pao-Pei (Precious Jewel) he had flown from Chengtu to Kai Tak. Pao-Pei was the last panda exported from China to a United States zoo before the outbreak of World War II.

Money kept Royal flying in China's perilous skies. "Sounds like these men are all alike and they don't really care about their homes or happiness as long as they make the almighty dollar," commented Maxine. In the spring of 1939, Sharp, Woods, and Royal, citing the extremely hazardous nature of their work, asked for a pay raise and an opportunity for future employment with Pan American Airways. During the previous eight months, Japanese fighters had shot at and forced down four passenger planes. "You don't have to be crazy to do a job like this," said W. L. Bond, "but it sure helps." CNAC more than doubled the pilots' monthly base salary from $450 to $1,000 for sixty hours' flying, five dollars each for the next ten hours, and twenty dollars for every hour flown above seventy hours. Royal often flew more than a hundred hours a month and earned more than $1,650 ($25,500 in 2009 purchasing power). "I'd like to get it while I can," he said.

In October 1939, Maxine, "crazy" due to the danger stalking her husband, left behind the stress of living in Kowloon and returned to the peace and quiet of southern California. Blissfully ignorant of Royal's constant scrapes, her state of mind improved in Los Angeles because she was not confronted by the daily details of his work and could sort of hope all was going well. Certainly, she enjoyed Christmas Day 1939 better not knowing that Royal flew into an ice storm, his air speed indicator and altimeter froze, and ice six to twelve inches thick lodged on his aircraft wings. As ice chunks fell off, the plane became unbalanced. "The throttles were vibrating back and forth like tuning forks," said Royal, "bruising and cutting my knuckles when I tried to grab them." He dropped to warmer air. When six hundred feet above Chungking, he circled until the ice melted, and then landed.[75]

Passengers caused problems too. Shortly after taking off from Hanoi, French Indo-China, Royal heard a "WHOOF PFFFFFF." He turned over the controls to his copilot, rushed into the passenger compartment, and discovered the emergency door was missing. A Chinese passenger, looking for cotton to stick in his ears, had mistaken the door for a cupboard, broken the seal, and turned the handle, causing the door to pop out. Royal grabbed the passenger's coat collar and shook a fist in his face. "Then thinking this fellow was nuts," said Royal, "I sat him down in his seat with the idea of tying him there when I noticed that the airplane was in a very steep angle. I was then somewhat alarmed cause with such a big load I was very careful not to climb too steeply. Then when I felt the whole plane quiver I ran to the cockpit pretty quick and I guess just in time because the airspeed was down to fifty and the plane stalls at sixty-five. Well sir I was moving faster than a bumble bee in a cloud of smoke when I pushed forward on the wheel and opened the throttles wide open. With such a load and since we were not very far above the ground it would have been serious had we fallen into a spin because I doubt there would have been enough altitude to straighten out."[76]

"Face" also complicated Royal's job. Taxiing down the Chungking runway with barely enough time to reach Kai Tak before fog was forecasted to arrive, he was directed to return to the airfield shack. His passenger, Finance Minister H.H. Kung, wanted to say good-bye to a visiting dignitary. Kung had graduated from Oberlin College (Ohio), earned an M.A. in economics from Yale University, and been awarded an honorary LL.D degree by Oberlin. In 1928, Chiang Kai-shek had appointed him Minister of Industry and Commerce. In 1932, Kung had negotiated with Italian Dictator Mussolini to send aviation instructors and sell military aircraft to China.

When Kung finished his farewell at the airfield shack, Royal told the ground crew he doubted the plane would arrive at Kai Tak ahead of the fog. The shocked Chinese said that Dr. Kung was the seventy-fifth lineal descendant of Confucius and his face must be saved for the honor of his ancestors. Royal made the flight and, fortunately, the fog held off long enough for him to land at Kai Tak with a few minutes to spare.[77]

More shocking than potential injury to Dr. Kung's "face" was Chiang Kai-shek's insistence that Royal be killed if he disobeyed an order. Royal was staying overnight in Chennault's Kunming quarters. The Gimo's secret service agents arrived and talked privately with the colonel. After they left, Chennault told Royal that he must land the next day at Kweilin. "Sorry, I can't do it," responded Royal.

"Why not?" Chennault demanded. "You will have an important general for your passenger. You must get there tomorrow." Royal complained that the Kweilin field was "humpty-dumpty with bomb holes." The two friends argued back and forth, Chennault insisting that Royal stop at Kweilin and Royal responding that only Chiang Kai-shek could make him go there. "Royal," said Chennault finally, "if you don't land at Kweilin, I'll kill you! I can't tell you why, but it is very important."

Although Royal thought Chiang Kai-shek resembled a minister or a YMCA secretary, the Generalissimo was cruel and brutal. He had been affiliated with a Shanghai criminal gang and killed a man in an argument. He had ordered every coolie working at an airfield executed because two had stolen gold coins that had fallen from a barrel and had sentenced to death the CAF pilots who had mistakenly bombed the American President Lines passenger ship *Hoover*. During World War II, the Generalissimo wanted the CNAC Chinese Managing Director shot because of a near accident, which was not his fault, but relented.

Responding to Chennault's threat (which never would have been carried out), Royal reluctantly agreed to stop at Kweilin. None of the passengers who boarded the plane, however, resembled a general. An elderly, scholarly looking gentleman; a middle-aged man; a beautiful woman; and two grim-faced goons, hands inside their coat sleeves, climbed aboard. Believing he had been double-crossed, Royal fumed all the way to Kweilin. If his plane had carried enough fuel, he would have flown directly to Hong Kong. Nevertheless, he obeyed Chennault's order and delivered the mysterious passengers to Kweilin.

When they next met, Chennault asked Royal how he had gotten along with the spies. Chennault explained that three of the passengers had been Japanese agents captured at Kunming and the other two had been Chiang's secret service agents. The Kunming warlord and British Hong Kong authorities, leery of Japanese reprisals, had refused to permit the execution of the spies in their jurisdictions, but the Kweilin warlord was willing. If Royal had not landed at Kweilin, Chiang's goons had orders to shoot the three spies in the plane.[78]

Fate intervened in another CNAC pilot's life. On October 29, 1940, Walter "Foxy" Kent, a happy-go-lucky redhead, took a flight originally assigned to Royal. Brash Foxy was a different breed of flyer than careful Royal. "All my life," said Foxy, "I've felt convinced that nothing would happen to me." When Japanese troops entered Peking, Foxy was inside the city walls. He disguised himself as a coolie, pushed a vegetable cart to the airport, and took off under the noses of Japanese soldiers. Making the last CNAC flight after the Japanese occupied Hanoi, Foxy confronted a diminutive Japanese officer in the airport terminal, called him a sawed-off runt, stormed out of the building, and took off.

Rather than wait for an all-clear signal and deal with grumpy passengers, Foxy liked to take off on schedule and land at an emergency field if he encountered enemy planes. On his fateful day, he spotted five Japanese fighters about one hundred miles northeast of Kunming and landed at the Chanyi emergency field. As he taxied off the runway in his civilian airliner, clearly marked on the wings "MAIL AND TRANSPORT," Japanese pilots strafed it and killed him with a 20-millimeter shell in the back. His stewardess, wearing a white nurse uniform, ran for cover and was wounded in the legs. A Japanese fighter returned, fired two bursts, and killed her. The attackers machine-gunned the DC-2 until the fuel tanks caught fire. Nine of the fourteen crew and passengers, including a mother and her ten-month-old child, died. Most were incinerated in the plane.

If Royal had been the pilot, the crew and passengers probably would have survived the day. He controlled what he could. He prepared meticulously, and calculated the odds for the best chance of a safe flight. Royal would have taken off after the Japanese fighters started returning to their base.

But Royal was a fatalist. Foxy was one of nine CNAC pilots. "Any one of us could have received the same dose from the Japanese as he did," commented Royal, "but it was his number that was up." Royal later said, "[y]ou get it when your time comes, whether you care or don't care. That is for someone else to decide."

Royal and Madame Chiang Kai-shek almost bought the farm on February 12, 1941. They took off from Kai Tak directly into a storm. When the plane bucked badly, Royal climbed to 16,000 feet, but Madame felt uncomfortable in the rarified air. Before dropping to a lower altitude, Royal took one sight on the moon and estimated his drift at an extraordinarily high twenty degrees. Three times, Royal tried to radio CNAC pilot Joey Thom, who had taken off forty-five minutes earlier, and warn him about seventy-mile-per-hour crosswinds, but Thom had turned off his radio to avoid detection by Japanese fighter pilots. Royal and Madame landed safely at Chungking, but Thom never arrived.

Two months later, Moon Chin found Thom's wrecked aircraft. Flying at an altitude of 6,000 feet, Thom had crashed into an unmapped 6,050-foot-high mountain. Moon believed Royal and Madame may have narrowly missed the same fate.[79]

Chapter 10

MY HERO ROY

(February – November 1941)

While Maxine worried about Royal's health and safety, American journalist Martha Gellhorn anointed him a hero. His performance on a routine (for him) Hong Kong-Lashio, Burma round-trip flight impressed Martha, who had recently reported on the Spanish Civil and Russo–Finnish Wars. She thought Royal was "the damndest aviator" she had ever seen and a genius. He validated her opinion by flying through a typhoon.

In late February 1941, Martha and husband, Ernest Hemingway, flush with cash from his *For Whom the Bell Tolls* novel royalties, arrived in Hong Kong to report on the Sino–Japanese War and British Far Eastern defenses. She created the impression that her "unwilling companion" hung around Hong Kong brothels and bars, gathering hearsay information for tabloid articles as she industriously investigated stories for *Collier's* magazine.

"Yes, I have to get out and dig for my stuff," Miss Gellhorn commented to Hugh Woods. "Ernest just sits around the house on his ass and writes and gets most of his ideas out of whore houses."

Macho Mr. Hemingway was impressed with the CNAC pilots' salaries and believed they were earning every penny and probably more. His wife saluted the airline as "China's life line for brains, money, and mail" without which no government could survive.[80]

Relying on a "favorable" (for China flying) weather report indicating a 500-foot ceiling, two miles visibility, and stormy weather,

Royal, Martha, and seven other passengers took off at 4:30 a.m. from Kai Tak on a "Flight into Peril." Martha likened the CNAC DC-2 to a flying beetle. Passengers sat on metal-frame canvas chairs, warmed themselves with coarse blankets, vomited into paper bags, and used a toilet behind a green curtain.

Half an hour after takeoff, the plane bucked a storm and Royal flew blind in clouds. Lightning flashed, frost covered the cockpit windshield, ice formed on the wings, and hail beat against the fuselage. The air speed indicator froze. Anticipating that this instrument might malfunction, Royal had practiced many hours comparing wind sounds through a slightly opened cockpit side window with the readings on his instrument panel air speed indicator. He opened the window an inch, listened intently, maintained adequate speed, and avoided going into a spin. "He became my hero within an hour of being air-borne," wrote Miss Gellhorn.

As Royal approached Chungking, a grayish-brown expanse of rubble, he struggled in 250 meters visibility to spot the island airfield, which was pocked with recently filled bomb holes. Flying upriver barely above rooftop level, he turned and landed. Martha and "Roy" spent the afternoon sipping tea in the primitive CNAC field office. They waited for a Kunming weather report, hopefully bad. In good weather, the Japanese bombed Kunming in the late afternoon killing thousands of civilians. Bombs had demolished Chennault's house, and shrapnel and tile fragments had littered his office. Royal wanted to avoid arriving in Kunming during a raid but also hoped to reach Lashio, 380 miles farther on, that night.

Even though he had not received the desired weather report, Royal decided to leave Chungking, fly low and slow, and arrive over Kunming at dusk. "Roy flew the plane, as if riding a horse, meandering along valleys," observed Miss Gellhorn.

"I go where I'm looking," he said. "You know there practically isn't a place you can land, on this whole trip." Nearing Kunming, Royal played peek-a-boo, swooping above mountaintops, checking the air space above the city and clouds, and dropping into valleys. "Yep," he said upon landing.

After refueling, Royal took off and flew along the Burma Road gorge. In average to bad weather, powerful drafts tossed the plane, which behaved like a runaway roller coaster. He touched down on the flare pot-lit Lashio field at 10 p.m., completing the 1494-mile journey in slightly more than twelve hours' flying time.

Receiving an all-clear signal the next day at 5:30 p.m., Royal took off and landed after dusk at Kunming. He and Martha rode rickshaws through the darkened, heavily bombed city. They saw a mile-long human chain passing water buckets to quench a major fire, a crowd waiting outside a movie theater to see *Kentucky* in Technicolor, and residents digging into the rubble of their bombed-out homes and shops. Martha rated Kunming in a class by itself compared with bombed Finnish cities. Royal opined that the Japanese Air Force used defenseless Kunming as a navigating and bombing training objective. "But he does not talk about what he has seen and where he has been," commented Martha. "If he talks at all, it is to tell you stories as jokes."

Before Japanese bombers returned, the DC-2 left Kunming for Chungking, where several high-level American and Chinese officials boarded for the last leg of the flight. As Royal landed at Kai Tak on the third night, several teary-eyed Chinese passengers clapped. In appreciation of the "extraordinary trip," Martha presented Royal a copy of *For Whom the Bell Tolls* inscribed by her and Ernest. Still impressed half a century later, Martha wrote the author: "Roy is worth a fine biography."

Looking drawn, Maxine greeted Royal and Martha at the Kai Tak terminal. Maxine had returned to Kowloon in late March 1940. Her second stay in the Orient proved more enjoyable than the first. She and Royal lived in an apartment staffed with four servants. Chuck Sharp and Hugh Woods shared an apartment above them. Sharp and his clique enjoyed drinking alcohol and gambling but Royal, a teetotaler, did not join their parties. Maxine hosted a tea for radical American journalist Agnes Smedley, who delivered an anti-Japanese lecture. Maxine also prepared dinner for Owen Lattimore, an American Far Eastern expert whose career Senator Joseph McCarthy later destroyed. In his spare time, Royal designed and built an experimental single-person watercraft that rode on a cushion of exhaust gases.[81]

But Hong Kong was a ticking time bomb. A million Chinese refugees were crammed in the Colony. Pill boxes and barbed wire rimmed the Repulse Bay beach where Royal and Maxine had honeymooned. Japanese nationals were quietly leaving. On May 6, Maxine and Ernest Hemingway boarded a Pan American Clipper and returned to the USA.[82]

Two weeks later, unlucky Hugh Woods, trying to evade Japanese fighters, made an emergency landing at Suifu. A Japanese bomb destroyed his DC-3's right wing. Royal flew in mechanics, parts, and tools and picked up Woods and his crew and passengers and took them to Chengtu. CNAC did not have a replacement DC-3 wing, but the DC-2 and DC-3 wing butt and center wing butt jigs were identical. Mechanics attached to the DC-3 fuselage a DC-2 wing that was five feet shorter than the DC-3 wing. The "DC 2 ½" was flown to Kai Tak for repairs, and CNAC continued operating with one DC-3 and four DC-2s.

Shortly after the DC 2 ½ operation, Royal flew young and attractive American journalist Annalee Whitmore, who, with Theodore H. White, coauthored *Thunder Out of China*, from Hong Kong to Chungking. Miss Whitmore, tired of writing Hollywood screenplays, had taken a job with a Chungking relief organization to evade the U.S. War Department prohibition against American female journalists working full-time in war-torn China. Stretching the truth a bit about his near participation in the MacRobertson Race, Royal told the adventurous young lady that he had flown the Prince of Wales around the world. Impressed by this story, she accepted his invitation to sit in the copilot seat. He told her that she must see Kweilin, one of the most beautiful places in China with its green-covered limestone mountains that, to him, from the air looked like millions of jammed together upside-down ice-cream cones. By the light of the moon, Royal landed at Kweilin. Somehow, the plane got stuck. While a coolie dug out a tire, Royal and Annalee enjoyed the scenery. They arrived in Chungking early the next morning. Waiting for journalist Mel Jacobs, her future husband, to come and get her, Annalee and Royal drank tea under an awning beside his plane. "Mel was a little put out," she recalled.[83]

It was soon Royal's turn to be "put out" by Old Man Weather. According to an emergency report, a severe storm was passing over Hong Kong, so Royal laid over at Kweilin the evening of June 29. He was flying the oldest CNAC DC-2, a seven-year-old relic with a fuselage rebuilt by Chinese mechanics. Two other CNAC pilots, Hugh Woods and beetle-browed Frank L. Higgs, prototype for "Dude Hennick" in Milton Caniff's *Terry and the Pirates* cartoon strip, joined him.

Although friends said the initials "F.L.H." stood for "Fly Like Hell," Higgs felt cautious the next morning without a Hong Kong weather report. Royal negotiated with his colleagues about taking off first. Frustrated by their comedic "Alphonse and Gaston" ("you go first; no, you go first") routine, needing to pass over Japanese bases in darkness and approach Kai Tak at daybreak, and believing the storm had passed over Hong Kong, Royal decided to take the lead.

At 3:00 a.m. Royal took off, planning to head south-southeast 325 miles until about seventy-five miles from Hong Kong, zigzag across the Japanese fighter patrol zone, and touch down precisely at daybreak. But a head wind held him back. Three hundred miles from Kai Tak, he noticed a strong drift and allowed for ten, then twenty and thirty degrees. He flew through strong counterclockwise winds. His Hong Kong bearings changed rapidly. The plane bobbed up and down like a cork in river rapids.

Searching for Hong Kong Harbor, Royal looked down a mile-wide hole in the clouds and spiraled the DC-2 through the smooth-as-silk eye of a typhoon. He dropped to 1500 feet above sea level before getting under the ceiling. Heavy rainsqualls drove the plane every which way with the force of a fire hose. After flying about a mile, the DC-2 leaped like a bucking bronco 300 feet straight up. Churning air currents smashed the plane unmercifully. Looking at the instrument panel seemed like trying to read a newspaper in a clothes dryer. During the next fifteen minutes, the plane covered ten miles with the air speed indicator registering 160 miles per hour. Huge waves smashed against rocky-shored islands and bashed British warships whose masts rolled in nearly one hundred-degree arcs.

On a normal approach, Royal would have turned ninety degrees toward Kai Tak after crossing downtown Hong Kong. Driven by a tail wind, however, he would have been blown off his approach if he turned too late and headed toward mountains without enough time and space to adjust power, bank, or turn, and avoid a crash. Taking into account the wind conditions, Royal must have turned earlier, perhaps as much as 120 degrees, and dealt with a crosswind.

Under full power, Royal approached Kai Tak at an altitude of 500 feet. "The rain was drowning the cockpit in a Niagara of water, in such solid sheets that I could only get an occasional glimpse of where I was going," he said. Water poured over the Kowloon sea wall. He was afraid that the runway, which fronted on the harbor, might wash away.

"Hong Kong wind thirty-five miles an hour," yelled the radio operator. Royal shouted that he did not believe him. The radioman checked and insisted that he was correct. Royal later discovered that the operator meant 135 miles an hour.

Taking advantage of a momentary lull in the rough air, Royal tried to land. Terrific gusts smacked the plane sideways, forward, back, up, and down. One second his wheels skimmed just above the water, the next, they dangled hundreds of feet above it.

Royal yelled at his copilot to raise the landing gear, which was dragging the plane, but the man was too terrified to respond.

"British weatherman say typhoon still here!" shouted the radio operator. "Blowing 113 miles an hour!"

Deciding he had exhausted his luck for the day, Royal headed to the widest part of Hong Kong Bay, turned into the wind, and climbed. Between 2,000 and 5,000 feet, he encountered extremely heavy rain. It felt like "riding in a speedboat, going at one hundred miles an hour through 30-foot waves—sideways, up and down, corkscrewing all over the sky."

As rain cascaded down the windshield in rough air at 6,000 feet, Royal regained control of his plane at 120 miles per hour throttled-down speed. At 10,000 feet, he climbed into comparatively smooth conditions and at 12,000 feet emerged into good flying weather above the clouds. Finally free from the typhoon's raw power, Royal flew north 200 miles to Namyung and landed in a ninety-mile-per-hour wind.

"That was the end of my experience with the typhoon," said Royal. "I felt as a tenderfoot might after just getting off the wildest of bucking broncos. My knees buckled under me as I walked across the rain-swept Namyung field."

Higgs and Woods, who had played it safe and stopped at Namyung, greeted him. "Hey, boy!" they yelled. "What goes? You look all in. Been working hard?"

"Sure have," replied Royal. "Just licked a typhoon."

In the opinion of an incredulous British air officer, Royal, who had flown through the eye, down the center, out one diameter, up the other diameter, and over the top of the typhoon, was the "only fool in existence who had luck enough to fly through and come out in one piece."

"There's an old saying," comments Louis Stannard, retired Pan Am pilot and author of the novel *China Diaries*, "that 'there are old aviators, and there are bold aviators, but there are no old bold aviators.' When Royal flew into the center of a typhoon and tried an approach to Hong Kong in hundred knot plus wind, he proved that the old axiom was for the rest of us and not him."[84]

Two months later, Royal flew Olga Greenlaw and her husband, Harvey, the American Volunteer Group (Flying Tigers) executive officer, from Hong Kong to Chungking. Taking off at 2:30 a.m. from Kai Tak in a DC-3, the sky "was inky black," reported Olga, "with rain pouring from low-scudding clouds—as unhappy a night for flying as you could imagine.... The first part of the flight was over Japanese-held territory and the goggle-eyed invaders had no qualms about improving their marksmanship on defenseless transports." These conditions delighted Royal. "They'll never find us in this stuff," he "beamed cheerfully." He circled blacked-out Hong Kong, flew blind at 13,000 feet to clear mountains, and skirted Canton to avoid anti-aircraft fire.

"It was sickeningly bumpy all the way to Chungking—for me, five and a half hours of torture," Olga recalled. She asked her husband whether Royal might miss the island field in the bad weather. "Oh, they don't crack up often," he replied. "Approaching [Chungking]," Olga said, "we could see the city plainly—a mass of ruins and destruction. Although the Japs were bombing it continuously and without mercy, the new capital of China carried on stoically."

In early October, Royal flew Generalissimo and Madame Chiang Kai-shek from Kweilin to Chungking. Madame Chiang, who was childless, chatted with Royal and advised him not to wait too long before starting a family. "The Madame certainly seemed to know a lot about me," Royal wrote Maxine. Madame was aware of his upcoming home leave and wanted to make sure he returned to China. She gave him money to shop for her and asked him to evaluate American public opinion about China and to prepare a report for her.

Later in October, Royal flew U.S. Army Brigadier General John Magruder and his staff from Hong Kong to Chungking. Magruder, head of the American Military Mission to China (AMMISCA), was responsible for observing Sino–Japanese War developments for U.S. Army Chief of Staff General George C. Marshall, overseeing the arming and training of thirty Chinese divisions and the deployment of the American Volunteer Group, and organizing U.S. Lend Lease supply operations.[85]

By November, China's treacherous skies finally wore down Royal. "Six years is a long time to spend in a land that is not home," he commented. Colonel Chennault had talked to Bond about Royal's need for rest and medical treatment for an abdominal infection. Although in June Royal had decided to remain in China because he was earning $1500 a month ($21,800 in 2009 earning power), by fall, he had changed his mind. During his last six months in China, he had flown 365 hours and 42 minutes (101 hours and 55 minutes on instruments).

Burned out and weak as a kitten on his last flight, Royal at first rejected a passenger's suggestion that he get some sleep. His Chinese copilot could fly level but not handle emergencies. Finally, Royal relented. "Head for that," he told the copilot, pointing to a mountain. "When you get to it, go around it." The copilot nodded and repeated the instructions. Royal dozed off. Awakening moments later, he saw the copilot starting around the mountain. Royal drowsed. Thirty minutes later, he awoke with a start. He looked outside and noticed the plane was flying around a mountain. By this time they should have flown beyond any high terrain. Suddenly, it dawned on him what was happening. "You idiot!" bellowed Royal. "What have you been doing?"

"Just what you say, boss," responded the copilot. "I keep flying round mountain."

Exhausted from chaotic flying, ill, and anxious to rejoin his wife, Royal returned to Kowloon the next day and prepared for his long-awaited vacation. He had logged 3,823 flying hours over China, French Indo-China, and Burma. "In all my six years of flying in China," he proudly remembered, "no airplane in my charge was damaged except for the bullet holes I got in the air and the few scratches that I got on a CNAC wing when a wheel broke through an underground cave at Kweilin."[86]

Chapter 11

GETTING IN HIS LICKS

(July 1937 – May 1942)

During their four years together, Claire Chennault and Royal developed a deep hatred toward the Japanese, whom they regarded as barbarians, for bombing innocent Chinese civilians and machine-gunning helpless pilots and passengers. Royal shared the popular American prejudice against the Japanese as "monkey people." He warned, "The honeybee is like the Japanese. He is a desirous and industrious little fellow. You cannot help admiring him for his aggressiveness and detailed organization, even when it comes to killing. But you cannot make him happy with a single pound of honey. Indeed, even as he puts it away, his frenzy reaches such a point that he will sting you badly if you do not give him more." Chennault and Royal wanted in the worst way to strike back at their enemy.

Shortly after their July 1937 reunion in Nanking, Chennault and Royal, as well as other American airmen, discussed bombing Tokyo. Chennault requested Chiang Kai-shek to provide them Martin B-10 bombers but was turned down because China's survival depended on U.S. aid and Chiang feared that involving American pilots in a raid on Japan might jeopardize his U.S. government support. "Oh well," said avid softball player Chennault, "it will be batter up sometime! We'll mow 'em down."

Royal did not give up on hitting back at Japan. In the fall of 1937, he wrote Chennault concerning "the mission that we discussed about where the nest stops for the night and the birds that roost there, etc."

He was concerned about keeping the project secret and obtaining a plane for bombing practice. Blissfully ignorant of Royal's scheme, the birds nestled undisturbed.

But Royal muffed his best opportunity to see Japan from the air. In early March 1938, Chennault provided him a copy of a memo about modifying a Douglas transport for extra fuel capacity, preparing airport runways, and obtaining blank leaflets for practice drops. Two days later, Mr. Donald asked Royal his price for a special mission. Madame Chiang Kai-shek turned down Royal's request to use *The Flying Palace*. On May 19, two Chinese pilots, flying Martin bombers, dropped propaganda leaflets on cities in western Japan. "Nuts. Guess I should have offered to do it for $5,000 instead of $20,000," Royal lamented. "Worth something just to make the trip."[87]

Reeling under Japanese air power, the Chinese government in October 1940 sent Chennault to Washington, DC, to help T.V. Soong procure American pilots and planes to defend Chungking, Kunming, and the Burma Road. In Royal's opinion, T.V., who *Time* magazine dubbed "the Morgan of China," was the most impressive member of the Soong Dynasty. "He was extremely prompt and resembled… a clean-cut, precise businessman of the Western World," wrote Royal. "He was well informed on a hundred subjects and could talk as intelligently about aerial navigation as he could about Chinese freight loadings."

T.V. was Chairman of the Board of China Defense Supplies, Inc. (CDS), a Delaware corporation set up by White House insider and wheeler-dealer Tommy "The Cork" Corcoran. President Roosevelt's uncle Frederic Delano was "honorary counselor." Thirty-three–year-old Harvard Law School graduate Whiting Willauer, who had worked as an attorney for the Civil Aeronautics Board, U.S. Department of Justice, and Federal Power Commission, was CDS executive secretary. With the passage of the Lend-Lease Act on March 11, 1941, CDS became the agent and conduit through which war materiel, planes, replacement parts, and fuel were leased, sold, and transferred to Nationalist China and CNAC.

President Roosevelt liked Chennault's plan for a "Special Air Unit" of 150 Lockheed Hudson bombers for striking Japan and 350 Curtiss P-40 fighters, all flown and serviced by American pilots and mechanics. But cooler heads prevailed. Secretary of War Henry Stinson and General George C. Marshall regarded bombing Japan as a "half-baked" idea that might provoke an attack on the United States, so the Roosevelt Administration agreed to provide China fighter planes, but not bombers. American fighter pilots and support personnel signed employment contracts with Central Aircraft Manufacturing Company (CAMCO), a front organization, and traveled to Kyedaw airfield in Burma to commence training under Chennault as the American Volunteer Group (AVG).[88]

In mid-May 1941, an American military mission under Brigadier General Henry B. Clagett, Philippine Department Air Force commander, arrived in Chungking to evaluate CAF combat readiness and Japanese Air Force tactics. CNAC Managing Director P.Y. Yang insisted on Royal as the mission pilot. Royal was very flattered that he had been chosen for this important and dangerous task. In two weeks, he showed his passengers approximately 200 airfields and potential airfield sites. Operating from Chungking, Kunming, and Chengtu, they visited the CAMCO aircraft assembly factory at Loiwing and landed at and inspected fields in Chekiang province, as well as other airdromes in Kwangsi, Kiangsi, and Honan provinces. Royal landed at Chuchow, approximately thirty miles from the Japanese lines, and at another field less than two hundred miles from Shanghai. His friends were amazed that he dared fly so close to the enemy, but the Chinese spy network warned the mission when Japanese planes taxied onto a field and took off and in which direction they flew. Wherever the mission stopped, the Japanese bombed soon after they departed. In his report, General Clagett identified the Chuchow field, 730 miles from Nagasaki, and Lishui field as promising advance bases for attacking Japan but also as vulnerable to land and air attack.

When Chennault returned from Washington, DC, in July, he stayed three nights in Royal's Kowloon apartment and brought news that the Roosevelt Administration had changed its policy. Chennault told Royal that the AVG was slated to receive twenty-four bombers immediately and forty-two more by the end of 1941.[89]

Royal's next job offer was even more a vote of confidence in his ability. Chennault recommended him for a brigadier generalship commanding the AVG bomber group that was projected to fly long-range, medium-speed Lockheed Hudsons in raids on Japanese shipping and factories. Royal deserved this position because of his familiarity with Japanese aerial combat tactics demonstrated in his report to MacArthur, unmatched knowledge of Chinese air fields, close working relationship with Chennault and high Chinese officials, and experience training the CAF bomber squadron.

In a letter to T.V. Soong, dated September 4, 1941, Chennault wrote, "One of the older CNAC pilots, who has been your personal pilot on a number of flights, is scheduled to return to the U.S.A. on leave about Dec. 1, 1941. He has stated to me that he will be available to lead a formation of bombers back along the Pan American route [Honolulu–Midway Island–Wake Island–Guam–Manila–Hong Kong] or north over the Alaska–Siberia route to any designated point in China, about the end of December 1941. He also states that he would be willing to accept command of the bombardment Group for subsequent tactical operations. Since this pilot is a very skillful navigator and is acquainted with most of the Chinese Airdromes, his services would be of great value to us."

The day after Chennault wrote this letter, White House aide and Lend-Lease Administrator for China Dr. Lauchlin Currie wrote Madame Chiang Kai-shek that the British government had agreed to the reallocation of thirty-three Hudson bombers to China by the end of the year and had arranged to make available 50,000 four-pound incendiary bombs. On November 5, Madame cabled Chennault that Currie had informed her "prospects good for deliverance of Hudsons by air."[90]

Before he departed Hong Kong for the U.S. on November 22, Royal talked to Madame Chiang Kai-shek and Chennault. Madame asked Royal to wake up America about the Japanese menace. "Tell them to send us as many planes as they want," she said. "Just give us two weeks' notice and tell us where they want the landing fields. We will be ready to welcome them."

"Tell 'em back in the United States," said Chennault, "that the showdown is coming pretty soon. Unless we get ready, our pants are going to be down plenty."

Chennault wanted Royal to recruit bomber pilots and crews in the U.S. and train them for flying over Chinese terrain. But the Japanese war machine foiled Chennault and Royal's dream of bombing Japan and Royal's opportunity to command the bomber wing. While forty-nine bomber and 118 fighter AVG personnel were en route to Burma, thirty-three Lockheed Hudson bomber crews were preparing to leave the U.S. for China and Royal was sailing on the American President Lines *President Coolidge* to the United States, the Japanese attacked Pearl Harbor, Wake Island, Guam, Manila, and Hong Kong. "The bombing of Honolulu," bemoaned Royal, "blew our plans sky-high. Our proposed line of flight ... to China was blasted. Our fondest dream, the bombing of Nagasaki, was not then to come true. However, in an indirect way, I got in my licks later."

Arriving in San Francisco on Christmas Day, Royal telephoned T.V. Soong, who told him to take a vacation while the Roosevelt administration reevaluated its Far Eastern military strategy. The Hudson (renamed Lockheed A-28-LO) bombers remained parked on the factory field in Burbank, California.[91]

Royal's hard-earned vacation did not last very long. Major Merian C. Cooper, Chief of Army Air Corps Intelligence for China, telephoned him in Los Angeles. During World War I, Cooper had founded and flown combat missions with the Kosciuszko Squadron, helping Poland resist a Russian Bolshevik invasion. More recently, Cooper had produced the epic film *King Kong* (1933) and the western classic *Stagecoach* (1939) directed by John Ford and starring John Wayne. "Leonard," said Major Cooper, "the information we want from you is so important we do not want to go ahead with our plans until you get here. Therefore, every day, every hour, every minute, might mean the success or failure of our mission. We will be holding up *a very big show* until you get here!" [emphasis added].

Major Cooper asked Royal to travel immediately at Army expense to Washington, DC. Simultaneously, Army Intelligence officers asked Pan Am management for information about Chinese landing fields. Pan Am vice president Harold M. Bixby telephoned Royal, explained that Pan Am as CNAC's parent company wanted credit for his assistance to the War Department, and said that Pan Am (expecting government reimbursement) would pay his and Maxine's travel expenses to Washington, DC. "After all," said Bixby, "being CNAC means you are also Pan Am, so hereafter, all your contacts with the Army should be through us."

Unknown to Royal, Pan Am president Juan Trippe and U.S. Army Air Corps commander Lieutenant General Henry H. "Hap" Arnold were competing for control of armed forces overseas air logistical support. The U.S. military air transport system was in disarray, while Pan Am, the nation's premier international airline, was strategically positioned worldwide. Pan Am Clippers crossed the Pacific Ocean, Pan Am Air Ferries operated from Miami, Florida, through Brazil to Africa, and Pan Am Airways–Africa, Ltd. linked the African coast with the Middle East. Trippe envisioned Pan Am as the aerial instrument for American global leadership and believed that World War II presented a golden opportunity for his airline. In the uncertain days following the

Japanese attack on Pearl Harbor, he exercised options on 50,000 shares of Pan Am stock. Trippe wanted the U.S. government to contract with Pan Am to operate all overseas military air-supply routes. In return for an investment of capital, he offered the government an ownership interest, but no control. He also wanted all other American airline overseas components merged into his Pan Am behemoth.

In the midst of this power struggle, Royal and Maxine arrived in Washington, DC, on Monday morning, January 12, 1942. "I fully expected Pan Am to rush me to the War Office as quickly as possible," related Royal. "Instead, I was sent to the Mayflower Hotel and told to stay under cover. Mr. Juan Trippe did not want the Army to know I was there until we had drawn up a plan of our own to present to the Chief of Staff.... I gathered that Mr. Trippe did not think too highly of the officers commanding our Air Force. Pan Am was going to show the Army how to conduct an air war. These ideas did not exactly fit mine but I said nothing.... If this bombing squadron headed for China to bomb Japan wanted me with them, than that is where I felt I should be and not mixed up with any politics."

As instructed by Chennault, Royal arranged a meeting early Tuesday morning with T.V. Soong. Royal also called General Arnold's office and said he was carrying a personal letter from a mutual friend, Frank Garbutt, who was related to Maxine by marriage and was a financial backer of aircraft manufacturer Glenn L. Martin. "A few minutes later Mr. Bixby called," said Royal, "wanting to know what in the Hell was the matter with me!! Why did I call outside when I had definite instructions to keep in hiding!" Bixby asked Royal whom else he had contacted besides General Arnold, and he revealed the T.V. Soong appointment. "Jesus Christ, God all mighty," exclaimed Bixby. "You have certainly upset the apple cart!! The Army has been calling here, raising hell with us because they know you are in town and haven't reported. Get over here to the Pan Am office just as quickly as you can!!!!"

At the Pan Am office Royal met with Bixby, John C. Cooper, Pan Am vice president and legal counsel (Major Cooper's brother), and Clarence Young, vice president and Pacific Division manager. Bixby told Royal he had placed Pan Am in an embarrassing position. Before Royal called General Arnold's office, Pan Am management had lied to Army officials and said Royal was not in town. "The damage has already been done," said Bixby. "Now you'll have to make some sort of an appearance but tell them nothing. Say you are sick and can stay only a minute, make up an excuse, but don't tell them anything they want to know. Mr. Trippe wants to take care of that himself after he talks to you. If you spill your beans now you will spoil all his plans."

Bixby accompanied Royal to T.V. Soong's office in the Chinese Embassy. In Bixby's presence, Royal could not discuss the AVG bomber group and Japan bombing plans. Waiting for a taxicab after finishing the meeting, Bixby explained Pan Am's predicament. President Roosevelt had issued an Executive Order delegating to the Secretary of War emergency power to nationalize all U.S. airlines. "The Army want[s] to take over Pan Am, lock, stock, and barrel," said Bixby. "Pan Am [i]s depending upon [you] to help [it] over the most difficult period in [its] history. What [you] say to the Army might make the difference of whether or not there [is] a Pan Am during the war."

Patriotic Royal was more concerned about winning the war than Pan Am's survival and potential huge profits. Even though he wanted Pan Am pilot seniority after the war ended and had a wonderful opportunity to ingratiate himself with the Pan Am upper echelon, Royal refused to permit his name and reputation and his Chinese aviation knowledge to be used in an underhand manner for one company's profit.

"Further, my disgust was growing more profound for this organization," said Royal, "that was trying to keep from our high command information which they evidently considered so important for their plans.... Furthermore, my pals in the Philippines were fighting for their lives. I couldn't give any help by hiding from the Army. To me Pan Am or any similar organization was not big enough to influence me into considering their interest paramount to that of our nation."

Unaware of Royal's attitude, Bixby asked him to prepare a detailed plan for Trippe's presentation to General Arnold. Pan Am wanted to use Royal's knowledge of landing fields to help procure a contract for flying supplies to China. Royal refused, explaining that the Army had contacted him first and his primary obligation was to his country.

"I was a stranger to all this Washington political wrangling," commented Royal. "I felt that if Pan Am was big enough to control the destiny of our nation I may as well pack up and go home." He decided to enter Presbyterian Hospital in New York City for treatment of his intestinal ailment. Before he could leave Washington, however, Captain Sy Bartlett telephoned and said the Army wanted to interview him.[92]

A week after arriving in the nation's capital, Royal conferred for more than an hour with Brigadier General Dwight D. Eisenhower, head of the Pacific and Far East section of the War Department War Plans Division. Eisenhower's rise up the Army chain of command had been tedious. After graduating from West Point in 1915, he did not see combat action during World War I. Ranked only a major, he had recently assisted MacArthur in trying to build a Filipino Army. Following the Pearl Harbor attack, General George C. Marshall had placed Ike in charge of Pacific Theater planning.

In meeting with Eisenhower and three other Army officers, Royal praised the AVG organization (now nicknamed the Flying Tigers) as thoroughly efficient and recommended sending one hundred fighter planes to protect the Burma Road. He also stated that the Japanese could easily conquer the Philippine Islands and Singapore within two weeks. His prediction about Singapore was close. The British unconditionally surrendered there on February 15, 1942. But the exceptional courage and stubbornness of American and Filipino troops made Royal's prophecy about the Philippines miss the mark. General MacArthur left the Philippines on March 11, Bataan surrendered on April 9, and the island fortress Corregidor fell on May 6, 1942.[93]

Upon learning of Royal's meeting with General Eisenhower, Trippe summoned the idealistic and independent-minded pilot. Even though he dearly wanted Pan Am seniority, Royal took the moral high road. "[Trippe] expressed his keen displeasure at what I was doing," said Royal. "He made it very plain that if I divulged to the Army everything I knew my value to Pan Am would be nil.... I expressed my opinion to the effect that as long as I did what I thought was right I could not be so very wrong." Trippe's foreboding parting words (a la Frye's comment to Royal about choosing between TWA and Jackie Cochran) were, "Well your man, I hope you know what you are doing."

Ignoring the imperious Trippe's warning, Royal kept four important appointments. He met with Army Air Section G-2 and assured his interviewers, as promised by Madame Chiang Kai-shek, that Chinese peasants anywhere in China in a week could build airfields with all-weather, mile-long, 200-foot–wide runways suitable for heavy bombers. He dined with Texas Congressman W.R. Poage and complained about his unpleasant experience with Pan Am officials. During a meeting with General Arnold, he was offered an Army Air Corps major commission but declined it because he would not be assigned to the China Theater.

As Bixby cooled his heels outside the door, Royal met for an hour in the State Department Building with Lauchlin Currie, who had been Royal's passenger in China. Currie was FDR's point man on the hush-hush AVG project and was later discovered to have been divulging classified White House information to Soviet intelligence agents. After shedding Bixby, Royal and Currie enjoyed dinner together. According to Royal, he and Currie worked "on plans which were just as vital to our government as what I was doing for the War Dept." In a subsequent memorandum to President Roosevelt, Currie urged "the establishment of an air freight service from Calcutta to northern Burma and China to maintain air and other operations in China." Currie also arranged for Royal's admittance to the U.S. Naval Hospital in Bethesda, Maryland.

But Pan Am management wanted to control Royal for publicity purposes and offered to pay his hospital expenses. Worn out by the Washington merry-go-round, Royal and Maxine traveled to New York City at the end of January 1942, and he entered Presbyterian Hospital. Royal's primary doctor was Bixby's personal physician. Upon his discharge in early February, Royal tried to pay the hospital bill but was advised that Pan Am would clear his account. He conferred with William Van Dusen, Pan Am public relations department head, and made several New York City radio appearances. He also met with Doubleday, Doran managing editor James Poling about publishing his memoir of his China experiences.

Acting quickly, Doubleday, Doran arranged with journalist Richard G. Hubler to revise Royal's draft and provide an introduction. Hubler divided the lengthy typewritten manuscript into chapters, added historical and biographical information, deleted repetitive or uninteresting material, and edited Royal's recitations of several conversations. In the introduction, Hubler described Royal as "a little, dark-haired, soft-spoken fellow with a talent for spinning yarns. He has an engaging grin and the knack of sideslipping through adventure as though he were a suburban commuter rather than an experienced pilot-adventurer... His forté is reliability." Hubler stated that *I Flew for China*, published in 1942, "is the tale of the last pioneers and of the last adventurers too" and a tribute to rugged individualism and adventurous spirit. The book also answered Madame Chiang Kai-shek's request to wake up America about the Japanese menace to mankind.[94]

After returning to California, Royal appeared on radio shows, pitching War Bonds and telling stories about the Flying Tigers and his

China experiences. At the Coconut Grove nightclub in Los Angeles he sat on the dais with movie actor Edward Robinson and actress Mary Martin and informed 400 Rotarians that Chennault and MacArthur "should receive immediate help at all costs." He also ferried B-24 bombers from the Consolidated Vultee Aircraft Corporation plant in San Diego to present-day Davis-Monthan Air Force Base near Tuscon, Arizona.

During the last week of March 1942, Royal traveled to Alameda Naval Air Station on San Francisco Bay and provided information to Lieutenant Colonel Jimmy Doolittle about Chinese airfields. Unknown to Royal, the Army Air Corps was planning a bombing raid on Japan launched from an aircraft carrier. After striking their targets, the raiders planned to fly approximately 1200 miles to Chuchow, refuel, and continue 800 miles to Chungking. On April 17, sixteen B-25 bombers lifted off the aircraft carrier *Hornet* 600 miles east of Japan. Doolittle's Raiders bombed Tokyo and other targets and headed for China. Short of fuel, not one bomber reached a Chinese airfield. Fifteen pilots ended their flights in East China or the China Sea, and one landed in the Soviet Union. Doolittle parachuted into a rice paddy fertilized with night soil in Japanese-controlled eastern China and traveled a thousand miles by foot, donkey, river boat, train, bus, and plane to Chungking.

Doolittle was flown out of China by Moon Chin. The raid was still a secret. En route to Calcutta, Moon received a message to pick up CNAC radio personnel at Myitkyina, Burma, which was about to fall to Japanese troops. Seventy-two passengers piled into the DC-3, which had a capacity of only twenty-one. When Moon took off, the plane barely cleared trees at the end of the runway. Observing the crowd unload in Calcutta, Colonel Doolittle said that had he known how many people were jammed into the old crate, he would have gone home the way he came. Moon asked Doolittle how he had gotten to China, and Doolittle replied "by way of Tokyo."

Although most war news following Pearl Harbor, with the exception of Flying Tiger kills, had been disheartening, the public announcement of the Doolittle Tokyo Raid boosted American morale and restored the Chinese leadership's faith in their ally. "We were losing face rapidly in China," Royal told the *Los Angeles Daily News* in late May 1942. "[T]he bombing congealed a situation that was rapidly getting out of hand. Our friends in China had been insisting that China's hope was the United States and at the same time we were losing battles one after the other and were virtually pushed out of the Orient. The bombing proved more than anything else that we had courage and that we meant to fight this war to a finish."

The day after the newspaper interview, Jim Doolittle wrote Royal: "This is just a note to thank you for your kindness in coming up to Alameda.... The information that you gave us was of extreme importance. You may justifiably feel that any degree of success that our mission attained was partially due to your cooperation."

Royal had played a minor, but important, role in a big show and indirectly gotten in a lick against the Japanese.[95]

Royal's first China flying assignment was from Sian at the end of the Silk Road. *(Author's Collection)*

Royal was personal pilot for both Chiang Kai-shek (left) and his kidnapper, the Young Marshal (right). ***(Museum of Flight/Brinkman)***

Madame Chiang Kai-shek commended Royal for his "competency, conscientiousness, courage and courtesy." *(John Korompilas)*

Manchurian Army officers presented Royal with an engraved silver cup honoring him because he "covered the whole land." (John Korompilas)

Royal and Communist soldiers wait for Chou En-Lai to take his first plane ride. *(Frank Evans)*

Chiang Kai-shek's DC-2, *The Flying Palace*, was as famous in China as the Lone Ranger's horse, Silver, in the U.S. *(John Korompilas)*

The Japanese destroyed the Boeing 247-D *Bai Ying* at Ichang.
(Frank Evans)

Colonel Claire Chennault roomed with Royal and selected him to lead the Flying Tigers Bomber Group. *(John Korompilas)*

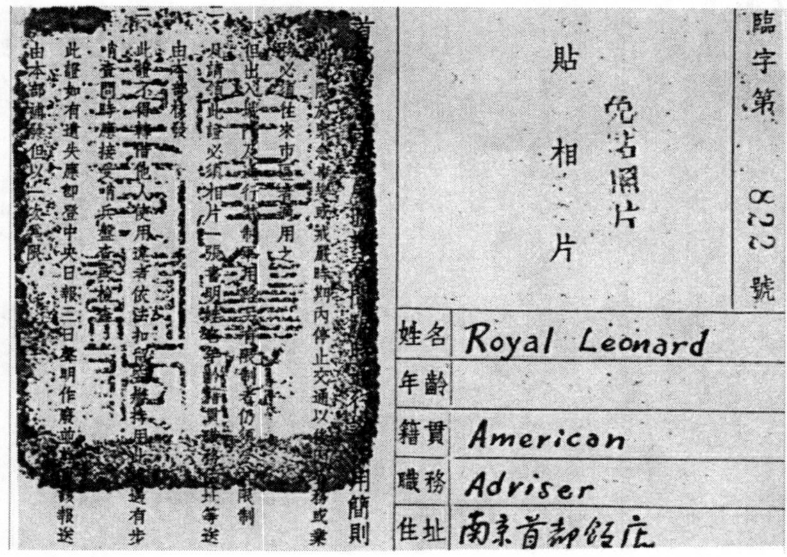

臨字第 822 號

貼 相 片

免貼照片

姓名	Royal Leonard
年齡	
籍貫	American
職務	Adviser
住址	南京首都飯店

Under Chennault's command Royal was an "adviser" to the Chinese Air Force. *(John Korompilas)*

Royal and Maxine Thayer married on September 17, 1938, in Kowloon Union Church. *(Frank Evans)*

Maxine saw a caravan transporting CNAC aviation fuel from Kunming to Chungking. *(John Korompilas)*

The Chungking island airfield, which resembled a mudflat in the Mississippi, often flooded in the monsoon season. *(John Korompilas)*

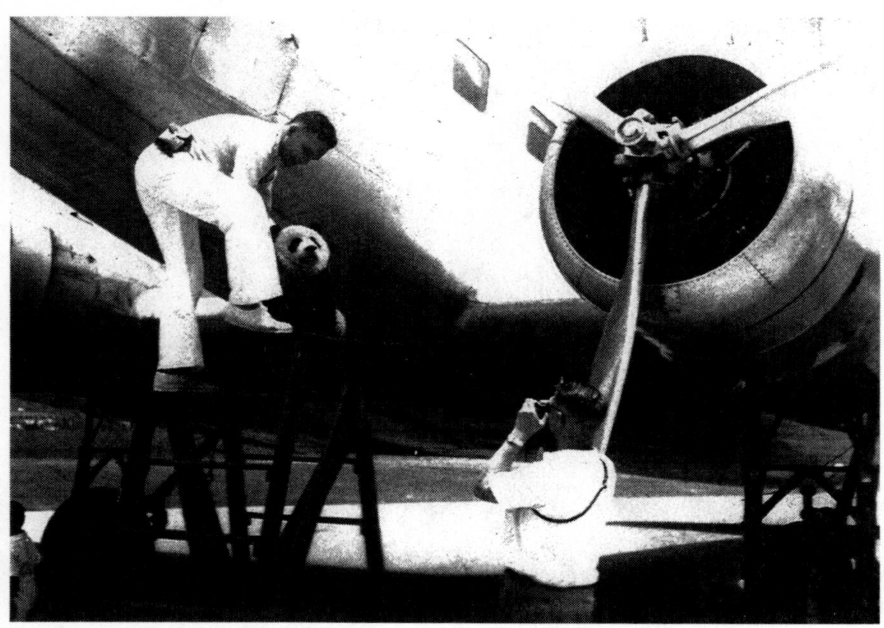

Royal flew the last panda to leave China before World War II destined for an American zoo. *(John Korompilas)*

China National Aviation Corporation (CNAC) fabricated the world's only DC- 2 & 1/2. *(Royal S. Leonard)*

Royal published his memoir in 1942. *(Public Domain)*

Royal was featured in a "Heroes of American Democracy" cartoon, 1942. *(Public Domain)*

Royal in 1943 was exhausted from flying the Hump, battling malaria, and fighting a mail-smuggling prosecution. *(Author's Collection)*

Air Transport Command
Dum Dum.

Attention: Captain Billotti

Dear Captain:

Please forward the following message to General Bissell and Roberts of ATC, Karachi:

(MESSAGE BEGINS) CAPTAIN ROYAL LEONARD FUGITIVE FROM JUSTICE HERE STOP NO LONGER CONNECTED WITH CNAC STOP WE REQUEST NO TRANSPORTATION BE GIVEN HIM ON OUR BEHALF STOP IF DEPARTED KARACHI NOTIFY CAIRO ACCRA ACCORDINGLY (MESSAGE ENDS) SHARP CNAC

CLS

CNAC Operations Manager Chuck Sharp wired military authorities that Royal was a "fugitive from justice." *(Gerrie Dubé)*

Royal returned to California in 1950 and became a businessman. *(Gerrie Dubé)*

Royal and Gerrie Johnson married on November 2, 1957. *(Author's Collection)*

Gerrie Leonard Dubé giving Royal S. Leonard a ring that belonged to his father. *(Author's Collection)*

Legendary Chinese–American pilot Moon Chin examining Royal's China scrapbook. *(Author's Collection)*

Chapter 12

SKYWAY TO HELL

(March 1942 – February 1943)

The sixty-four–dollar question was whether Royal would return to CNAC. He was disgruntled over his Washington, DC, encounter with Pan Am president Juan Trippe, as well as past-due salary and vacation pay and unreimbursed travel and hospital expenses. Unlike with Chiang Kai-shek's Headquarters Transport Squadron, Royal's financial experience with CNAC had been less than satisfactory. He had waited several months before receiving the thousand dollars promised for rescuing the CNAC DC-2 from Japanese fighters at Lungwha Field in August 1937. His first regular paycheck for October 1938 had been made out incorrectly and he had not been able to cash it until six months later. His initial $1200 monthly salary had been reduced to $450 once he had trained Sharp for mountain night flying. And it was too late to file a claim under his health insurance policy for his Presbyterian Hospital bills that Pan Am had promised, but failed, to pay. In late March 1942, Royal resigned from CNAC.

Responding to Royal's resignation letter, Bond wrote, "CNAC, and myself personally and particularly hope you will return to China. CNAC needs you. We need your flying skill and more particularly your *integrity and character*. The situation in China means a greater need for CNAC than ever, both for China and the United States.... I say get back in step, relax, take care of yourself and get a good rest and then I hope you will get back to China as quickly as you can because you are needed out there and there is no one who has ever done a better job out there" [emphasis added]. Bond also mentioned that Royal must return to

China to collect his four-month vacation pay. Chiming in from his Chinese Embassy office, T.V. Soong urged Royal to rejoin CNAC and "continue the splendid work you have done in the past."

After a month passed without a response, Bond offered Royal irresistible bait—an opportunity for postwar Pan Am pilot seniority. Although Pan Am management maintained that CNAC pilots were not entitled to this status, Royal and seven colleagues, based on their exceptional service, had been provisionally transferred to the bottom of the Pan Am junior pilot seniority list. Upon completion of their CNAC employment and specific approval of their individual qualifications and records, they would be eligible for transfer into the Pan Am junior pilot classification with seniority accrued from September 1941. "CNAC is going to be a great outfit [,] Royal [,] and PAA is going to be the greatest and most interesting airline in the world," wrote Bond. "I am sure that your PAA seniority standing is going to be of inestimable value to you one of these days and I want to see you hold on to it." Knowing Royal's yen for money, Bond pointed out that CNAC pilots were probably the highest paid in the world and were not subject to U.S. income tax. Caucasian captains could earn $2,000–$2,500 a month ($26,300–$32,900 in 2009 purchasing power). Concluding the sales pitch, Bond laid it on: "You have showed me a wonderful lot of loyalty and you have earned the best.... What I am trying to say [,] Royal [,] is that you do not owe me or CNAC anything.... You have a place reserved for you right out in front of the parade, you have a place reserved for you in PAA's list, places which you have earned."

After haggling with the Pan Am administrative office over his expense account and Pan Am finally paying his hospital and doctor bills, Royal yielded to Bond's blandishments and rejoined CNAC. Like Juan Trippe, Royal was confident Pan Am would prosper after the war, and he dearly wanted Pan Am seniority. He and Maxine needed his overdue salary and vacation pay. And he earnestly hoped while working for CNAC to continue planning with Chennault to bomb Japan. In *I Flew for China*, Royal emphasized an altruistic reason for returning—to help the Chinese people in their fight against Japanese aggression:

> I had gone away from California to do a job and had wanted to earn money. I came back from the job carrying something I had not expected to find anywhere. Least of all, in China. I had found friends in a strange land, friends to whom I could not talk without thumbing through the missionary's guide of "One Hundred Best Characters" in the

> Mandarin language. But friends we were, in spite of the abyss of custom and language and training. I wondered what it was that bridged the chasm. What secret weapon against the world did we have in common? Even now I cannot tell. That escapes me. Perhaps one of the reasons why I am now going back to China is to find out. Sometimes I think it is because I was the pupil and China the teacher. I realized that they were struggling desperately for freedom, the right to live the best life they saw, not the worst that some overlord saw for them.[96]

Before Royal returned to the Orient the Hearst newspaper chain published a "Heroes of Democracy" cartoon featuring a "daring young Californian" who, flying Chiang Kai-shek, won many races "against Death" and whose numerous "obituaries were premature." In a *Los Angeles Examiner* interview, Royal protested that any heroism attributed to him consisted mostly of "running away from bombs."

In late May 1942, Royal traveled to Miami, Florida, for familiarization training on the B-25 bomber and to await CNAC flying orders. His complexion was yellowish, and his joints ached. His gall bladder, infected with pus cells, was drained twice. On a more pleasant note, Martha Gellhorn, who was living in Florida with Mr. Hemingway, helped Royal polish his book manuscript. They made contact through her hotel telephone operator, who took his messages and forwarded her responses. "Maybe she is afraid," Royal wrote Maxine, "of what her old man might say if [she] communicated with me direct." Royal forwarded Maxine a letter from Martha, commenting, "thought you would like to know how I am getting along with my girl friend."

Between June 25 and July 12, 1942, Royal piloted a B-25 bomber 12,000 miles from Miami to Tehran, Persia. He arrived in Calcutta, India, on a passenger plane bearing unspecified "excess baggage" for Madame and Chiang Kai-shek. He reported to CNAC headquarters as the airline under cost plus contracts with the U.S. Army and China Defense Supplies commenced freight operations with Lend-Lease C-53s and C-47s and passenger service with its DC-2 and two DC-3s. Operation of a Chinese government and U.S. corporate-owned paramilitary airline in the China–Burma–India (CBI) military theater was a politically sensitive issue with the American high command, but it was part of the price for keeping China in the war and tying down Japanese armed forces.[97]

In Calcutta, Royal and his best friend, CNAC operations assistant Robert Pottschmidt, rented an apartment in a mansion called Rainey

Castle. Royal entertained visitors by balancing in a chair on its hind legs and reading aloud from a newspaper or magazine. Another housemate, Al Oldenburg, regarded Royal as "standoffish" and quiet because he did not associate much with the younger pilots. Oldenburg thought Royal, who had a yellowish complexion, was a hypochondriac because he complained about flare-ups of malaria. Royal had contracted this malady as a teenager. His tiredness, high temperature, and hand pain were symptoms of malignant malaria attacking his gall bladder. Each attack cycled through an uncontrollable shivering stage, followed by a fever raging up to 105 degrees Fahrenheit and profuse sweating. Unfortunately, quinine, the principal drug treatment for the disease, affected Royal adversely. He was prescribed Atabrine, which immediately relieved his hand pain but bothered his eyes, making objects appear yellowish.

Even for a pilot in the best of health, flying the Hump from northeastern India (Assam) over the Himalayan mountain range between the Salween and Mekong River valleys to Chungking and Kunming was a death-defying challenge. "Some of the boys," wrote Theodore H. White and Annalee Whitmore Jacoby in *Thunder Out of China*, "called it the Skyway to Hell; it was certainly the most dangerous, terrifying, barbarous aerial transport run in the world." U.S. Army Air Transport Command (ATC) pilots branded the Hump route "The Aluminum Highway" for plane wrecks strewn below them. CNAC Captain J. Gen Genovese described the Hump as "a pilot's Hell—where there's not enough air to breathe, where there's ice on your wings and your de-icers don't work ... and where snow-capped mountain peaks rise up out of nowhere to smash you and your plane to frozen, undiscoverable pieces." According to U.S. Army Lieutenant General William H. Tunner, the "weather on the Hump changed from minute to minute, from mile to mile. One end was set down in the low, steamy jungles of India; the other in the mile-high plateau of western China.... Unfortunately it seemed that when the weather was good in India, it was terrible in China."[98]

Flying the Hump in the monsoon season, Royal dealt with the most extreme weather conditions in his arduous career. Between mid-May and mid-October, rainfall in northeastern India averaged 200 inches. Theodore H. White described the monsoons as "black, solid masses of rain and wind that flick a plane about as if it were a feather." According to former CNAC pilot E.C. Kirkpatrick, "the thunderstorms were god-awful. You'd be upside down half as much as you'd be right side up. The instruments would all go whammo at the same time." In the words of historian Bliss K. Thorne, each rainy-season trip was like "a long dull ache with occasional flashes of pain—like a three-hour tooth extraction: steady hurt, relief when it was over, then wonder how another could be withstood."[99]

Royal first flew across the 17,000-foot–elevation southeastern end of the Hump on the shorter 520-mile route from Dinjan, India, to Kunming that CNAC and ATC pilots used when bad weather grounded Japanese fighters based in northern Burma. After he had made a few flights, Royal checked out several former Flying Tiger pilots who had joined CNAC.

When good weather enabled Japanese fighter pilots to prey on unarmed transports crossing the southeastern end, CNAC and ATC pilots used the longer and more difficult 720-mile route over the 18,000-foot–elevation northwestern Hump end which was beyond Japanese fighter range. Often, in poor visibility conditions, they climbed above clouds to avoid crashing into unseen 20,000 feet and higher peaks. Sometimes they flew under the weather through mountain gaps. In Pimaw Pass, Japanese soldiers shot at planes whose wing-tip clearance was barely fifty feet. Commenting on the choice between smashing into mountains and encountering Japanese fighters, Royal wrote, "Strange isn't it, that what is considered a dangerous practice seems tame when there is a greater danger to consider."

In late October, Royal arrived at the CNAC Dinjan field during a Japanese bombing raid. He turned back to an Army field, refueled, and decided to fly to Chungking because the weather was clear. As he flew north of the usual route and just above 19,000-foot peaks, his radio compass failed. Using celestial navigation, he landed at Chungking two hours after dark.

As CNAC senior pilot, Royal usually flew a DC-3 on the 1340-mile passenger-airmail night route between Calcutta and Chungking via Kunming. "Royal was the kind of pilot people would say I would like to fly with him," commented E.C. Kirkpatrick, "meaning I trust him."

The arrival of one of Royal's passengers exacerbated a personality conflict between two key CBI theater command figures. On December 7, 1942, Billy Todd, a Red Cross worker, landed in Kunming without military orders. "What are you doing here, girl? And who are you?" asked Brigadier General Chennault, surprised to see a woman in slacks getting off a plane. Billy explained that she had come to set up a Red

Cross facility for China Air Task Force (CATF) personnel. Delighted by the news, Chennault invited her to lunch.

A few days later, Billy was summoned to a conference with Chennault and Brigadier General Clayton Bissell, commander of the U.S. Tenth Air Force based in India. Chennault and Bissell were bitter enemies. They had clashed in the early 1930s over fighter tactics at an Army Air Corps School where Bissell was an instructor and Chennault a student. Hap Arnold had promoted Bissell to brigadier general one day ahead of Chennault, so Bissell outranked Chennault. Bissell had the gall to order Chennault not to contact Chiang Kai-shek without Bissell's permission.

"She goes!" said Bissell after listening to Billy's story.

"She stays!" retorted Chennault.

After a heated discussion, the generals compromised on a three-week trial period. Billy cleaned a building, named it the "Victory Club," recruited twenty-five young Chinese women who spoke English, and stayed in Kunming for the duration of the war to the delight of American pilots and ground personnel.

Another of Royal's passengers slightly ruffled British–American relations. U.S. Navy Commander Milton Miles, dressed in khaki shorts and a pullover sweater, was the first passenger aboard the plane at Dum Dum Airport in Calcutta. Miles commanded the Sino-American Co-operative Organization (SACO) working with Chinese guerillas behind Japanese lines and setting up weather stations to gather information for the U.S. Pacific Fleet. Knowing seats were unassigned, Miles sat down and started reading a newspaper.

"This is my seat," said a tall, impressive man, draping his coat over Miles' newspaper.

"You dropped your coat, sir," said the surprised Miles. "I'm a passenger here, myself."

An aide to the interloper informed Miles that he was talking to Sir John Travers, head of a British parliamentary mission to Chungking.

"I'm very glad to meet you, Sir John," said Miles, rising to his feet. "I'm the Rear Duke Miles, myself."

"Rear Duke! Rear Duke!" responded Sir John. "Never heard of a Rear Duke!"

"I believe he's pulling your leg, sir," said the aide as Sir John selected a different seat.

Royal overheard the conversation and broadcast a word by word description of it over his radio. When the plane landed at Dinjan, a row of vehicles was drawn up along the runway. Hugh Woods, who, after several close calls with Japanese fighters, had developed a heart condition and now was managing CNAC Dinjan ground operations, opened the aircraft door. Miles thought Woods was welcoming the British dignitary.

"Is the Rear Duke Miles inside?" asked Woody to many guffaws.

A true blue-blood, Lady Violet Seymour, wife of the British Ambassador to China, praised Royal for flying her "so magnificently" from Calcutta to Chungking. Coming over the Chinese capital, Royal occasionally saluted the lady by making a loop over the British Embassy. He sometimes dined with her and the ambassador. She worried about Royal habitually rubbing his arms to ease pain and the effect of malaria drugs on his outlook.

Royal's attention to detail kept him and his passengers alive. Trying to find Chungking one night, he missed the island field. He reshot the location using his sextant and chronometer and determined that the map designation was ten miles off.

"Roy could fly anything anywhere" commented former CNAC and Flying Tiger physician Lewis "Doc" Richards. "He conducted his life like he was going to live forever. Most of the pilots lived like they were going to die next week."

Colleagues told an apocryphal story about Royal's obsession with safety. When in the company of a Calcutta lady of the night, he kept an eye on his watch and always left in adequate time to make his preflight aircraft check.

"Royal said that he took a lot of ribbing from the other pilots because he was so cautious," recalled his sister Alice, "but it paid off. A lot of them were dead in not too short a time."

Chinese crew members understood the vagaries of Hump flying. "[A] new pilot arrives with a full bag of luck and an empty bag of experience," said a radio operator. "He must quickly fill his bag of experience before the bag of luck is empty." Another crew member pointed out that an "old captain has better luck."

Approximately one in three CNAC pilots who made a significant number of Hump flights did not survive. The casualty rate for less-experienced ATC pilots was higher. In three years, 1,314 crew members were killed and 345 were listed as missing, and 501 aircraft were lost.[100]

Always concerned about safety, Royal clashed with CNAC operations manager Chuck Sharp and vice president W.L. Bond over securing bars of tin and wolframite (concentrated tungsten ore used in making high-grade steel) to prevent sliding and damage to fuselages; providing, inspecting, and repacking parachutes; and removing rubber wing de-icers in the summer to prevent disintegration from the heat. Bond admitted that "during the war we have been unable to keep organized and systematized as a result of which many careless practices have grown up." CDS official Whiting Willauer, who was supervising CBI Lend-Lease operations, rated tying down cargo as one of Hump transport's most serious problems. Royal particularly criticized Sharp for the use of Indian jute fiber rope that broke easily.

After Sharp left on home leave in November 1942, Royal requested Bond's permission to work on his own time in the CNAC shop on a cargo tie-down system. Bond, however, reluctant to undermine the authority of his roommate and personally selected operations manager, declined the offer. When CNAC pilots Joe Rosbert and George Huang returned to Dinjan in transports with fuselages badly damaged from loose 110-pound tin ingots shifting during severe turbulence, their colleagues concluded that unsecured cargo had cut the control cables on Orin Welch's plane and caused his fatal crash.

Royal had not survived this long by going along with unsafe airline practices. He still did not know how to hold a rung on a corporate ladder, let alone climb the next one. Even though he was primarily flying passenger planes, he reacted like a union representative concerned about his fellow pilots' safety rather than a senior pilot seeking a promotion.

"Up until this moment," said Royal, referring to Rosbert and Huang's experiences, "there had been no clue as to what happened. All the pilots refused to fly until CNAC had more consideration for their safety. Mr. Bond asked me to go with him to Dinjan to help build up the morale. My reply was that I could not conscientiously tell the boys it was safe to fly as long as CNAC continued to operate in an extremely dangerous manner. Many dangers could be eliminated by a little forethought."

Eventually, CNAC installed a tie-down netting system like that used on ATC aircraft.[101]

Loner Royal showed CNAC junior birdmen tricks of the trade. Harking to his mail pilot days, Royal told Peter Goutiere, when his instruments malfunctioned while flying in clouds, to hang a pencil on a string above the cockpit windshield so its swinging would indicate whether his plane was banking. He also taught Goutiere to keep the C-53 direction finder (DF) outside antenna in a cross-wise position (contrary to manufacturer specifications) so if it froze he could turn the plane and locate his air field destination by listening for the radio beam. If the antenna was kept in the manufacturer specified straight-ahead position and froze, a pilot could not find the radio directional beam. "One time my antenna froze and afterward I thanked Roy for his warning," said Goutiere.[102]

Clever tricks could not overcome the handicap of using low-altitude engines in overloaded planes at high altitude. However, an engine accessory was available that might alleviate the problem. "17,000 feet is often the limit of these overly loaded airplanes with low-altitude engines," explained Royal. "While struggling for more altitude, a friendly updraught would relieve our anxiety by boosting us up to 23,000 feet. Some vertical currents would be more than our rate of climb instruments could measure, possibly six or seven thousand feet per minute. During the next few minutes a sinking mass of air would hold us down to 13,000 feet in spite of wide open engines. Under those conditions we would often be faced with the dilemma of what to do when the nearness of 15,000 foot ridges accelerated the turbulence so much that turning around would be a dangerous maneuver. Every pilot concerned is still asking: 'Why is it necessary to fly over the highest terrain in the world with low altitude engines when supercharged engines can be had?'"[103]

CDS executive Whiting Willauer also believed Hump transport performance could be improved by using two-stage superchargers driven by gears obtaining power from engine crankshafts that enabled planes to operate with full power at high altitude and fly farther on one engine. Not involved in CNAC internal politics, Willauer insisted on Royal as the pilot for two-stage supercharger altitude and performance tests.

Royal was definitely the best-qualified CNAC or ATC pilot for this assignment. Ever since seeing Cap Theodore's Curtiss Pusher, Royal had wanted to be an aeronautical engineer rather than a pilot. He had done engine performance tests for T&WA. He had figured out a plausible explanation for the Wiley Post–Will Rogers crash. He had worked with Jack Northrop, Donald Douglas, and the Loughead (Lockheed) brothers and their engineers but felt inferior around them because he did not have an engineering background. He had studied physics and engineering texts to make up for his lack of formal education.

"Royal was a borderline genius on mechanical things," recalled Doc Richards. "Royal was the complete pilot," explained former CNAC pilot Fletcher Hanks. "He analyzed everything. He was excellent in preparation of a flight. He had a wide knowledge of airplanes. He was used as a test pilot because he had a greater knowledge of engines than ninety-nine percent of the others."

But Royal was not a unanimous choice for the two-stage supercharger test pilot job. Although Bond favored conducting the tests, Willauer sensed that Royal "was under a cloud" with him. Bond viewed Royal as a bad organization man with a chip on his shoulder vis-à-vis CNAC and Pan Am. Royal regarded himself as on loan from the Chinese government and was primarily loyal to the Chinese government majority ownership, rather than the Pan Am minority management. He was probably the Chinese government's eyes and ears inside CNAC day-to-day operations. He was also close to General Chennault and ATC officers and was working on a manual for ATC pilots detailing CNAC Hump-flying procedures. According to Willauer, Bond was "being crazy" about the manual project because Bond viewed CNAC and ATC as competing airlines and believed ATC officers in the spring of 1942 had withheld cargo so CNAC could not start Hump flights ahead of the Army.

Royal, who had flown for two of the most progressive U.S. airlines (Western Air Express and TWA), participated in planning for two trans-ocean airline projects and for an international air race, pioneered use of celestial navigation on U.S. commercial passenger flights, and engaged in high-level labor-management negotiations, was somewhat critical of Bond who had no airline experience prior to joining CNAC. Willauer believed Bond was capable of managing an eight-plane passenger airline but not a major freight operation.

Royal was very critical of Sharp. Bond acknowledged that Sharp's difficult temperament and tactlessness hampered his effectiveness. For example, Bond reported that Sharp "jumped right down Bissell's throat with hob-nailed shoes and spurs on" rather than firmly and courteously making his point in a letter to the Tenth Air Force commanding general.

Bond and Sharp were trying to operate an airline under the worst imaginable conditions and Royal was a perfectionist about flying under any conditions. To Royal, there was only one way to operate an airline, the right way. His bosses moaned about Royal wasting time checking his aircraft before taking off, but in three and a half years, Royal had damaged only one CNAC plane when its wheels sank into a muddy runway. Royal did not think much of Sharp whose plane had been wrecked when an engine caught fire.

Royal functioned in a CNAC no-man's land. "Royal was a single-minded person," said former pilot Ray Allen. "He had a lot of connections and knew a lot of people in the Chinese government. He didn't associate much with the younger fellows." Another former pilot confirmed this impression. "Royal was senior to the wheels in the company," recalled E.C. Kirkpatrick. "He was also a better pilot in many instances. His personality was somewhat against him. He was one of the older pilots, but he didn't get along with the old boys. He didn't divulge much."

Willauer was worried about Sharp's lack of imagination. Stubbornly and unrealistically insisting that the engines in use on CNAC Hump transports were adequate, Sharp, unable to grasp the potential long-run benefit of two-stage superchargers, wanted the tests delayed, arguing that CNAC could not spare a plane for test purposes. "Chuck was like a bull," said pilot George "Hogleg" Robertson. "He never changed his mind." Willauer believed that Sharp opposed the tests because he disliked Royal and Frank Sinclair, the Douglas Aircraft Company technical adviser to CDS. In Royal's opinion, Sharp objected to the tests because he regarded Royal's efforts to improve CNAC Hump performance as a personal insult.

When Sharp left on home leave, Bond approved the test flights. In late December 1942, CNAC mechanics installed S3C4G two-stage supercharger engines on the CNAC twin engine C-53 identified as number 48. The C-53 was a DC-3 passenger plane that had been converted to a transport by adding a plywood floor and enlarging the side door.

"It was only after considerable persuasion," stated Willauer, "that I got Bond to agree that Leonard would be the pilot to fly the tests which I want to pull off for the ATC. His excuse was that Leonard's time for the month of January would be exceeded if he did. (That would mean extra pay for him, and jealousy from the other pilots. These are all considerations with which I have some sympathy from the viewpoint of a commercial operation, but with which I have none from the viewpoint of establishing a real air route.) I fear that if

Leonard does not run the tests, *the 'best foot' may not be put forward*" [emphasis added].[104]

The most important Hump two-stage supercharger test flight occurred on January 31, 1943. Willauer invited British Embassy press attaché Erik Watts along as a passenger because all two-stage supercharger engines under U.S. production were allocated to England and British officials would have to be persuaded to release some for use over the Hump. Watts had indicated that he would try to convince Ambassador Howard Seymour to recommend the release if the tests were successful.

Willauer also invited Colonel Edward H. Alexander, recently named ATC India–China Wing commander, to accompany them in order to obtain his endorsement for installation of two-stage supercharger engines on Army twin-engine transports. Alexander, however, declined the invitation because he was expecting the secret and imminent arrival of certain notables, including General Hap Arnold, whose staff pilot got lost crossing the Hump and whose plane arrived at Kunming three and a half hours late and almost out of fuel.

Willauer showed Royal's test data to Colonel Alexander and discussed with him whether a test flight should be attempted on a day that all other aircraft were grounded due to ice storms. Even four-engine Consolidated C-87 Liberators, faster and with more range and a higher ceiling than C-53s, were not flying that day.

"Finally, Roy and I," related Willauer, "decided we might as well try the trip ... because it would be the real demonstration of what these engines installed in a Douglas plane could actually do. In other words, we deliberately set out to fly when the C-87s or other Douglases wouldn't."

With the C-53 overloaded by a ton and a quarter, Royal took off from Dinjan and headed for Chungking. He climbed steadily to 15,000 feet, put on high blower, and rose through an ice storm to 20,000 feet. At 24,000 feet, the plane disappeared into clouds.

Based on experience, Royal expected to climb above the clouds in less than a minute. Despite wide-open motors, churning turbulence forced the plane down to 21,000 feet. Winds buffeted the C-53 from every direction. Drafts lifted it to 25,000 feet, dropped it to 19,000, and bounced it to 25,000 feet. The three and a half ton cargo broke loose and repeatedly smashed against the ceiling and floor with sickening thuds and shudders. "It was like," commented Royal, "walking a tight wire in a tornado."[105]

Royal worried his strength would fail. His arms and legs ached from struggling to keep the plane upright. He dared not look away from his instruments long enough to locate any nearby mountains or check the rear compartment for damage because he might lose track of the rate-of-climb instrument. If the instrument hand made a complete turn, it would show level when actually measuring 4,000 feet per minute vertical velocity up or down.

Royal was unsure of his exact location. The violent blasts increased in turbulence, and the plane repeatedly plunged and leapt. The lowest temperature on the outside thermometer scale was thirty below, and it registered at the bottom. Until the plane got on top of the weather, Royal could not be sure he had cleared the highest peaks. If he was directly on course, he would miss 25,000-foot–high Minya Konka by fifty miles, but possible 110-mile-per-hour crosswinds narrowed his margin of error. His effort to climb seemed futile.

Forced down to 19,000 feet, Royal decided that his best chance was to turn south to lower terrain. Hoping his drift estimate was not too far off, he changed course for Kunming. When the radio operator tried to get a Kunming bearing, however, he heard nothing.[106]

Cruising at 24,000 feet, Royal turned over the controls to copilot Gordon Poon, removed his oxygen mask, tied a knot in the intake tube, and walked to the lavatory in the rear of the fuselage. He strained to dislodge a 190-pound radio thrown against the bathroom door, used the toilet, and then struggled back to the cockpit. He had to sit down next to Willauer behind the radio operator. Willauer shook his hands a few minutes and shoved him into the pilot seat.

Even after putting on his oxygen mask, Royal still felt dopey. It took him five minutes to figure out what was wrong. He had forgotten that he had tied a knot in the intake tube and was trying to suck air from a shut-off hose. Finally understanding his predicament, he untied the knot, resumed inhaling oxygen, and revived.

Now Royal decided to change course from Kunming to Chungking, his original destination. After a four-hour battle, he finally saw the sun for a few minutes, took a sextant sight, and determined that he was nearing Chungking. Finishing the last hour and a half of the flight on instruments, he sighed with relief as he touched down on the island field.[107]

"It was rough as Hell" recalled Willauer. "In fact, Roy said that the turbulence on this trip was almost as bad as that which he encountered when caught in the typhoon off Hongkong.... This was undoubtedly the worst storm of the year, and certainly the fact that the ship got through on those circumstances ought to prove the point that a Douglas plane can carry an overload at 23 to 24,000 feet in any kind of condition under which one would ever expect to fly in this region."

In total, Royal tested the two-stage supercharger engines for more than one hundred hours. Colonel Alexander was favorably impressed with the results showing that the engines operating on high or low did not use excessive fuel, run too hot at high altitude, or exceed the maximum head temperature. Bond strongly recommended the installation of two-stage superchargers on future CNAC planes.

Subsequently, all CNAC and ATC C-47s and C-53s were equipped with two-stage supercharger engines. "At about 12,000 feet you shifted it in just like shifting a car to high gear," recalled former CNAC Captain Jim Dalby. The extra power provided a much more comfortable 25,000-foot ceiling.

"After flying with these engines for a few hours it makes a pilot wonder if he is not skating on thin ice, so to speak," commented Royal, "when he flies the [H]ump with low altitude engines."

No longer were Hump pilots dependent on underpowered, low-altitude engines for flying overloaded planes on the Skyway to Hell.

Less than seven months after Royal's last two-stage supercharger test flight, a Japanese fighter shot down C-53 number 48. Captain Sam Anglin, his copilot, and the radio operator were killed.[108]

Chapter 13

LONE RANGER OVER TOKYO

(January 1942 – October 1943)

Battling Hump monsoons, winds, and ice storms and evading unseen mountain peaks and lurking Japanese fighters satiated most CNAC pilots' appetites for flying, but not Royal's. Utilizing his two-stage supercharger engine test flight and Clagett military mission experiences, Royal conspired with Madame Chiang Kai-shek and Brigadier General Claire Chennault to bomb Tokyo. Lieutenant General Joseph Stilwell, CBI Theater commander, and his subordinate Chennault, China Air Task Force (later U.S. Fourteenth Air Force) commander, disagreed over whether ground warfare or air power could defeat Japan most effectively. To make a point in this strategic debate, Chennault was willing to end-run the U.S. armed services chain of command and strike a quick blow against Japan under the auspices of the Chinese Commission on Aeronautical Affairs, headed by Madame Chiang.

Chennault wrote Maxine and explained his and Royal's motivation for wanting to bomb Tokyo ASAP: "After all that happened since Hongkong days, I wonder if you realize yet why I had to come back to China and, in the same manner, why Roy has to stay here. It is hard to put this into words, but I am sure that we both felt at that time that we had a job to do and that it was *the kind of a job that no one else could do as well as we could.* You will remember that I knew that war between Japan and the U.S. was inevitable and that I also knew that we were not prepared for it. I felt that it was up to me to make such preparations as I could in China and to be right on the job so that the Japanese could not surprise us. I am still looking forward to the time when we will be able to take the war out of China into Japan—that will be full compensation for all of the sacrifices and privations which I have suffered during the past six years" [emphasis added].[109]

During his U.S. home leave, Royal had advocated bombing Japan. In January 1942, a month and a half after Pearl Harbor and three months before the Doolittle Raid, Royal had told Army Intelligence: "They [the Japanese] feel so secure now that they have depleted their home defenses. If we sent just ONE plane up there, they would get stirred up and hysterical. Two or three raids on Japan proper would do more to make them bring their stuff back than anything else that could happen."

Chennault's friends in Louisiana had raised funds to buy a Lockheed 414 bomber for the Flying Tigers. In February, Chennault cabled T.V. Soong that conditions were favorable for long-range bomber surprise attacks on Japan and requested that Soong arrange for Royal to have the Lockheed 414 modified, employ a copilot, and fly the plane to China. If more than one plane was purchased, Chennault wanted Royal to lead a formation.

In May 1942, Royal told a *Los Angeles Daily News* reporter, "Japan still can be bombed as a daily routine from bases in China. Not an armada, you understand, but a limited amount of planes per day."

Early in the summer of 1942, some deactivated Flying Tiger pilots were incorporated under Chennault's command into the 23rd Fighter Group of the U.S. Tenth Air Force China Air Task Force (CATF) charged with protecting Hump transports from Japanese fighters. When Royal made his first Hump flight to Chungking in mid-July, he arrived at night, slept under the wing of his plane, and left early the next morning without meeting Chennault. The brigadier general immediately sent Royal a short note indicating that he wanted to talk to him. In a late-July memorandum to Tenth Air Force commander General Clayton Bissell, Chennault reaffirmed his conviction that if the CATF were significantly strengthened, he would drive the Japanese Air Force from China, cut communication lines between Japan and Malaya, and ultimately bomb Japan.[110]

While American marines were fighting on Guadalcanal in the South Pacific, Royal planned a Tokyo bombing raid. More ambitious than Chennault, he wanted to strike Tokyo before the Japanese Air Force had been defeated in China. Royal believed he and close friend

Robert Pottschmidt, also a skilled celestial navigator, had the right stuff for the job. Royal thought an unarmed C-53 carrying three crew members, 2,000 gallons of fuel, and one ton of small firebombs could drop its payload from 20,000 feet over Tokyo and return to China.

Royal identified two potential Mainland China–Tokyo routes. He favored the longer 3100-mile Sian–Tokyo–Chuchow route because the Japanese would not expect a raid originating from Sian and because strong tail winds at high altitude on an almost due eastern course would save fuel and simplify celestial navigation. Although the 2750-mile Chuchow–Tokyo–Chuchow route was shorter, Royal feared the takeoff closer to Japanese lines would be detected. He believed, however, that a plane leaving Chuchow at night in November might not be discovered if lucky enough after daybreak to fly through 300 to 400 miles of cloud cover.

In touting his plan to the Commission on Aeronautical Affairs, Royal played on Chinese pride. "I can not think of a better way to show that the Chinese have what it takes than such a mission as this," he commented. He pointed out that the Chinese would receive credit for first bombing Tokyo from the Chinese Mainland, as well as forcing the Japanese to use fighters for home defense instead of against Chinese and American armed forces in the CBI and South Pacific. The Chinese could also demonstrate that effective bombing was possible in poor weather conditions. In late 1942, Royal submitted a report on the project to General Chennault. After discussing it with T.V. Soong, Chennault told Royal that the outlook for implementation of their scheme looked "very good."

During overnight stops on his twelve Dinjan–Kunming two-stage supercharger test flights in January 1943, Royal stayed with Chennault and they discussed their scheme. Royal hoped the first bomb dropped on Tokyo would "be, figuratively speaking, the one which will dislodge the trigger rock and set in motion the avalanche that will eventually crush Japan." He wanted to use either one or three C-53s with supercharged engines. He proposed modifying the Commission on Aeronautical Affairs C-53 with supercharged engines and obtaining two similar planes from the United States. Royal suggested that Chiang Kai-shek transfer him to the Headquarters Transport Squadron and send him to the U.S. to supervise aircraft modifications and lead the planes to China. He estimated that an eastern China base could be outfitted in six months with sufficient materiel for a Tokyo raid. While ferrying supplies, Royal would train crews under conditions simulating a

Tokyo flight. They would fly at night, navigate at high altitude, and develop bombing accuracy by dropping navigator flares that illuminated on water contact.[111]

As Royal and Chennault plotted their clandestine mission, Chennault's U.S. Air Force plan moved through Washington channels. In his February 4, 1943, revised "Plan for Employment of China Air Task Force in China," Chennault outlined a three-step approach. The CATF would achieve air superiority in eastern and southeastern China, undertake intensive offensive action over Hankow, Hanoi, and Formosa, and "advance its units into those fields within range of JAPAN and continue its attacks, now upon JAPAN proper."[112]

Between March 9 and April 2, Royal and Chennault met several times in Chungking and discussed their plan. Chennault offered Royal a commission as a major, but he declined, probably because he was earning more than $2500 tax-free a month and a major with less than three years service and one dependent was paid $370 a month. Royal could double his money playing the illegal currency-exchange game. In the Chinese black market, he converted U.S. dollars into CN at the rate of one U.S. dollar to sixty CN. In Calcutta, he could get one dollar for 30 CN, doubling his money.

CNAK-ers razzed ATC pilots about their pay differential in the "C-NAC Cannonball" song:

Hear the mighty engines

Hear the captain call

I'm headed back to Dinjan

On the C-NAC Cannonball

....

The mighty mountains are rough

The Army boys do say

The Army gets the medals,

And C-NAC gets the pay

If Royal had enlisted in the U.S. Air Force, Chennault would have assigned him to the 308th Bombardment Group. "Special flights would then be worked out," Chennault wrote Royal on a USAF letterhead, "from time to time as conditions permitted." The 308th Liberator heavy bomber (B-24) squadrons, based at Kunming, were flying aviation fuel and other supplies from India to China. And Chennault indicated that he would transfer Royal under Chiang Kai-shek's command when his services might be needed.[113]

Promoted to major general in command of the Fourteenth Air Force (who also called themselves Flying Tigers), Chennault in early May 1943 presented a Japan bombing plan to President Roosevelt, Prime Minister Churchill, and their chiefs of staff at the Trident Conference in Washington, DC. Upon returning to China in late July, Chennault discussed the clandestine project with Madame Chiang Kai-shek, who said "everything had been approved by the highest authority [probably Chiang Kai-shek]."

Unfortunately for Royal, the War Department withdrew Chennault's authority to issue officer commissions to civilians. In July 1943, Chennault advised Royal to return to the U.S. and apply for a commission through the Chief of Army Air Forces. Chennault was also concerned about Royal's health and, as "a friend of long standing," strongly urged him to seek proper medical attention and get some much-needed rest in the U.S. Chennault wanted Royal, if he obtained a commission, to request to fly a B-24 to the China Theater. "In view of the fact that the project was approved here," Chennault further advised, "I do not think it necessary or appropriate to mention it to the man in Washington [probably General Arnold].... I want you to feel that the question of your return to military service is purely one for you to decide and I do not want you to base your decision upon my desire to have you return. I am confident that I will be able to carry out certain plans without regard to individuals. If I cannot do these things with one man, I will find someone else who can. With this understanding, I repeat again that I would like to have you in my command and that I am sure you will have considerable action."

On August 21, 1943, Chennault wrote that he was "positive" Royal could obtain a commission and be assigned to China. "Since I am not in a position to order you to accept a commission," Chennault concluded, "I do not feel that I can do any more in the matter."[114]

Despite the recently revealed execution of three Doolittle Raid members and announcement of the Japanese government policy to execute pilots captured after bombing Japan as "enemies of humanity," Royal still wanted to go ahead with the Tokyo bombing raid. But a personal legal problem doomed his and Chennault's secret project. Royal told Maxine he "fully expected to be under Claire and do things worth while, but I am afraid that considering the dirt Sharp has set in motion

I am going to be so busy fighting the British that there won't be a chance to help China fight the Japs."[115]

Neither Chennault nor Royal executed their and Madame Chiang Kai-shek's plan or received full compensation for their sacrifices and privations. General Arnold retained control over, and excluded Chennault's Fourteenth Air Force from, long-range Japan bombing missions. In mid-June 1944, Twentieth Strategic Air Force B-29s took off from Mainland China and bombed the Imperial Iron and Steel Works at Yawata.

Could Royal have flown to Tokyo in an unarmed plane, dropped firebombs, and survived? "Royal was a different type of person," said his long-time colleague Moon Chin. "He didn't drink at all. He never said much. He was always writing notes, reading a book, or playing with his sextant. He did everything according to the way engineers do. He did a lot of things other people can't do."

According to Flying Tiger ace and CNAC pilot Dick Rossi, Royal "was an inventive type of guy and was frequently coming up with some ideas or theories. Royal had good ability as a pilot and was a serious student of navigation. Generally, we thought he had a few peculiarities. He marched to a different drummer."

Royal S. Leonard, not yet conceived at the time his father yearned to play Lone Ranger over Tokyo, wonders whether his father could have bombed Tokyo and returned alive. But, as another China aviation colleague, Jim Bledsoe, said about Royal, "He knew how to stay alive!"[116]

Chapter 14

INTERNATIONAL INCIDENT

(April 1943 – August 1948)

On April 20, 1943, CNAC vice president W.L. Bond asked Royal to smuggle a company letter past British–Indian customs-censor officers in order to avoid its censorship. As fate would have it, Finance Minister H.H. Kung's daughter Rosamonde also asked Royal, who regularly carried messages and personal items for her family, to take two parcels and letters in his personal baggage. Needless to say, Royal quickly obtained Bond's permission to accommodate her.

Sensing a trap (as he later explained to ALPA founder and President David Behncke) at the Dum Dum Airdrome customs shack, Royal presented the company letter to customs-censor officer Deatker, who read and passed it. Then Deatker did something unprecedented in Royal's experience. He searched Royal's dispatch case and seized Miss Kung's letters containing derogatory information about Sharp and newspaper clippings illegal to mail under the censorship law. He also confiscated an innocuous letter from Dr. Campbell, a Canadian medical missionary, that had cleared customs on a previous Calcutta–Chungking flight, shaken loose in Royal's dispatch case, and never been delivered.

As soon as Deatker released him, Royal telephoned Miss Kung and said her letters had been seized. Upon arriving at Chungking, Royal immediately reported the incident to Doctor and Madame Kung, with whom he often dined. "This all seems strange to me," fumed the formidable, hard-willed Madame Kung, whom John Gunther described as powerful and cunning as any person in China. "Possibly Rosamonde could be criticized for not abiding by the rules. She should have sent all her letters in the diplomatic bag. However, the officer in accepting her note did not act very nicely. Certainly! Certainly! .... I cannot understand what is the matter with the British. Do they think they can treat us in this manner and then expect the leaders of China to react kindly towards them on the day of reckoning when they want Hong Kong back?"

The next day the British-Indian chief censor invited Miss Kung to lunch, apologized, and returned her letters.

During the next two weeks, the British–Indian customs, censor, and prosecutor offices assured Royal that the matter was an unfortunate incident and had been dropped. In the meantime, Sharp returned from home leave and heard about the derogatory references to him in Miss Kung's letter. Sharp probably believed that Royal was her source of information. Ever since Maxine and Sharp had been neighbors in the Kowloon apartment complex, she had told Royal not to trust Sharp, but he had ignored her warning. In mid-May, friends in the customs office warned Royal that at Sharp's instigation mail-smuggling charges would be filed against him after Bond left on home leave. Up to this time, CNAC had dismissed three pilots for smuggling contraband, but none for smuggling mail.[117]

Convinced that he had been set up for refusing to cooperate with Pan Am president Juan Trippe in Washington, DC, Royal contacted Bond, did not mention that he had cleared the company letter, and said that Deatker had searched his personal baggage and found it. Royal told Bond that he had a subpoena, which he did not, and intended to hold him as a material witness. Under the Defence of India Rules, a person convicted of mail smuggling was subject to a heavy fine and up to five years imprisonment. Bond was aware that Sharp in a company memorandum had warned all CNAC flight crew members about this law. Eager to return home, Bond provided Royal a letter accepting responsibility for the incident:

> Several weeks ago, on the occasion in which you had your difficulty, I gave you one or two letters from myself to the Managing Director, which I asked you to take up personally. Any difficulties made over this is my fault. I gave these letters to you to be handled this way partly because there was not sufficient time to go through the Censor, partly because I did not want them censored. These letters

> pertain to a request from the Royal Air Force that we train several of their pilots for flights over the "hump". While I recommended that this request be granted, I made certain comments, in the strictest affairs of CNAC, in which I think no one else would be interested. I trust that you have no further difficulties in connection with this.

On May 24, 1943, the British customs office filed criminal charges, based on information from the Intelligence Office, alleging Royal had been apprehended carrying three uncensored letters. Friends in the censor's office told Royal that Bond had informed British–Indian authorities he was carrying the company letter. Royal certainly did not think the Kungs had betrayed him.[118]

Upon learning of the mail smuggling prosecution, Chinese government officials requested that Royal travel to Chungking to discuss the matter. On July 1, he described his predicament to Minister and Madame Kung. Intimating that they wanted Sharp reassigned, the Kungs acted decisively on Royal's behalf. Chinese Vice-Minister of Foreign Affairs K.C. Wu spoke to a British–Indian government representative and requested dismissal of the mail-smuggling charges. British Ambassador Seymour added his political clout and asked that the case be dropped. Convinced that Royal was "in no way guilty of a deliberate breaking of the law" and his price was "beyond any petty-truancy," Lady Violet Seymour contacted the Viceroy of India about dismissing the prosecution. Sparing no effort on his behalf, Chinese officials retained a law firm to represent Royal in the British–Indian court.

To forestall intrigue between Royal and his Soong Dynasty and British diplomatic friends, Sharp removed Royal from the Calcutta–Chungking passenger service and assigned him to the Dinjan–Kunming freight run. As senior pilot, Royal felt insulted. On standby status for company orders to return to the U.S. and fly a transport back to India, Royal believed Bond and Sharp, regardless of the prosecution outcome, planned to send him home and fire him. He also feared they would try to ruin his reputation in U.S. aviation circles.

With Bond in the United States, Dr. Arthur Young, the American Economic Adviser to Nationalist China and one of two American CNAC Board of Directors members, became involved in the matter. Young had earned a PhD in economics from Princeton University and an LL.B from George Washington University. As a U.S. State Department economic adviser, he had prepared diplomatic instructions that assisted Pan American Airways in obtaining Latin American landing rights. His services were especially useful to CNAC in obtaining U.S. dollars for daily operations.

Due partly to the "Leonard affair," Young believed that high Chinese officials regarded CNAC negatively and he feared that CNAC was losing their unqualified support and also losing ground in its rivalry with the 100% Chinese government-owned Central Aircraft Transport Company (formerly Eurasia). Young telegraphed Bond that the Leonard–Sharp dispute threatened "important CNAC interests" and perhaps involved "a repercussion on American–Chinese relations and relations between India and China." Young and Managing Director C. F. Wang regretfully concluded that, for the overall good, Royal had to be withdrawn from China, but recognized that the matter had to be handled delicately because his competence as a pilot was unquestioned and Chinese officials would not regard him as disloyal for complaining to them as CNAC majority owner rather than to American management.

In Washington, DC, Joseph W. Ballantine, Chief of the State Department Division of Far Eastern Affairs, noted "stories unfavorable to CNAC started by Leonard and by the Aviation Commission, which stories have reached the highest circles of the Government and which those circles seem to believe in a certain degree. *Intimations have been given that the company should transfer Sharp to some other post*" [emphasis added].[119]

Caught in the choppy cross currents of American, Chinese, and British–Indian diplomatic affairs, Royal sought advice from Tenth Air Force commander Major General Clayton Bissell. On July 26, Royal boarded an Army plane, expecting to meet General Bissell that afternoon at his New Delhi headquarters and return the next day in time for a July 28 court appearance. Royal told General Bissell about his problems with Sharp and Sharp's refusal to repair an ATC transport that Bond had agreed CNAC mechanics would overhaul. General Bissell advised Royal to return to Calcutta, clear up the matter, and "under no circumstances to leave under a cloud." Unfortunately, the plane on which Royal was scheduled to return to Calcutta was damaged in a minor accident and his flight was canceled. His attorney obtained a continuance of the court date.

The Leonard–Sharp dispute now reached the point of no return. On July 29, Royal wired Sharp from New Delhi and requested his long-awaited U.S. travel orders to fly a new transport back to India.

Sharp, who believed Royal was prejudicing General Bissell against him, concluded that Royal intended to flee India and avoid prosecution. Sharp fired from the hip and cabled General Bissell:

> CAPTAIN ROYAL LEONARD FUGITIVE FROM JUSTICE HERE... NO LONGER CONNECTED WITH CNAC... WE REQUEST NO TRANSPORTATION BE GIVEN HIM ON OUR BEHALF... IF DEPARTED KARACHI NOTIFY CAIRO ACCRA ACCORDINGLY.[120]

Upon his return to Dum Dum airdrome on August 1, four British–Indian policemen arrested Royal. Unsuccessful in contacting the American Consul-General, Royal reached Chinese Consul-General Pao, who arranged his release into Chinese custody, guaranteed his bail, and provided him a place to stay at the Chinese Consulate. Sharp, unaware that Bond had requested Royal to smuggle the company letter, told Pao he had fired Royal for continually smuggling letters despite many warnings and intended to make him an example for the younger pilots. Royal telephoned Sharp, who confirmed his firing. Sharp told Royal he did not like Royal's attitude in the court case because he should have pled guilty and avoided complications for CNAC.

After discussing Royal's case with Chiang Kai-shek, Finance Minister Kung angrily summoned Dr. Young, threatened to liquidate CNAC if its operational problems were not resolved, and ordered Young and Managing Director C.F. Wang to conduct an investigation of CNAC operating problems and the mail smuggling prosecution. Royal, who was undergoing treatment at the Calcutta School of Tropical Medicine, and Sharp were ordered to fly to Chungking and explain their conduct. When Sharp arrived on August 9, the Chinese secret service, pursuant to Chiang Kai-shek's orders, tailed him. When Royal arrived, Young, whom Royal called "Urgent Arthur," tried to arrange Royal's affairs so he could not contact Dr. Kung, but Royal evaded Young and reported directly to Kung who became furious with Young.

After meeting with Royal and Sharp, Dr. Kung ordered Sharp detained in Chungking for the duration of an investigation, countermanded Royal's dismissal because it had not been approved by the Chinese government majority ownership, and reinstated Royal at full pay. Kung even suggested that Royal sue Sharp for defamation in a Chinese court. In the recent Sino–American treaty, signed January 11, 1943, the United States had renounced extraterritorial rights in China, and Americans could now sue and be sued under Chinese law. Upon further reflection, however, Kung changed his mind because the lawsuit might attract too much attention and complicate matters even further.[121]

Physically ill and mentally exhausted, justifiably believing Sharp was trying to ruin his career, and always stubborn when convinced he was right and others wrong, Royal returned to Calcutta and appeared in court on August 17. Charges pertaining to the Rosamonde Kung letters were dismissed, leaving the legal issue whether Royal had violated the censorship law when he failed to declare the missionary's letter that had previously passed censorship and cleared customs. Testimony was offered showing that British–Indian customs-censor officers were lax in performing their duties and allowed CNAC pilots to carry documents without declaring or submitting them for inspection. The matter was continued.

The Chinese government investigative hearing convened on August 25 in Chungking. Royal and Sharp testified before a board consisting of the Chinese Customs Administrator and Vice-Ministers of Finance and Communications, as well as present and former CNAC Managing Directors and Economic Adviser Young. The board concluded that CNAC had taken suitable action to curtail smuggling and that Royal had no compelling evidence against Sharp. After nineteen days of detention, Sharp returned to Dinjan to deal with a mechanics work stoppage.[122]

Striving to avoid publicity that might embarrass China's "big bugs," Young, who regarded the matter as "vitally important to the status of the company and its part in the war effort and to the future of business cooperation between the United States and China," worked with the British–Indian Government External Affairs Department to discharge the mail-smuggling prosecution. Young believed the defense tactic of discrediting the British–Indian customs and censor officers was harmful to British–American relations. Royal played his ace card and showed Acting American Consul-General John MacDonald a copy of Bond's letter accepting responsibility for not declaring the intra-company communication. Royal pointed out that CNAC management would be very embarrassed if it were disclosed he had been set up with the British–Indian censors for smuggling a letter he had declared and Miss Kung's letters had been seized instead.

In Washington, DC, Bond disingenuously explained to Alger Hiss, special assistant to the State Department Chief of the Division of Far Eastern Affairs (and another Soviet informant), that the letter was meant to apply only to intracompany procedures and not

British–Indian regulations (which were the basis for the CNAC policy and Sharp's memo about mail smuggling).

On September 23, the prosecutor, pursuant to a U.S. State Department request and British–Indian government instructions, petitioned for withdrawal of the smuggling charges based on "reasons of state and no ground of public policy." The prosecutor did not have much of a case because the missionary's letter had been previously cleared. It was understood that Royal could not join the ATC in India, which barred him from accepting Brigadier General Edward H. Alexander's offer of an advisory position, but could serve in China under General Chennault or the Commission on Aeronautical Affairs.

On October 10, Royal, departed India for the U.S. on an ATC transport. Less emotionally involved than other principals in the incident, Arthur Young, who had been running interference for CNAC with Chiang Kai-shek, described Royal as "over-strained." Bond, smack between Sharp and Royal, thought Royal was "a mental case." Bixby, who seems to have kept the incident from coming to Juan Trippe's attention, believed Royal suffered from a "persecution complex." On October 20, Bond cabled Bixby to cancel Royal's precious Pan Am seniority status. Ill and exhausted, Royal had been downed by company politics rather than an unseen mountain or a Japanese fighter.[123]

Upon returning to California, Royal took care of his health. He underwent a long-overdue surgery for an abdominal condition that had been interrupting his sleep. He wrote General Chennault that he had never realized how much energy he had been expending trying to subdue a constant feeling of physical irritation.

After dealing with his illness, Royal tried to take care of Pan Am and CNAC. He contacted Consolidated Vultee Aircraft Corporation, indicated that the Chinese government wanted to terminate its relationship with Pan Am, and inquired whether Consolidated was interested in obtaining international landing rights in China, starting a passenger service, and taking over operations when the Pan Am subsidiary's contract with the Chinese government expired. General Sales Manager Frank A. Learman told Royal that his company would need to discuss any proposal with a Chinese government representative, and Royal said he would contact Rosamonde Kung, who was in New York City.[124]

In early 1944, Royal filed separate wrongful employment termination and libel lawsuits in Los Angeles Superior Court against Pan

Am, CNAC, and their officers. Juan Trippe was personally served in Los Angeles, and Pan Am was served as a corporation doing business in California. Royal wrote Chennault that the actions were commenced "following the advice of a certain man in a special Govmt. office in Washington." Sharp had boasted he would ruin Royal and prevent his employment by U.S. airlines. In early 1945, Richard S. Mitchel, managing director of Consairway, the ATC South Pacific Wing, told Royal, who was flying as a copilot between northern California and Australia, that he would not be checked out as a pilot as long as he was suing Pan American Airways.

Apparently blacklisted in the U.S. commercial airline industry, Royal worked as personal pilot for U.S. Ambassador to Peru William D. Pawley between July 1945 and January 1946. They had met in the late 1930s when Pawley was managing the CAMCO aircraft assembly and repair factory at Loiwing in western China. Royal was unhappy with Pawley, who wanted him single-handedly to fly a C-47, which normally carried a crew of three, from Miami, Florida, to Lima, Peru. Pawley also wanted him to perform mechanical work, load the baggage, and clean the passenger compartment. "The last minute I said NO!!!" related Royal. Pawley hired a copilot but wanted Royal to land at night without flares at an out-of-the-way place in Panama. Royal again said "NO." Bothered by arm pain, Royal quit his job with the ambassador.[125]

Determined to defeat Royal's lawsuits, CNAC executives arranged the alteration of a State Department memorandum. CNAC attorney Gordon Tweedy asked Calcutta Consul-General MacDonald to prepare a statement about Royal's New Delhi visit with General Bissell, review the document with Tweedy, and send it to the State Department for release to Pan Am. MacDonald completed the memo but forwarded it to Washington before Tweedy could scrutinize it. MacDonald stated that the Chinese Consul General had advised the magistrate about the New Delhi trip and the trial date had been postponed. This memo confirmed that Sharp's wild charge branding Royal a fugitive from justice was untrue and defamatory. At CNAC management's insistence, MacDonald wrote State Department officials in Washington, DC, and requested deletion of the damaging sentence about the postponement, which was redacted in a copy provided to Bond but not in the original document preserved in State Department records.[126]

The wrongful employment-termination trial against Pan Am commenced on March 5, 1947, in Los Angeles Superior Court. Royal probably testified that Pan Am vice president H.M. Bixby in Washington, DC, told him "being CNAC means you are also Pan Am," Pan Am executives represented him to the Army Air Corps as a Pan Am technical expert, and Pan Am paid his Los Angeles–Washington, DC, travel expenses and New York City medical bills. He also may have testified that Bond wrote he was "entitled to the status of a Captain" with Pan Am and that a CNAC roster identified his prior service as "PAA." A newspaper article reported that Royal claimed he "was farmed out" by Pan Am. Neither Sharp, who did not return from China in time, Bond, who was still affiliated with Pan Am and CNAC, nor Pan Am vice president Bixby, who was based in New York City, appeared as witnesses. They had not been served with process and probably wanted to avoid submitting to California jurisdiction in the libel lawsuit. The jury rendered a $6,515.31 ($62,600 in 2009 earning power) verdict against Pan Am.

The judge, however, granted a motion for a new trial on the grounds of insufficient evidence to justify the verdict and the verdict being against the law, probably because Pan Am never directly employed Royal, and Sharp, as CNAC operations manager, wrongfully terminated him. Rather than risk another trial, Pan Am, recognizing CNAC and Sharp's liability, settled. In connection with the wrongful-termination case, Bond acknowledged that Sharp had failed to obtain the required majority owner Chinese government's approval before discharging Royal. As for the libel action, Sharp's "fugitive from justice" charge was untrue and Royal had been damaged because he could not find employment with an U.S. commercial passenger airline. On August 4, 1948, the lawsuits were dismissed. The settlement terms are not known. Pan Am had indicated willingness to resolve both cases prior to trial for $2,500 and subsequent to trial for $3,500.[127]

Finished with Pan Am and CNAC, Royal still felt he owed an obligation to a friend in China.

Chapter 15

STANDING BY FOR THE YOUNG MARSHAL

(December 1936 – June 1950)

During his time in the Orient following the Sian kidnapping, freedom-loving Royal never forgot the Young Marshal and his plight. Royal, who was five years younger than his former employer, considered the Young Marshal his friend. "I was never treated as his servant or as an aerial chauffeur," recalled Royal. "I was treated by the others as though I were none the less than a general." During their year together, the Young Marshal and Royal had played golf and tennis, hunted pheasants, and competed at rifle marksmanship. On their last flight in December 1936, Royal recalled, the Young Marshal "talked just as a father might talk to a son, and the next minute he reminded me of a son confiding in his father." In February 1938, Royal dined with the Young Marshal's wife and discussed his fate.

Royal was not the only person who remained loyal to the Young Marshal. In the fall of 1940, Donald left China partly because Chiang Kai-shek refused to free the Young Marshal. The next year, T.V. Soong urged Madame Chiang to persuade her husband to release the Young Marshal. A Manchurian-exile group in Hong Kong advocated the Young Marshal's release to help fight the Japanese. "I do not think that the Young Marshal will ever again appear alive," Royal stated in early 1942, "but the program he initiated will keep China alive."

After the Japanese surrender in 1945, Chiang Kai-shek staked his political future on regaining control of Manchuria, which the Japanese had occupied for fourteen years, and deployed his best troops and equipment there against the Chinese Communists. Several of Chiang Kai-shek's advisers recommended releasing the Young Marshal, who was a national hero for forcing resistance to the Japanese, to assist in retaking Manchuria. No other political figure, Chiang or Mao Tse-tung included, was as popular as the Young Marshal in Manchuria. "I think he is the strongest personality today in China," said Donald, the westerner most knowledgeable about Chinese affairs. "You will hear more of him." When General George C. Marshall in late 1945 and early 1946 was attempting to mediate between the Nationalists and Communists and bring about a democratic coalition, Madame Chiang Kai-shek spoke to him about freeing the Young Marshal. "But I never would mention it any way to the generalissimo," said General Marshall, recognizing the importance of face, "because this fellow had taken him prisoner and I didn't think I ought to stick my finger in that pot at all." During a Nationalist and Communist conference in the spring of 1946, Mao demanded the Young Marshal's release. On December 12, 1946, the tenth anniversary of the Sian kidnapping, Chou En-lai repeated the demand.[128]

As Royal's wrongful termination case was proceeding to trial in Los Angeles, Manchurians were expecting the Young Marshal's discharge from custody at the end of his ten-year prison term. Chiang Kai-shek, however, refused to release the Young Marshal. The Gimo was unwilling even to discuss freeing and returning to political power the man who had rebelled against him, whom he held responsible for his kidnapping and public humiliation, and whose action, he believed, had prevented the defeat of the Communists. The Young Marshal had become a "nonperson, deprived of all rights."

Chiang Kai-shek eliminated any possibility of the Young Marshal's reemergence with a semi-autonomous power base; the Gimo realigned the three prewar Manchurian provinces into nine and appointed minor Manchurian politicians, mostly former Japanese collaborators, as provincial governors under a high commissioner. The Young Marshal's younger brother, General Chang Hseuh-Szu, as well as former Manchurian Army and disbanded pro-Japanese Manchukuo Army units, went over to the Communists.

In May 1947, the U.S. Consul General advocated sending the Young Marshal to Manchuria "as an additional step toward winning defections from the Communists of native guerilla forces." In August, the U.S. assistant military attaché evaluated the Nationalist position in

Manchuria as desperate, indicated that most Manchurians wanted the Young Marshal in an important position, and recommended that the U.S. government pressure Chiang Kai-shek to appoint the Young Marshal to a leadership role. By the end of the year, the U.S. Consul General regarded the Young Marshal's restoration to power as the only hope for the Nationalists to hold Manchuria. The Manchurian capital, Mukden, fell to the Reds on October 31, 1948.

As the Young Marshal languished in Chiang's custody, the Red Army repeatedly defeated the Nationalist Army. On January 21, 1949, the day before the Nationalist commander in Peking surrendered, Chiang Kai-shek stepped down as President of China. He had transferred his family circle, key high government officials, Blue Shirts, the Young Marshal, Palace Museum treasures, and the government gold reserve, as well as half a million of his best troops, to the island of Formosa. His successor, former vice president Li Tsung-jen, offered amnesty to political prisoners and ordered the Young Marshal released, but Chiang refused to free him. According to Royal, many Formosans reacted very positively to Li Tsung-jen's announcement of the Young Marshal's release.

Formosans, who were a mix of aboriginals, Hakka Chinese, Dutch, and Japanese, regarded themselves as Taiwanese, not Chinese, and despised the Nationalists. Under Japanese rule between 1895 and 1945, Formosan industry and agriculture prospered, and the Taiwanese enjoyed a higher standard of living than the Mainland Chinese. After the Nationalists took over in 1945, the island economy collapsed as relatives and cronies of Chiang's Governor-General Ch'en Yi, the rapacious former warlord of Fukien province, filled government positions, appropriated businesses, sold military supplies, occupied the best houses, hoarded and smuggled rice, allowed the public health system to deteriorate causing cholera and bubonic plague epidemics, and engaged in a reign of terror. In February 1947, Ch'en brutally suppressed a Formosan rebellion and executed, by subsequent Nationalist government admission, as many as 28,000 Taiwanese. "We think of the Japanese as dogs and the Chinese as pigs," said some Taiwanese. "A dog eats, but he protects. A pig just eats." One month after the massacre, the U.S. Consulate in Taipei reported that some Taiwanese were considering resisting the Nationalists and wanted the United Nations to intervene.

Upset by the tyrannical and corrupt Nationalist regime on Formosa, the Truman Administration and Congress started looking for an alternative to Chiang Kai-shek. In August 1947, General Albert C.

Wedemeyer, who had succeeded Stilwell as Chiang Kai-shek's Chief of Staff and commander of U.S. armed forces in China, reported that the Taiwanese might be receptive to a United States guardianship or United Nations trusteeship. In mid-1948, U.S. Ambassador to China John Leighton Stuart believed the U.S. as a trustee under UN auspices should hold Taiwan for the Chinese people. In January 1949, a U.S. National Security Council paper recommended the U.S. develop and support a local non-Communist Chinese regime that would provide decent government. In March, Secretary of State Dean Acheson leaned toward encouraging a revolution against Chiang and establishing a UN trusteeship but realized a Taiwanese revolution could not succeed on its own against Chiang's military might.

Trying to determine whether there was a viable independence movement that might request UN intervention, the State Department sent special envoy Livingston Merchant to Formosa. He did not find one. The Formosan League for Re-emancipation (FLR) based in Hong Kong and headed by the Liao brothers, who held PhDs from U.S. universities, was of dubious strength on Formosa. Merchant suggested recommending to President Li Tsung-jen that Ch'en be replaced as governor-general by Taiwan defense commander General Sun Li-jen, who held degrees from Purdue University and Virginia Military Institute, had fought effectively in Burma during World War II, and was deputy commander in chief of the Chinese Army.[129]

Royal had his own candidate for a regime change on Formosa. After finishing the jury trial in Los Angeles, he had set up Royal Leonard, Inc., a California corporation engaged in aviation consulting, and traveled on business to Hong Kong, Shanghai, Tokyo, Okinawa, Calcutta, Bombay, Karachi, Bangkok, Manila, and other parts of the Far East. He helped organize and was employed by Jardine Aircraft Maintenance Company (JAMCO), a subsidiary of the British conglomerate Jardine, Matheson & Co., and arranged its purchase of a complete aircraft engine overhaul plant. He also was a sales representative for U.S. aircraft manufacturer Glenn L. Martin Company.

In early 1949, Royal wrote Texas Congressman W.R. Poage about a role for the Young Marshal on Taiwan. Royal regarded the Generalissimo as "a stupid, arrogant, blundering fool" for allowing the Communists to take over Manchuria, rather than freeing the one leader who might have prevented its loss. He believed the Young Marshal still had enough prestige to make all Chinese factions listen to reason. Royal convinced Poage that the Young Marshal could help strengthen Chinese opposition to Communism, but other Congressmen to whom Poage spoke dismissed the Young Marshal's influence as of no importance.

In February 1949, Royal tried to visit the Young Marshal but could get no closer than fifteen miles from his place of incarceration in the rugged northern Formosan mountains. Royal contacted Governor-General Ch'en about visiting the Young Marshal and was told that only Chiang Kai-shek could grant permission. No visitors were allowed except, occasionally, Jimmy Elder, the Young Marshal's boyhood friend and current financial adviser. "The Gimo seems to be determined not to let him free as long as they are both living," commented Royal.[130]

In April, Royal started flying part-time between Hong Kong and Formosa as a copilot for Central Air Transport Corporation (CATC), managed by the enterprising former CNAC pilot, Moon Chin. The airline was operating fourteen C-47 and twenty-three C-46 transport planes over twenty-seven scheduled Chinese domestic and overseas routes. Royal impressed CATC check pilot Leonard Lam as a born pilot, smart and alert, good planning and judgment, quick to detect and respond, and smooth flying. But CATC routes were shrinking. Shanghai fell to the Communists on May 25 as Communist troops occupied more and more of Mainland China.

In June, Royal wrote his sister that he was "still standing by for the Young Marshal, but he probably will not get his freedom until the 'Gimo' is really finished and that could be a year from now." Royal also confidentially informed Glenn L. Martin Company that he was "on a standby basis" for the Young Marshal. In July, Royal attended a two-week U.S. Army conference in Japan dealing with the defense of Hong Kong. During August, Royal spent a week on Formosa, but his activities are unknown.

"The Defection," the final blow to U.S.–Nationalist Mainland China civil aviation ventures, occurred on November 9, 1949. Chinese pilots, including Gordon Poon, copilot on Royal's January 31, 1943, Hump two-stage supercharger test flight, fled from Kai Tak to Communist-held territory in two CATC and ten CNAC planes. Royal had flown one of the hijacked CATC aircraft to and from Formosa the previous day. In Peking, the Communist People's Republic of China (PRC) Premier Chou En-lai—Royal's airsick Sian Incident passenger—welcomed the defectors.

In Kowloon, Moon Chin called a CATC pilots meeting and asked his men what they wanted to do. "You couldn't trust anybody," said

Moon. "You didn't know what side anybody was on. Pilots will go anywhere for money." Moon stated he was not returning to Mainland China and advised his pilots not to do so.

After the meeting, CNAC pilot E.C. Kirkpatrick encountered Royal in the Peninsula Hotel barbershop. Royal asked E.C. if he wanted a Mainland China flying job. "Royal had a lot of connections," recalled E.C. "He was trying to set up something. I said we'll talk some other time. Later we talked. He tried to discourage me [from flying for the Communists]. I said I wasn't interested."

CATC and CNAC suspended flights from Kai Tak, leaving only Claire Chennault and Whiting Willauer's Civil Air Transport, Inc. (CATI) supplying the few remaining Nationalist Mainland China enclaves.

Like other Americans with business interests in Hong Kong, Royal tried to stay in the good graces of the Chinese Communist leadership. Juan Trippe, for example, sought to have Pan Am positioned advantageously whichever side won the Chinese civil war because he wanted Pan Am to operate in Mainland China. CNAC and CATC management expected a new partner upon the fall of the Nationalists because the Chinese government was their majority owner. JAMCO planned to overhaul aircraft for the Chinese Communists. "Incidentally, the story gets to me from various sources," Royal wrote his sister, "that the Commies, who now are calling themselves the liberating party, have quite a bit of respect for me because of my battle with Pan Am. The Commies do not like them." Royal advised Glenn L. Martin Company that the Communists wanted to buy Curtiss-Wright C-46s, which were unavailable, and indicated that they might be interested in purchasing Martin twin-engine model 2-0-2s.[131]

After Chiang Kai-shek resumed the Nationalist presidency on March 1, 1950, Royal continued to correspond with Congressman Poage, who had asked him whether he thought the U.S. should support Chiang Kai-shek or try to control Formosa through another leader. Royal recognized that the Young Marshal, so long in confinement, could not suddenly come forth as the conquering ruler, but believed his name was a symbol commanding respect because he was universally admired by and a legendary figure among all Chinese. Royal reported that Formosa was "a glowing tinder" that might "set off a real explosion." He advised Poage that the Taiwanese were fed up with Chiang and did not want Communism but would accept any leader, even Communist, to get rid of Chiang and would not realize their mistake until they were crushed by Communist oppression. Royal believed a free election on Formosa under United Nations supervision and without Blue Shirt intimidation would establish the Young Marshal's potential as a national leader.

But Royal realized Chiang Kai-shek would block any effort to return the Young Marshal to a position of influence or power. "The Gimo," he stated, "is shrewd enough to know that if the American people get to know the Y[oung] Marshal, the Gimo would then be thoroughly and completely eclipsed. This possibility, he is closely guarding against. He has done a most thorough job of making sure this will never happen. He is torn between a complex containing this fear and the knawing memory of the fact that had it not been for the Young Marshal's intervention, the Gimo would have been killed in Sian." Royal was afraid that any public show of support for the Young Marshal, however, might result in the Young Marshal's death. His fear was not unfounded. Chiang's special service operatives had brutally murdered Chiang's other kidnapper, General Yang Hucheng, after thirteen years in custody.[132]

When the Korean War broke out on June 25, 1950, the Truman Administration decided it had no choice but to stick with Chiang Kai-shek. Realizing the U.S. government would not force Chiang to release the Young Marshal, Royal decided to free him and, in so doing, bring him worldwide attention as a potential Chinese leader and provide him another opportunity to change the course of Chinese history. "Royal was kind of a recluse," recalls Angela Shrawder who, with her CNAC pilot husband, Gerry, often socialized with Royal in Kowloon and heard him discuss the Young Marshal. "Royal was an icon who had done all these things."

As an accomplice in his scheme, Royal recruited Old China Hand Arthur Duff, who resembled the Young Marshal and spoke a northern Chinese dialect. After the Japanese occupied Hong Kong, Duff, who was operating a General Motors truck agency, hid in a Chinese home that was searched four times. In January 1942, he escaped on a small fishing boat and was transferred to a pirate vessel. Chinese guerillas attacked and killed the pirates and guided Duff through Japanese lines into Mainland China. During World War II, Duff had served as a U.S. Office of Strategic Services (OSS) operative and helped set up a clandestine supply system for American submarines in the China Sea. Duff and Royal had worked together as agents for Bendix Aviation Corporation, attempted to obtain a Sperry Gyro Company agency, and tried to sell airplane parts to Philippine Airlines.[133]

Outlining the scheme, Royal told Duff he had visited the Young Marshal (which he had not) and confirmed that the Young Marshal wanted to escape. Royal would obtain permits to visit the Young Marshal, pick up Duff at Kai Tak, and fly 500 miles east to Formosa. In the early evening, they would drive to the Young Marshal's place of incarceration and bribe his Blue Shirt guards to leave them alone. Duff and the Young Marshal separately would enter the bathroom and put on clothes similar to those the other was wearing. When Royal and the Young Marshal left the compound, Duff, his hair dyed like the Young Marshal's, would shake their hands and wave good-bye. Hopefully, the guards, imbibing cognac, would ignore them. Duff would get in bed. Optimistically, the guards would not discover the ruse until the next morning. When questioned, Duff would say he had been drugged and would feign anger at Royal for duping him. By that time, Royal and the Young Marshal would have flown to Kai Tak and the Young Marshal, using Duff's passport, would have cleared British customs.

But Duff, who had narrowly escaped death several times, weighed his slim chance for fleeting fame against the likelihood of immediate death and declined to participate. "Either we all escape, or no one escapes," said Duff.

Royal proposed another scheme. On a holiday, Royal and Duff would join the Young Marshal at his dining room table. Royal, drinking water, would toast the Young Marshal, Duff, and the guards. Duff would ask the Young Marshal to use the bathroom, and the Young Marshal would escort Duff past the bathroom and out the back door to a hidden car. Duff would get behind the steering wheel, and the Young Marshal would lie down on the backseat. Finishing the toasts, Royal would walk toward the bathroom, exit through the back door, and jump in the car. Duff would drive half a mile to an airfield. Royal would take off and fly south 730 miles to the Philippines, where they would offload the Young Marshal at a small airfield, bribe immigration officials, and rely on friends to help him enter the United States.[134]

Unknown to Royal and Duff, the Young Marshal would not have tried to escape. "It was a rebellion," said the honorable Young Marshal, referring to the Sian kidnapping, "and I had to take responsibility for it." According to his son-in-law Tao Peng, "the Young Marshal would have said no if asked whether he wanted to escape. His main intention was to right what he had done wrong. Political right or wrong was a different matter from personal honor. He was wrong in revolting against a superior, so he didn't complain about being imprisoned."[135]

In August 1950, Royal gave up trying to free the Young Marshal and returned to Los Angeles. Fletcher Bowron, the former judge who had rendered the paternity judgment against Royal, was serving a fourth term as city mayor. Unfortunately, Royal and Maxine's marriage had foundered. In twelve and a half years, they had spent more time apart than together. When they legally separated in March 1951, she valued their community property at $350,000 ($2,890,000 in 2009 purchasing power). Their divorce became final two years later.

Having lost round one to TWA president Jack Frye, round two on a phantom TKO to Pan Am president Juan Trippe, and round three to Chuck Sharp backed by corner man W.L. Bond, the only U.S. airline flying job open to Royal was as a C-46 copilot with the Flying Tiger Line, Inc., founded by former Flying Tiger and CNAC Hump pilot Robert Prescott. Royal started with the airline, which was ferrying supplies to American Far Eastern military bases, on June 20, 1951, and terminated on April 11, 1952. Although Royal held a commercial pilot license until 1959, his widow, the former Gerrie Johnson, whom he married on November 2, 1957, does not recall him flying again.

Stymied in commercial aviation, Royal built and managed residential rental properties, owned an aluminum-magnesium foundry, operated a trucking company, and worked two small gold mines. Like his Frye, Trippe, and Bond relationships, Royal's business dealings were contentious. "Royal was a very likable person and full of funny stories," recalls Gerrie, "but don't do any business with him. He'd expect twice or ten times as much in his favor. He'd talk on the phone about a business deal, get in an argument, and hang up laughing." He was constantly involved in business litigation. When a financial institution attempted to repossess a compressor from his foundry, Royal resisted physically. In quieter moments, he patented a baby nursing bottle and invented and marketed "Modern Plastic Rough-Weather Boot*Leggers," which provided rain protection over men's pant cuffs and shoe tops.

Wasted by liver and colon cancer, Royal Leonard, age 57, died June 21, 1962, in a Glendale, California, hospital bed. A journalist wrote that he was "a guy who has had all of the adventure and excitement that you and I, as Mr. Average American, can find only in our fantastic reveries of thrill and excitement." He took calculated risks blind flying CAM-12, evaluating the Lockheed Orion, and making the death-defying Hump two-stage supercharger test flight. He survived coping with cantankerous mail planes, lurking Japanese Zeros, hidden Himalayan peaks, and the world's worst flying weather; and never used a parachute. He idealistically dreamed and schemed about bombing Tokyo and rescuing the Young Marshal. As a lone pilot against a big corporation, he stood up for his principles and often paid a price for his convictions. Royal Leonard merits recognition for his role in U.S. aviation and Chinese history. He certainly does not deserve to be forgotten.[136]

EPILOGUE

The Kelly Field classmate who lured Royal to China and the TWA chief pilot who fired him died in the same plane accident. During a Boeing 307 Stratoliner prototype demonstration flight on March 18, 1939, pilot Julius Barr crashed with passenger Harlan Hull, who was evaluating the aircraft model for possible purchase by TWA.

Jackie Cochran was recognized as the world's best woman pilot. In 1938, she won the Bendix Race. During World War II, she founded and commanded the Women's Air Force Service Pilots (WASP) ferrying service. After the war, Royal, Maxine, and their son Royal S. visited Jackie and Floyd Odlum at their ranch near Indio, California. Jackie was the first woman to fly faster than the speed of sound and, later, twice that speed. She won the Harmon Trophy, awarded to the year's outstanding female pilot, fourteen times. Jackie died August 9, 1980.[137]

W.L. Bond oversaw the CNAC transition from Hump wartime operation to Mainland China peacetime service. In December 1947, Pan Am promoted him to vice president for the Orient. A year later, Bond and Royal accidentally met and dined in the Peninsula Hotel coffee shop. In 1950, Bond retired to his Virginia farm. Between 1978 and 1980, he wrote a self-serving memoir entitled *Wings for an Embattled China* that ignored his recommendation of Royal for Pan Am seniority and unfairly evaluated Royal on the basis of his stormy relationship with the CNAC American minority ownership and management rather than on flying skill. Bond also besmirched Royal's part in the Hankow evacuation, forgetting his own letter to a Pan Am executive praising Royal's performance. Bond, however, acknowledged that his manuscript had "limited" value "as a historical or reference work" because he wrote it forty years after the events without refreshing his memory from documents. The bitter mail-smuggling prosecution, a vexing incident in which Royal unfairly blamed a fatal crash on CNAC management, and the unfavorable jury verdict against Pan Am had poisoned Bond's attitude toward Royal. W.L. Bond died July 16, 1985.

"Desk Flyer" Chuck Sharp was amply rewarded for his loyalty to American management. After World War II, the Chinese government wanted a more amenable CNAC operations manager and pressed for Sharp's removal. Pan Am granted Sharp pilot seniority. He flew Latin American routes, retired in 1968, and died January 14, 1974. Not one CNAC Hump line pilot was awarded Pan Am seniority. When recruiting pilots for CNAC, Pan Am officials promised after the war that they would be members of the family. "If so," opined unlucky Hugh Woods, "they were treated as illegitimate members."[138]

Madame Chiang Kai-shek enjoyed a long life. Upon learning of Royal's death, she wrote his widow: "But I do wish you to know that the President and I have always held Mr. Leonard in high regard. He was an excellent pilot, and was ever faithful in the performance of his duties. His devoted service to us will be long remembered." Madame Chiang sent Christmas cards to Maxine until Maxine's death in April 1990. During Madame Chiang's final years, her niece Rosamonde Kung, whose parcels and letters had been seized by the British–Indian customs officer, was her principal companion and care supervisor. In October 2003, Madame Chiang Kai-shek, age 105, died in New York City.[139]

Royal's Hump test-flight passenger, Whiting Willauer, transitioned from CATI executive overseeing the supplying of anti-Communist forces in China to U.S. diplomat thwarting the spread of Castro-style Communism in Central America. In 1954, Willauer resigned as CATI president and accepted the U.S. Ambassadorship to Honduras. That year, Willauer helped direct the CIA-sponsored coup against the leftist Arbenz government in Guatemala. Royal's former employer William Pawley acted as special State Department liaison with the Pentagon for the venture. After serving as Ambassador to Costa Rica, Willauer died of a heart attack at his Nantucket summer home on August 6, 1962.[140]

The Young Marshal lived for six and a half decades after he and Royal parted at the Nanking airfield. In 1961, Chiang Kai-shek built a modern home for the Young Marshal and kept him under virtual house arrest. The Young Marshal studied Ming Dynasty history and attended Sunday Baptist services with Chiang and Madame Chiang in their private chapel. When Chiang Kai-shek died in April 1975, the Young Marshal wrote a couplet:

With mutual affection and esteem,

we are blood brothers;

Yet political disputes made us

almost enemies.

After the Gimo died, Madame Chiang occasionally lunched with the Young Marshal; he believed she had dissuaded her husband from executing him. Following the death of Chiang Kai-shek's son in 1988, the Taiwanese government released the Young Marshal. By this time, his chief guard, who had been a Blue Shirt lieutenant at the start of his assignment, was a major general. In 1991, the Young Marshal visited relatives in the United States. He told historian-journalist Harrison Salisbury that he had "embarked on a new crusade—to bring Beijing and Taiwan into a united China." He never returned to Mainland China, however. The Young Marshal died, age 103, on October 14, 2001, in Honolulu, Hawaii.

According to Chinese premier Chou En-lai, the Young Marshal and Yang Hucheng for their action at Sian "will be remembered by the Chinese people for a thousand years to come." Quite a contrast to the legacy of Royal Leonard. When shown Royal's picture more than a half century after last seeing him, the ninety-three–year-old Young Marshal did not recognize him. He remembered his longer-time American employee, Julius Barr, but not his admirer, staunch friend, and erstwhile savior, *Forgotten Aviator Royal Leonard.*[141]

ACKNOWLEDGMENTS

A very special thanks to Royal's family—his widow Gerrie Leonard Dubé, son Royal S. Leonard, sister Alice Evans (deceased), nephew Frank Evans, brother Morris Leonard (deceased) and sister-in-law Elizabeth Leonard—for sharing their stories, providing and granting permission to publish documents, and, most importantly, remaining patient with the author on his long sojourn.

Special thanks also are owed to CNAK-ers Ray Allen, Moon Chin, Dr. Reg Farrar (deceased), Peter Goutiere, Fletcher Hanks (deceased), E.C. Kirkpatrick (deceased), Bill Maher, Al Oldenburg (deceased), Robert J. "Catfish" Raines (deceased), Dr. Lewis Richards (deceased), Dick Rossi (deceased), Gerry (and Angela) Shrawder, and Felix Smith, as well as webmaster Tom Moore, for their assistance.

John Korompilas has been very generous in allowing me to utilize his Royal Leonard memorabilia collection.

Nancy Allison Wright and Robert Willett provided me copies of invaluable documents uncovered in their research.

Many others have assisted me, and I will list them by general subject matter:

<u>Formative years</u>: Donald J. Barrett, Asst. Director for Public Services, USAF Academy, Colorado Springs, CO; Dr. Robert S. Browning, III, Office of History, Kelly AFB, TX; Roger Conger (deceased), Waco, TX; Sean Perrone, University of Wisconsin–Madison Division of Archives, Madison, WI; Mark W. Ridley, Historical Research Center for Air Force History, Bolling AFB, AL; Virgil Vaughan, Denver, CO; and Richard J. Veit and Ben Rogers, Baylor University, Waco, TX.

U.S. commercial flying career: Richard Sanders Allen, Lewiston, ID; John Amendola, Jr., Bellevue, WA; Edward G. Betts (deceased), Pacific Palisades, CA; Teddy Durrer and Henry Wydler, Swiss Transport Museum, Lucerne, Switzerland; Phil Edwards, National Air & Space Museum Library, Washington, DC; Rudy Eskra, Fred Weisbrod Museum, Pueblo, CO; Eleanor M. Gehres, Western History Room, Denver Public Library, Denver, CO; William R. Gulley, Jr. and Curtis Hansen, ALPA Archives, Wayne State University, Detroit, MI; Ted Hereford, Newport Beach, CA; William A. Hooper, Jack Connors, and Jack Ramsey (deceased), New England Air Museum, Windsor Locks, CT; Fred Jacob (deceased), Glendale, CA; Capt. Elrey B. Jeppesen (deceased), Englewood, CO; William T. Larkins, Pleasant Hill, CA; Paulette D. O'Donnell and Marie Force, Delta Air Lines, Atlanta, GA; Dennis Parks, Janice Baker, and Katherine Williams, Museum of Flight, Seattle, WA; and Edward Peck, Louisville, KY.

Pre-World War II China flying: Dr. Dauril Alden, Seattle, WA; Jim Bledsoe, Oceanside, CA; Robert Fausel (address unknown); Harry Gann (deceased), McDonald Douglas Archives, Long Beach, CA; Jon Halliday, London, England; Frank Havelick (deceased), Torrance, CA; Allen W. Hughes, Sunnyside, CA; Peter Moreira, Halifax, NS; Tao Peng, Los Altos, CA; Malcolm Rosholt, Rosholt, WI; P.Y. Shu, Palo Alto, CA; Sebie Smith, Montgomery, AL; Dr. Paul G. Spitzer, Corporate Historian, Boeing Co., Seattle, WA; Louis Stannard, Willow Spring, NC; Kasey Sutter-Mueller, Newhall, CA; and John Williams (deceased), San Diego, CA.

Post-Hump activities: Virginia (Duff) Black, Pacifica, CA; Dr. Keith Eiler (deceased), Hoover Institution, Palo Alto, CA; Bob Keefer, Sacramento, CA; and Leonard Lam, Kowloon, Hong Kong.

Archival Assistance: National Archives personnel have patiently provided invaluable guidance, especially Kenneth D. Schlessinger, as well as Rebecca Lentz Collier, Joseph Dane Hartgrove, David A. Pfeiffer, Sally Schwartz, John Taylor, and Mitchell Yokelson. Other helpful archivists and librarians include Thomas W. Branigar, Dwight D. Eisenhower Library, Abilene, KS; Caroline Harzewski, Pan American World Airways, Inc. Special Collection, Richter Library, University of Miami, FL; Jean Holiday, Mudd Library, Princeton, NJ; Carol A. Leadenham, Nick Siekierski, and Lisa Nguyen, Hoover Institution Archives, Stanford, CA; Susan Palmer, Kroch Library, Cornell University, Ithaca, NY; Raymond Teichman, Franklin Delano Roosevelt

Library, Hyde Park, NY; Ray Wagner, San Diego Aerospace Museum, San Diego, CA; and Elwood White, USAF Academy, CO.

A debt of gratitude is owed to the reference librarians at the Arden-Dimick Library, Sacramento Main Public Library, and California State Library, Sacramento, CA, and Shields Library, University of California, Davis, CA, who responded unflinchingly to a myriad of unusual inquiries.

General Acknowledgments: Kind friends and family members contributed immensely to improving this book bit by bit. My wife, Carolyn, read the manuscript many times and made valuable suggestions, as well as dealt with word processing problems. My son, Shawn, and Nancy Allison Wright recommended significant improvements to an early draft. Dr. Louis L. Tucker and Felix Smith provided valuable counsel about strengthening the final chapters. My niece, Katy Warren, suggested editorial changes and conquered formatting problems. Neighbors Jim and Jane Hagedorn and Dal Darracq; niece and nephew, Amanda and Geoff Froh; and friends Tony Crawford, Peter Moreira, Louis Stannard, Robert Willett, and Tom Williams also made welcome suggestions. Jennifer Garland assisted with photographs.

Any errors and omissions are due to the author's foibles and failings.

NOTE ON ORIGINAL SOURCES

Royal's scrapbooks contain newspaper clippings and photos covering his boyhood through 1939. He kept appointment book pocket diaries in 1931, 1937, and 1938.

Between December 1936 and June 1950, Royal typed hundreds of letters to his wife, sister, brother, and friends. He kept carbon copies, and the recipients saved originals. During her two stays in Hong Kong, Maxine wrote regularly to her mother and kept carbon copies.

In 1937, Royal started writing a 500-page manuscript, mainly about the Lockheed Orion defects, MacRobertson and Bendix races, and early experiences in China. Different segments are in the possession of his widow, Gerrie Dubé (GDP), and son, Royal S. Leonard (RSLP). The manuscript is initially cited as "Leonard unpublished manuscript (n.d.)" and subsequently as "Leonard unpublished mss. (n.d.)."

A portion of the *I Flew for China* book manuscript has been preserved. The extant 149 manuscript pages in possession of Royal S. Leonard cover the same events as *I Flew for China*, pages 5 through 111. The manuscript is initially cited as "*I Flew* manuscript, RSLP" and subsequently as "*I Flew* mss., RSLP." The book is cited as "*I Flew*."

After Royal was prosecuted for mail smuggling, he wrote a 139-page "Summary of the Leonard Case" about his difficulties with Pan Am management in Washington, DC, and the events leading to, and the course of, the prosecution. In an addendum, he typed copies of letters and documents that are accurate when compared with extant originals. The "Summary" in the possession of his widow is cited as "Leonard Defense, GDP."

The Pan American Airways Legal Department maintained extensive files dealing with Royal's lawsuits for wrongful-employment termination and defamation covering the years 1942 through 1947. The Pan American Historical Foundation (PAHF) provided the author complete copies of these files but contributed only a portion to the Pan American Airways Collection in the University of Miami Richter Library. Pan Am Airways Collection documents are cited as "PAC," and copies of documents provided by PAHF and only in the author's possession are cited as "PAM."

Royal's pilot logbooks have been lost or destroyed.

Documents are quoted verbatim except for spelling and grammatical corrections or as otherwise indicated by [brackets].

Documents from private collections are cited with the date in parentheses and documents from institutional archives are cited with the abbreviation for the institution in parentheses.

With a few exceptions, the author uses the Wade-Giles system (e.g. Sian) for spelling Chinese names and places because this system was used in his sources. In 1958, the Chinese government introduced the Romanization system designated Pinyin (e.g. Xian).

ABBREVIATIONS

AEP	Alice Evans Papers, in possession of Frank Evans, Milpitas, CA
ALPA	Airline Pilots Association Collection, Archives of Labor and Urban Affairs, Wayne State University, Detroit, MI
ANYP	Arthur N. Young Papers, Hoover Institution Archives, Palo Alto, CA
CLCP	Claire L. Chennault Papers, Hoover Institution Archives, Palo Alto, CA
CNAAF	China National Aviation Association Foundation
FAA	Federal Aviation Agency, Oklahoma City, OK
FRUS	*Foreign Relations of the United States*
GDP	Gerrie Dubé Papers
JADP	J. Arthur Duff Papers, Hoover Institution Archives, Palo Alto, CA
JCP	Jacquelyn Cochran Papers, Dwight D. Eisenhower Library, Abilene, KS
JKC	John Korampilas Collection, Folsom, CA
LBCP	Lauchlin B. Currie Papers, Hoover Institution Archives, Palo Alto, CA
MLP	Morris Leonard Papers in possession of Elizabeth Leonard, Wichita, KS

NARA	National Archives & Records Administration, Washington, DC
PAC	Pan American World Airways, Inc. Records, Special Collections Division, University of Miami Libraries, Coral Gables, FL
PAM	Pan Am Historical Foundation Records copies, provided to and in possession of author, Sacramento, CA
RSLP	Royal S. Leonard Papers, Chatsworth, CA
SKHP	Stanley K. Hornbeck Papers, Hoover Institution Archives, Palo Alto, CA
TVSP	T.V. Soong Papers, Hoover Institution Archives, Palo Alto, CA
TWP	Theodore White Papers, Harvard University Archives, Cambridge, MA
WLBP	W. Langhorne Bond Papers, Hoover Institution Archives, Palo Alto, CA
WWP	Whiting Willauer Papers, Dept. of Rare Books and Special Collections, Princeton University Library, Princeton, NJ

End Notes

Chapter 1

[1] "Two Denver Mail Planes 'Lost' in Fog," *Denver Post* (Dec. 5, 1928); "Division No. 2 Sends Report Lost in the Fog!" Western Air Express, *The Dashboard Record* (Jan. 1929): 17–18; "Stearman Biplane Proves Popular," 3 *Western Flying* (Aug. 1927): 21; U.S. Dept. of Commerce, Aeronautics Branch: Information Division, *Airway Bulletins* No.145: "Lowry Field" (Aug. 5, 1927) and No. 279: "Alexander Airport" (Jan. 24, 1928); Lt. Commander F.W. Weed, U.S.N., "The Fight with Fog," 4 *Western Flying* (March 1928): 25–26, 91; Lt. Theodore C. Lonnquest, U.S.N., "Aircraft Instruments," 25 *Aviation* (July 9, 1928): 107, 129–134; Wesley L. Smith, "How I Fly at Night," XIX *The Journal of the Society of Automotive Engineers* (Sept. 1926): 228–233; J. Earle Miller, "Mystery of Port of Missing Planes Solved?" *Popular Mechanics* (Mar. 1928): 360–363.

[2] Capt. E.A. Underhill, "Pilots under the Hood," 10 *Western Flying* (Sept. 1931): 19 ["Not more than one per cent …"]; "Denver Air Mail Pilot Killed in Crash," *Denver Post* (Dec. 11, 1927); "Denver Air Mail Flier Killed as Plane Crashes in Heavy Fog," *Rocky Mountain News* (May 9, 1929).

[3] Wisconsin State Board of Health, Bureau of Vital Statistics, Certification of Birth Record [April 3, 1905]; Morris Leonard to author, May 29, June 29, Aug. 10, Sept. 19, and Dec. 22, 1989, Jan. 23, Feb. 12, Mar. 6, and Apr. 13, 1991; "There were": author interview of Morris Leonard, Hemet, CA (Feb. 16, 1990); Frank Tallman, *Flying the Old Planes*: 33–38; Peter M. Bowers, *Curtiss Aircraft 1907–1947:* 36, 41; "I'll go up": Royal Leonard, *I Flew for China*, xiii; ibid xii (hereafter cited as

I Flew); unidentified clippings in Royal Leonard scrapbook entitled "P.T.A. Carnival is Big Success at High School," "1400 Miles in Four Days on Motorcycle Waco Boy's Record," "Waco to Milwaukee in 3 Days on 32 Gallons of Gasoline Is Record of Last Week's Trip" and "Schott-Riley Win City Bike Titles in Races Sunday" (n.d.), John Korompilas Collection (hereafter cited as JKC); "the acrobat": William C. Ocker and Carl J. Crane, *Blind Flight in Theory and Practice:* 31; Royal Leonard Waco High School Transcript, May 31, 1923, Waco Independent School District, Waco, TX; Waco High School *Daisy Chain* (1923); Royal Leonard notebook journal, June 7, 1923–April 30, 1926, JKC; Royal Leonard (hereafter "Leonard") to Morris Leonard (n.d.), Morris Leonard Papers (hereafter cited as MLP).

[4] A. Scott Berg, *Lindbergh*: 53, 57-58; "Learn to Fly," *Popular Mechanics* (Jan. 1926): 87; http://www.measuringworth.com/powerus/ (hereafter cited as measuringworth.com); Leonard notebook journal, May 1 and July 3, 1926, JKC; Morris Leonard to author, May 29, Sept. 19 and Oct. 4, 1989; author interview of Morris Leonard, Hemet, CA (Feb. 16, 1990); Royal Leonard University of Wisconsin-Madison Transcript, University of Wisconsin-Madison Archives, Madison, WI.

[5] Enlistment Record of Royal Leonard, March 3, 1928, Colorado Division of State Archives and Public Records, Denver, CO (hereafter cited as Enlistment Record); Alice Evans telephone interview by author (Oct. 9, 1989); "The West Point of the Air," *Popular Mechanics* (Apr. 1930): 561–562; Brooks Field Section, *The Flying Cadet* (Aug. 1927): 18–19, 47, 64; Manning Ancell with Christine M. Miller, *The Biographical Dictionary of World War II Generals and Flag Officers: The U.S. Armed Forces* (1996): 379, 451; Martha Byrd, *Chennault, Giving Wings to the Tiger:* 30–31; Joseph P. Juptner, "Consolidated 'Trusty', PT-1," 1 *U.S. Civil Aircraft:* 197–199; "Never Hesitate!": Leonard notebook journal, Apr. 8, 1927, JKC; Berg, *Lindbergh*: 73–74, 77–79; Brooks Field Section, *The Flying Cadet* (Aug. 1927): 18–19, 64; Leonard to Morris Leonard (Nov. 7, 1927) (in author's possession, Sacramento, CA); Alexis Klotz, *Three Years off This Earth:* 18; "Growing Wings for the Army," *Popular Mechanics* (Oct. 1928): 642–647 [Royal's solo flight picture]; Sally Nash email to author, May 7, 2010; unidentified clipping from Royal Leonard scrapbook entitled "Born Aviators Alone Survive Severe Test," JKC; "My plane!": *I Flew*: xiii–xiv; unidentified clippings in Leonard scrapbook entitled "Flyers Here Are Healthy, Exams Show," "Flying School Students to Graduate" and "19 Take Exams for Air Corps Commissions," JKC; Royal Leonard Army Air Corps

Second Lieutenant Commission (Jan. 24, 1928), JKC; "Our Sphinx": Kelly Field Section, *The Flying Cadet* (Feb. 1928): 18; ibid 25, 38–39.

[6] Klotz, *Three Years:* 24; T&WA employment verification for Royal Leonard (n.d.) in author's possession, Sacramento, CA [hiring date April 23, 1928]; Enlistment Record; Clarence M. Young, Director of Aeronautics, to Mr. Royal Leonard (n.d.) [Transport License No. 2627], Royal Leonard Airman File, Federal Aviation Agency, Oklahoma City, OK (hereafter cited as FAA); *I Flew*, xiv; R.E.G. Davies, *Airlines of the United States since 1914*: 43, 65-66, 89; "I flew": *Pueblo Chieftain*, May 14, 1928; Lt. W. V. Davis, Jr., "Where Are We?" 4 *Western Flying* (Sept. 1928): 62 [describing "aerial navigation" as "avigation"]; Juptner, "Stearman – 3CB," 1 *U.S. Civil Aircraft*: 143–145; U.S. Dept. of Commerce, Aeronautics Branch: Information Division, *Airway Bulletin* No. 140 for Cheyenne, WY (July 25, 1927) [highest recorded wind velocity 82 mph]; Leonard to Morris Leonard, Oct. 16, 1928 and Jan. 8, 1929, MLP; "I can believe": Rudy Eskra (Fred E. Weisbrod Memorial Museum, Pueblo Airport) telephone interview by author (June 20, 2000); "Of course": Leonard to Morris, Oct. 16, 1928, MLP; *I Flew:* xvi–xvii; U.S. Dept. of Commerce, Aeronautics Branch: Information Division, *Airway Bulletin* No. 160 for Pueblo-Cheyenne Airway (Aug. 16, 1927); James G. Woolley, "Operation of Western Air Express," 25 *Aviation* (Nov. 17, 1928): 1561–1562; "highest": "Airmail Goes Thru Daily in Spite of Storms, Dark," *Colorado Springs Gazette & Telegraph* (Dec. 9, 1928); "He sprinkled": Alice Evans telephone interview by author (Oct. 3, 1993); "Doolittle, James Harold," 6 *American National Biography* (1999): 744–745; "Simulated Landings, Take-Offs in Fog Made by Lieut. Doolittle," 27 *Aviation* (Oct. 5, 1929): 718, 724.

[7] Unidentified newspaper clipping in Leonard scrapbook entitled "Engine Trouble Unknown On Denver Airline" (n.d.), JKC; "Airmail Goes Thru Daily in Spite of Storms, Dark," *Colorado Springs Gazette & Telegraph* (Dec. 9, 1928); *Denver Post* (Dec. 9, 1928); Leonard to Morris Leonard (Oct. 16, 1928), MLP; Klotz, *Three Years:* 30–31; measuringworth.com; "I don't know": Eskra telephone interview by author (June 20, 2000); Application for Federal Recognition as a National Guard Officer and for Appointment in the Officers Reserve Corps (Aug. 21, 1928) and Leonard to Hon. Wm. Adams, Gov. of Colorado (Apr. 14, 1929), Enlistment Record; Fred E. Jacob, *Takeoffs and Touchdowns: My Sixty Years of Flying*: 11–21; "Royal was": Jacob interview by author, Glendale, CA (Feb. 3, 1991); Berg, *Lindbergh*: 86–89; "neglected": Charles A. Lindbergh, Pilot, Report of North Bound Mail Flight – St. Louis to Chicago (Sept. 16, 1926): 3, Federal Aviation

Administration, File 805.0, RG 237, National Archives and Record Administration (hereafter cited as NARA); Kenneth S. Davis, *The Hero: Charles A. Lindbergh and the American Dream:* 126–127, 132; Charles A. Lindbergh, "And Then I Jumped," *Saturday Evening Post* (July 23, 1927): 6–7, 59–60.

Chapter 2

[8]"First Coast Trip," *Kansas City Star* (June 2, 1929); "The New Fokker Passenger Liners," 4 *Western Flying* (May 1928): 56, 129; "Get that kid": Morris Leonard to author (Mar. 6, 1990); *I Flew:* xv; "Jess": Western Air Express, *Dashboard Record* (Jan. 1930): 21; "From the Log Book," *Dashboard Record* (Nov. 1930): 21; unidentified clippings entitled "'Big Boy Jess' LEAVES," "Abandoned Pup is Air Minded" and "Jess Grounded" in Leonard scrapbook, Gerrie Dubé Papers (hereafter cited as GDP); "Bear Mascot at Airdrome in Alameda Takes Master Safely on Flying Trips," *Oakland Tribune* (Dec. 27, 1930); "Big Boy Jess" lyrics: Robert J. Serling, *The Only Way To Fly: The Story of Western Airlines, America's Senior Air Carrier:* 107–109; American Society of Composers, Authors and Publishers (ASCAP), *Biographical Dictionary, 4th ed.* (1980): 541; "No": *I Flew*: 6; Alice Evans telephone interview by author (May 19, 1994); "Pilots Instructed in Use of Radio," *Los Angeles Times* (June 11, 1930); unidentified newspaper clipping in Leonard scrapbook entitled "Flying Fireman," JKC.

The dynamic duo of Royal and Jess preceded flamboyant racing pilot Roscoe Turner and his lion cub, Gilmore, who was born February 7, 1930, and took his first plane ride April 13, 1930 [Carroll V. Glines, *Roscoe Turner, Aviation's Master Showman*: 124–127].

[9] W.G. Herron, "The New Air Mail Act," 7 *Western Flying* (June 1930): 40–43; Davies, *Airlines of the United States since 1914*: 114–117; "Transcontinental & Western Air," 24 *Aero Digest* (Feb. 1934): 26–27; Robert Serling, *Howard Hughes' Airline: An Informal History of TWA*: 16–18; "Doings in the Industry," 11 *Western Flying* (June 1932): 36; George E. Hopkins, *The Airline Pilots: A Study in Elite Unionization*: 52, 79, 113; George E. Hopkins, *Flying the Line: The First Half Century of the Air Line Pilots Association*: 3; "Frye, William John," 8 *American National Biography*: 529–530; "Frye, William John (Jack)," *Dictionary of American Biography*, Supplement VI (1980): 220–222; "Chest Expansion Airline," *Fortune* (Apr. 1945): 132–136; "To do his bidding":

Leonard unpublished manuscript (n.d. – probably May 1937): 224–225, Royal S. Leonard Papers (hereafter cited as unpublished mss. and RSLP).

[10] "the biggest, most costly": Oliver E. Allen, *The Airline Builders*: 103; ibid 102; "The Fokker F-32 Transport Monoplane," 27 *Aviation* (Nov. 9, 1929): 926–930; "is an expression": unidentified newspaper clipping in Leonard scrapbook entitled "Pilot Royal Leonard Promoted," JKC; "Two Largest Landplanes Will Reach City Tuesday," *Los Angeles Times* (Apr. 6, 1930); "a novel": "Plane Radios Yule Cheer to World," *Oakland Post-Enquirer* (Dec. 19, 1930); Serling, *Only Way*: 127–128; undated *L.A. Times* clipping in Leonard scrapbook entitled "Huge Plane Becomes Filling Station," JKC; Frank Evans telephone interview by author (Nov. 16, 2009).

[11] Major C.C. Moseley, "Hitch Your Airport to the Stars," *Aviation* (Nov. 1935): 16–18; "Mail Pilot Walks on Tight Rope as Practice," *Glendale News-Press* (May 6, 1932); "'Airplane Watchers' on Job," *Pasadena Star-News* (Dec. 8, 1930); U.S. Dept. of Commerce, Aeronautics Branch, *Airway Bulletin* No. 1017: "Grand Central Air Terminal" (June 3, 1930); "He flies": Alice Evans telephone interview by author (May 19, 1994); "In Pursuit of the S.A.T.R," 12 *Western Flying* (Dec. 1932): 11, 16–18; "I did acrobatics": Leonard to Morris Leonard (Dec. 27, 1931), MLP.

[12] Richard S. Allen, *The Northrop Story, 1929–1939:* 13–28, 134–137; copies of T&WA Accident Reports numbers 46 (Mar. 3, 1932) and 59 (May 20, 1932) in possession of Ed Betts, Pacific Palisades, CA; Serling, *Howard Hughes' Airline*: 27–28; U.S. Dept. of Commerce, Aeronautics Branch, *Airway Bulletin* No. 98: "Wichita Airport" (Apr. 25, 1930); "I wondered": Ted Hereford telephone interview by author (May 28, 1995).

[13] Richard S. Allen, *Revolution in the Sky:* 132–133, 214–218, 220–223 [accident total does not include Post-Rogers crash in modified Orion or eight Spanish Civil War Orion losses]; "TWA Cuts 90 Min. from Mail Time,"13 *Western Flying* (Aug. 1933): 28; Terrance A. Geer, "The Lockheed Orion 9D," 16 *American Aviation Historical Society Journal* (Spring 1971): 40–43; "I was," "All," "It really was," "I might" and "If you": Leonard unpublished manuscript (n.d.):, 8-10; ibid 7, 11-15 (hereafter cited as unpublished mss.), GDP; Hopkins, *Airline Pilots:* 113; *FAA Statistical Handbook of Aviation* (1959): 76; "It was": Ted Hereford telephone interview by author (May 28, 1995); T&WA Management and Pilots Executive Council Meeting Minutes, Kansas City, MO

(June 13, 1933): 25, GDP; "Under the": Leonard unpublished mss. (n.d.): 19, GDP.

[14] "Plane into River," *Kansas City Times* (July 29, 1933); Leonard unpublished mss. (n.d.): 15–18, GDP; Ted Hereford telephone interviews by author (May 28 and Oct. 15, 1995) [confirming engine-switches location]; Bryan B. and Frances N. Sterling, *Will Rogers & Wiley Post: Death at Barrow*: 102–111, 145, 174–178, 189–193, 293–295; Teddy Durrer, Swiss Transport Museum to author (Oct. 21, 1998); Geer, 16 *AAHSJ*: 41; "controls to be used": Pacific Automotive, Ltd. parts list in Sterling, *supra*, 105–107; Dr. Reba Neighbors Collins, *Will Rogers & Wiley Post in Alaska:* 55; Gordon S. Williams, "Ballast for Wiley Post," *Air Enthusiast Twenty-eight* (1985): 74–78; Gordon S. Williams Photo Collection negative scanning by Katherine Williams (Nov. 2, 2006), Museum of Flight, Seattle, WA [A photograph taken ten days before the crash shows the cockpit seat back, Post's right shoulder, upper arm, and elbow, and nearby controls, but a partition across the lower cockpit blocks view of any controls below his right elbow.]; Jack Connors, Engine Curator, New England Air Museum [Pratt & Whitney Archives], to author, Apr. 3, 2001; "No matter": Leonard, unpublished mss. (n.d): 18, GDP.

[15] "Chest Expansion of an Airline," *Fortune* (Apr. 1945): 199; Jacobs, *Takeoffs and Touchdowns*: 64–65; Phil Cohan, "Wrong Way Corrigan Revisited," 3 *Air & Space* (June/July 1988): 46–52; "Howard looked": author interview of Jacobs, Glendale, CA (Feb. 3, 1991); "I sure": Leonard to Morris Leonard (Dec. 27, 1931), MLP; Ted Hereford telephone interview by author (Aug. 26, 1995); "Offer of Navigation Course," 1 *The Air Line Pilot* (Oct. 1932): 4; Leonard unpublished mss. (n.d.): 2, RSLP; "In summing": Royal Leonard, "Check by Sextant – How Celestial Navigation May Be Used in Checking Dead Reckoning of an Air Liner," 13 *Western Flying* (May 1933): 12; ibid 10-11; Morris Leonard telephone interview by author (date unrecorded); Davies, *Airlines:* 111–112, 156–164; Leonard unpublished mss. (n.d.): 52, 54–55, GDP.

Chapter 3

[16] "the most significant": Terry Gwynn-Jones, *Farther and Faster: Aviation's Adventuring Years, 1909–1939:* 251; "greatest race": "Mildenhall to Melbourne," *Time* (Oct. 29, 1934): 48; "race of the century":

"Off to 'Down Under'," 33 *Aviation* (Oct. 1934): 311; ibid 312; Jacqueline Cochran and Maryann Bucknum Brinley, *Jackie Cochran*: 7-18, 22-99; "Odlum of Atlas," *Fortune* (Sept. 1935): 50–55, 102, 104, 106, 109–110; William M. Leary, Jr., *Aerial Pioneers: The U.S. Air Mail Service, 1918–1927:* 230; Frye Memo to Leonard re Trans-oceanic service (Jan. 2, 1934); Leonard unpublished mss. (n.d.): 26, 28, 77–81, 110, 115–116, 137–138 (GDP); Leonard unpublished mss. (n.d.), 263–266 (RSLP); Francis X. Holbrook and John Nikol, "Harold Gatty and the Bridging of the Pacific," 29 *Aerospace Historian* (Sept. 1982): 176–182; code names: Odlum cable to Turner, Oct. 2, 1934, Bx 2, London-Melbourne Air Race 1934 Cable File 4; Odlum cables to Turner, June 1 and 2, 1934, Bx 2, London-Melbourne Air Race Cable File 1, Jacquelyn Cochran Papers, Dwight D. Eisenhower Presidential Library, Abilene, KS (hereafter cited as JCP).

[17] Leonard unpublished mss. (n.d.): 87–97, 111–114, 116–121, 134–135 (GDP); Bertha Leonard to Jackie Cochran (July 25, 1934) and Leonard to Wesley Smith (June 3, 1934), Bx 2, Leonard File 1 (JCP); Hopkins, *Flying the Line:* 83.

[18] "quiet, calm": Serling, *Hughes' Airline:* 21; "'Great Loss' Felt by T. & W. A. Boys on West Coast," 1 *The Air Line Pilot* (Sept. 1, 1932): 1; "I thought": Leonard unpublished mss. (n.d.): 142; ibid 86–87, 98–111, 122–132, 135–136, 138–141, 143, 151–156, 184–185, 231, GDP; "Royal was": Hereford to author (Aug. 1995); Leonard Report (c. Sept. 1934): 1–33, RSLP; "U.S. Pilots and the $50,000 race," 14 *Western Flying* (May 1934): 20; "Such a": Leonard unpublished mss. (n.d.): 147; ibid 146, 148–151, 1-D to 48-D, RSLP; measuringworth.com; Bruce Brown, *Gatty: Prince of Navigators*: 157.

[19] Cochran and Brinley, *Jackie Cochran*: 104–106; Royal and Jackie quotes from Leonard unpublished mss. (n.d.): 158-61; ibid 156, 162-163, RSLP; Affidavit of Vera Mankinen (Dec. 5, 1934), Bx 2, Leonard File 2 (JCP); Glines, *Roscoe Turner*: 172.

[20] "I was," "Gee" and "Why you": Leonard unpublished mss. (n.d.): 166, 168 and 171; ibid 163-165, 167, 169-170, 172, RSLP; Affidavit of Vera Mankinen (Dec. 5, 1934), Bx 2, Leonard File 2 (JCP); "would talk": "Forced Landing of Plane Here," *Tucumcari (NM) Daily News* (Oct. 2, 1934); Cochran and Brinley, *Jackie Cochran:* 109–110; *I Flew:* xviii–xix; "HeeBeeGeeBee": Charles Mendenhall, *The Gee Bee Racers:* 112; ibid 109; "As I looked": Leonard unpublished mss. (n.d.): 203–205, RSLP; "Would the": Cy Caldwell, "That Air Race to Australia," 24 *Aero Digest* (Mar. 1934): 31; "Kingsford-Smith, Sir Charles

Edward," *Webster's Biographical Dictionary, 1st ed.* (1962): 822.

21 Cochran and Brinley, *Jackie Cochran*: 110–113; "NO RADIO": Leonard unpublished mss. (n.d.): 204–205, RSLP; "The 11,323-Mile MacRobertson Race from London to Melbourne within 71 Hours," 24 *Aero Digest* (Nov. 1934): 20–22.

22 Gwynn-Jones, *Farther and Faster:* 255; "Mildenhall to Melbourne," *Time* (Oct. 29, 1934): 48–49; "Of course": Leonard unpublished mss. (n.d.): 208-209; ibid 216–221, 224–227, RSLP; "two of the best": "From England to Australia," 14 *Western Flying* (Nov. 1934): 10; measuringworth.com; "Satisfactory": Cochran to Maurice Garner cable (Nov. 7, 1934); Smith to Leonard [London] cable (Jan. 14, 1935); Leonard to Cochran cable (Feb. 3, 1935), Bx 2, Cables File 5 and Leonard File 2 (JCP); Carl Solberg, *Conquest of the Skies: A History of Commercial Aviation in America:* 236–237; State of California Dept. of Health Services Certificate of Birth 35-002917 (Jan. 3, 1935, amended Nov. 29, 1935).

Jackie Cochran's verifiable "race of the century" costs, including $63,065 for two planes, Royal and Wesley's $700 salaries for six months, their $4,000 travel advances, $2,600 for five control point station manager salaries, $1,500 for five refueling stands, $1,400 for the *Q.E.D.* transfer payment to Pangborn, $900 for Royal's Darwin–Sydney charter flight, and additional $1,500 expense money for a station manager who was "fleeced" by a confidence man in Paris totaled $87,365 ($1,400,000 in 2009 earning power). Unverifiable costs include passage to and from Europe for Odlum, Jackie, Royal, Wesley, five station managers, and Ed Granville and his mechanics; *Q.E.D.* shipping; travel for Royal and five station managers to stations; spare Gamma parts and shipping to stations; attorney Mabel Willebrandt, London agent Turner, and insurance fees; 154 or more trans-Atlantic cable charges; "an ogre" of U.S. telephone calls; two mapmaking assistants' salaries; and Jackie's Darwin special assistants, marquee, tub, and other accoutrements [Receipt to Cochran from Leonard, July 24, Chase National Bank cable transfer, Aug. 22 and Cochran cable to Turner, Aug. 31, 1934, Bx 2, Leonard File 1 and Cable File 2 (JCP); measuringworth.com.]

Chapter 4

23 "nationally known" and "America's testing laboratory": "Eight Ready for Air Race" and "Bendix Race Cash Put Up," *Los Angeles Times*

(Aug. 29 and 21, 1935); Don Dwiggins, *They Flew the Bendix Race:* 24; Mendenhall, *Gee Bee Racers:* 105–109, 118, 165–167; Cochran and Brinley, *Jackie Cochran:* 109; "Granville, Miller & DeLackner Model R-6H," 25 *Aero Digest* (Oct. 1934): 45–46; "big green elephant": Leonard unpublished mss. (n.d.): 179; ibid 296–297, RSLP; chapter title from Dwiggins, *Bendix Race:* 52; "Don't ask me": Joe Christy, "Shady Lady of the Skies," *Argosy* (Dec. 1961): 62, copyright permission, Col. John Doolittle, Ret.; Gwynn-Jones, *Farther and Faster:* 167.

[24] Complaint, Florence G. Suddarth v. Royal Leonard, filed March 30, 1935, and Receipt for Exhibits, Aug. 6, 1935 ["hush note" not listed], Los Angeles County Superior Court action no. D-130763, L.A. County Courthouse, L.A., CA; measuringworth.com; "romantic airport affair": "Blonde Sues Plane Racer," *Los Angeles Times* (Aug. 3, 1935); "Court Will View Child in Parentage Dispute," "Suddarth Baby Shown in Suit Over Parentage" and "Flyer Held Father of Baby Girl," *Los Angeles Times* (Aug. 5, 6 and 7, 1935); *Glendale News-Press* (Aug. 3, 6, 7 and 9, 1935); Affidavit of Royal Leonard on Motion to Reopen Case for Further Proceedings (Aug. 29, 1935), p. 3, quoting Plaintiff's Exhibit A (Suddarth to Royal, April 24, 1934), L.A. Co. Sup. Ct. action no. D-130763; Leonard unpublished mss. (n.d.): 64–67, GDP; unpublished mss: 278–279, RSLP; measuringworth.com; "perfect image": Leonard to Maxine Thayer (Aug. 12, 1935), RSLP.

[25] "The fact," "Lady Luck" and "They found": Leonard unpublished mss. (n.d.): 180 and 304; ibid, 299-303, RSLP.

[26] Mendenhall, *Gee Bee Racers*: 117; "Bendix Dash Aces Poised," *Los Angeles Times* (Aug. 30, 1935); David M. Goodrich to Leonard (Sept. 6, 1935), GDP; unidentified newspaper clipping in Leonard scrapbook entitled "Cecil Allen Falls to His Death at Start of Dash," JKC; "None of us": Leonard unpublished mss. (n.d.): 304–305, RSLP; "It's too": "Bendix Race Cash Put Up," *Los Angeles Times* (Aug. 21, 1935); measuringworth.com; Dwiggins, *Bendix Race*: 62.

[27] "The drama": unidentified clipping in Leonard scrapbook entitled "9 Planes Hop; 1 Cracks Up at Start," JKC; Don Dwiggins, *Hollywood Pilot: The Biography of Paul Mantz:* 93–94; "Bendix & Thompson," *Time* (Sept. 9, 1935): 31; "Gee" and "You crazy": Leonard unpublished mss. (n.d.): 309 and 312; ibid 306-308, 310-311 and 313–314, RSLP; "Bendix Racer Killed Near Los Angeles," "Roscoe Turner and Roy Leonard Refuel Planes Here in Bendix Race, Leonard is Forced Out" and "Serious Trouble Forces Leonard to Remain Here," *Wichita (KS) Beacon* (Aug. 30 and 31, 1935); Chief of the Air Corps, *Handbook of*

Service Instructions for the Model R-1340-47 Engines and Associated Models (1939): 17; Dwiggins, *Hollywood Pilot:* 93–94; "Tragedy and Rain," *Cleveland Plain Dealer* (Aug. 31, 1935); "Was it 'Old Man Jinx'": Leonard, unpublished mss. (n.d.): 314, RSLP; George J. Marrett, *Howard Hughes: Aviator:* 21–22; John T. Chapin, "Sky Conqueror," 7 *Wings* (Aug. 1977): 32–41.

[28] Affidavits of L.T. Riley and A.H. Zeiler, M.D. (Aug. 30, 1935) in Support of Motion to Reopen Case for Further Proceedings, Affidavit of Florence G. Suddarth (Nov. 7, 1935), Findings of Fact and Conclusions of Law (Sept. 13, 1935) and Minute Order (Nov. 15, 1935), L.A. Co Sup. Ct. action no. D-130763, L.A. Co. Courthouse, L.A., CA; Leonard to Maxine Thayer (Aug. 31, 1935), RSLP; Leonard pocket diary (Feb. 16, 1938), JKC; "thanks for all": Leonard to Maxine Leonard (Feb. 20, 1940), RSLP.

Royale Regina died Sept. 17, 1938. Royal completed his court-ordered child support payments in 1940 [State of Calif. Dept. of Health Services Standard Certificate of Death no. 38-053452, Sept. 19, 1938; Satisfaction of Judgment, entered June 25, 1940, L.A. Sup. Ct. action no. D-130763, L.A. Co. Courthouse, L.A., CA].

Chapter 5

[29] "Would": *I Flew:* xix; ibid 4, 13–14; "Don't anyone tell": Kelly Field Section, *The Flying Cadet* (Feb. 1928): 14; Barr and Chiang quotes from "Thrills-Suspense-Hardships-Humor Mark Adventurous Sky Trails of the Late Julius Barr over War-Torn China," 8 *The Air Line Pilot* (Apr. 1939): 4; Baitsell, *Airline Industrial Relations:* 105; measuringworth.com; "Had a pearl diver": Leonard, unpublished mss. (n.d): 327; ibid 326, RSLP; "I told": *I Flew:* 5.

[30] John K. Fairbank, *The Great Chinese Revolution:1800–1985:* 217-239; Arnold J. Toynbee, *Survey of International Affairs 1936:* 876–883, 899–902, 908–909; Tien-wei Wu, *The Sian Incident: A Pivotal Point in Modern Chinese History:* 44–45; Chinese Ministry of Information (comp.), *China Handbook 1937–1945:* 213–214, 217; William M. Leary, Jr., *The Dragon's Wings: The China National Aviation Corporation and the Development of Commercial Aviation in China:* 101; Martha Gellhorn to Charles Colebaugh (Mar. 1, 1941), Bx 349, Crowell Collier Collections, New York Public Library; "so": Gen. and Mme. Chiang

Kai-shek, *The Account of the Fortnight in Sian When the Fate of China Hung in the Balance:* 45; ibid 44.

[31] John Gunther, *Inside Asia* (1942 War Ed.): 224–229, 245–249; Howard L. Boorman (ed.),"Chang Hseuh-liang," 1 *Biographical Dictionary of Republican China:* 61–66 [birth date 1898]; Gen. D.E. Swinehart, "Aviation in North China," 24 *Aviation* (Mar. 12, 1928): 636, 648; "My first impression": *I Flew:* 21; Nym Wales [Helen Snow], "Notes on the Sian Incident, 1936": 35, Nym Wales (Helen Snow) Papers, Bx 17, Notes on the Sian Incident Folder, Hoover Institution Archives, Stanford Univ., Stanford, CA.

[32] *I Flew:* 1–3, 14–16, 21–22, 27–28; "Boeing Transport Model 247-D," 24 *Aero Digest* (Nov. 1934): 42–43; Leonard to Morris Leonard (May 12, 1936), MLP; "No more bullet holes," "Sometimes" and "covered": *I Flew*: 24, 29 and 50.

[33] Leonard and Li [not Yii] conversation, "It was impossible," "Over and over," "After a few" and "It was": *I Flew:* 61, 55–56, 68–69, 233 and 38; ibid 8-9, 36-37, 39-40, 44-45, 58-60, 232; Gunther, *Inside Asia* (1942 War Ed.): 246; "It was almost" and "It looks just": Leonard to Alice Evans (Oct. 21, 1936), AEP.

[34] "Chiang Kai-shek," Boorman, 1 *Biographical Dictionary*: 319–329; Leonard to Alice Evans (Apr. 24, 1936), AEP; Theodore H. White and Annalee Jacoby, *Thunder Out of China:* 124–125; "He was": *I Flew:* 49; ibid 47.

[35] "showed" and "I looked": *I Flew for China* manuscript (hereafter cited as *I Flew* mss.)*: 66–67*; *I Flew* mss.: 429–434, RSLP.

[36] Jung Chang and Jon Halliday, *Mao, The Unknown Story:* 180–181; Leonard to Maxine Thayer (Nov. 6, 1936), RSLP; "The road," "It was," "It reminded," "We no can do" and "The Young Marshal": *I Flew:* 69, 70, 72 and 74; ibid 71 and 73; "However": *I Flew* mss., 452; ibid 439-451, RSLP.

[37] *I Flew*: 13, 41–44, 49, 52; Leonard to Alice Leonard, Jan. 17, Feb. 19, Oct. 4 and Dec. 6, 1936, and Apr. 14, 1937, AEP; "a political prisoner": *I Flew* mss., 401, RSLP.

[38] "one of the most sensational upheavals": *I Flew* mss., 474, RSLP; "the most dramatic event": Chang Kuo-t'ao, *The Rise of the Chinese Communist Party 1928–1938: Volume Two of the Autobiography of Chang Kuo-t'ao:* 474; "Gunther, John," 9 *American National Biography:* 730–731; "one of the most unusual dramas": Gunther, *Inside Asia* (1942 War Ed.): 249.

Chapter 6

[39] "I wondered": *I Flew* mss. : 423–424, RSLP; cf. Jay Taylor, *The Generalissimo: Chiang Kai-shek and the Struggle for Modern China:* 117–123; Chang, *Mao:* 175–177; Luo Ruiqing, et al., *A Turning Point in Chinese History: Zhou Enlai and the Xi'an Incident—An Eyewitness Account:* 22–37; Wu, *Pivotal Point*: 47, 56; James Bertram, *First Act in China: The Story of the Sian Mutiny*, 106–110; Jonathan Spence, *The Search for Modern China:* 416–417; Laura Tyson Li, *Madame Chiang Kai-shek, China's Eternal First Lady:* 106; Agnes Smedley, "How Chiang Was Captured," *The Nation* (Dec. 31, 1937): 180–182; Xu Youwei and Philip Billingsley, "Behind the Scenes of the Xi'an Incident: The Case of the *Lixingshe*," 154 *The China Quarterly* (June 1998): 287–290; "We passed" and "Chiang Kai-shek": *I Flew:* 34–35 and 77; "Guess he": Leonard to Maxine Thayer (Nov. 6, 1936), RSLP.

[40] "Even if" and "[E]xcept" quotes combined from Ruiqing, *Turning Point*, 46 and Wu, *Pivotal Point*, 71; Ruiquing, *Turning Point*: 46–50; Leonard unpublished manuscript about Sian Incident (n.d.): 12–13, RSLP.

[41] "From that moment" and "Not until": *I Flew:* 82-83 and 84; ibid 79-81, 85; Mi Zanchen, *The Life of General Yang Hucheng:* 1–73; Wu, *Pivotal Point:* 22.

[42] Ruiquing, *Turning Point*: 50–52; Wu, *Pivotal Point:* 79-80; "the special care": *I Flew:* 88; ibid 89-90; Zanchen, *Yang Hucheng:* 126, 240; unidentified clipping in Morris Leonard scrapbook entitled "Pilot Sends News from Nanking, China," MLP.

[43] "Soong, Mei-ling," Boorman, 3 *Biographical Dictionary:* 146–147; Gunther, *Inside Asia* (1942 War Ed.): 202–203, 225–228, 230–233; "Missimo": Hannah Pakula, *The Last Empress: Madame Chiang Kai-shek and the Birth of Modern China:* 244; Earl Albert Selle, *Donald of China:* 320–327; *I Flew* mss.: 494–496, RSLP; *I Flew:* 91–92, 95.

[44] "U.S. Flier 'Detained' by Chiang's Troops," *New York Times* (Dec.17, 1936); "Hey," "Orders" and "Well": *I Flew:* 96 and 99; ibid 95, 98; *I Flew* mss.: 496–504, RSLP; Chang, *Mao:* 184–185; Ruiqing, *Turning Point:* 52, 57–64; "Zhou Enlai," 12 *The New Encyclopaedia Britannica:* 913; Jonathan Haslam, *The Soviet Union and the Threat from the East, 1933–41:* 80–81; Wu, *Pivotal Point:* 102–104; Leonard to Dwight D. Eisenhower (Dec. 13, 1952), GDP.

The Communist passengers' version of their uncomfortable flying experience was translated for the author by T.Y. Sung, Sacramento, CA from excerpts of two Chinese-language Chou En-lai biographies provided courtesy of Jon Halliday.

45 "Night after night": *I Flew*: 102–103; Chiang and Madame Chiang Kai-shek, *Fortnight:* 86–87; Wu, *Pivotal Point:* 140; Ilona Ralf Sues, *Shark's Fins and Millet*: 105; Boorman; "Ho Ying-ch'in," 2 *Biographical Dictionary*: 79–84.

46 "Are you ready," "Nobody," "To them" and "Maybe": *I Flew:* 105, 107, 108 and 109; ibid 103, 106; "I could hardly realize": *I Flew* mss.: 513, RSLP; Zanchen, *Yang Hucheng:* 140–143.

On Jan. 13, 1937, U.S. Ambassador to China Nelson T. Johnson interviewed Royal about the Christmas-day flight. Nelson commented: "... his description of the circumstances in which the departure was made from the flying field in Sian I find highly interesting, particularly the hurried flight, without the dramatic speeches which were later reported. These, therefore, would seem to have been the sort of convenient fabrications in the nature of amendations of actual events so rarely possible to publicize with such success" [Johnson, U.S. Embassy, Nanking, Cover Letter with Memorandum of Conversation (Jan. 13, 1937), No. 344, dated Feb. 6, 1937, to Secretary of State, U.S. State Dept. Decimal File (1930-1939) 893.00/14038, RG 59 (NARA); Leonard pocket diary (Jan. 13, 1937), JKC].

47 "Now be," "I knew then" and "Everybody concerned": *I Flew:* 109, 110 and 112–113; "It meant": Felix Smith, *China Pilot: Flying for Chiang and Chennault*: 93; Chang, *Mao:* 188; "was begging": Reminiscences of Sebie Biggs Smith, 49, in Oral History Collection of Columbia University, New York City; Wu, *Pivotal Point*: 152–153.

Chapter 7

48 "Certainly" and "The Young Marshal's principles": *I Flew:* 115 and 116; ibid 111-14; measuringworth.com; Wu, *Pivotal Point*: 155; Baitsell, *Airline Industrial Relations:* 105; Charles Drage, *The Amiable Prussian:* 45–51, 88–104, 106, 108–109; author interview of Moon Chin, Hillsborough, CA (Mar. 6, 1999); Leonard pocket diary (Feb. 12, Apr. 3–7, 13, May 7, 24, 29–31 and June 2, 1937), JKC; Berater Stennes Order to Der Pilot Leonard (Mar. 22, 1937), RSLP; Leonard to Alice

Evans (Apr. 14, 1937), AEP; Jonathan Fenby, *Chiang Kai-shek: China's Generalissimo and the Nation He Lost:* 254–255.

49 "For the love," "boots-on" and "Well": *I Flew:* 116, 176 and 117; ibid 118-19, 175 and 177; Leonard pocket diary (July 20 and Aug. 8, 1937), JKC; Byrd, *Chennault:* 30–31, 36–72; Sterling Seagrave, *The Soong Dynasty:* 359; Arthur Young, *China and the Helping Hand, 1937–1945:* 24–25.

50 Leonard pocket diary (Aug. 13 and 14, 1937), JKC; "China-Japan," *Time* (Aug. 23, 1937): 19–20; Jack Samson, *Chennault*: 22–24; Chennault, *Way of a Fighter:* 44–46; Toynbee, *Survey of International Affairs 1937*: 214; "Chinese planes": *I Flew:* 165; ibid 164; "Not one": Leonard to Fred Jacob (Sept. 26, 1937), MLP.

51 "Like the report" and "I would have gladly": *I Flew:* 166; ibid 167; measuringworth.com; "It sure seemed funny": Leonard to Fred Jacob (Sept. 26, 1937); Leonard to Morris Leonard (Aug. 22, 1937), MLP; "Guerilla Airline," *Southern Flight* (Dec. 1943): 54; Leonard pocket diary (Aug. 15, 16 and 17, 1937), JKC.

52 Gene Gleason, *Hong Kong:* 24–25, 39, 158–159; Martha Gellhorn, "Time Bomb in Hong Kong," *Collier's* (June 7, 1941): 31; Young, *Helping Hand:* 27–28; "Guess": Chennault, *Way of a Fighter:* 51; Byrd, *Chennault*: 79–80; Leary, *Dragon's Wings:* 114; Leonard and airport manager quotes from *I Flew:* 171; ibid 164, 167-170, 172; Leonard pocket diary (Aug. 18 and 22, 1937), JKC; Leonard to Jacob (Sept. 26, 1937), MLP.

53 "Japan-China," *Time* (Sept. 6, 1937): 19; *I Flew:* 130–131; Leonard pocket diary (Aug. 29, 1937), JKC; Leonard and Madame Chiang quotes from *I Flew:* 132; ibid 131, 143; "Well, I couldn't": Leonard to Jacob (Sept. 26, 1937), MLP.

54 Royal Leonard American Adviser Pass (JKC); "It is": Leonard to Jacob (Sept. 26, 1937), MLP; "All of us": *I Flew:* 132; "As for blind flying": *I Flew*: 162; ibid 144-147.

55 *I Flew:* 144–145, 147; P. St. John Turner, *Heinkel, an Aircraft Album*: 74; Leonard pocket diary (Sept. 15, 1937), JKC; Leonard to Fred Jacob (Oct. 2, 1937), MLP; Chennault to Leonard (Sept. 6 and 24, 1937), Leonard Memos to Chennault (Sept. 15 and 18, 1937), and Leonard Memos entitled "General Outline of Training Program for Bomber Pilots," "Night Flying" and "Camera Obscura" (n.d.), GDP; Leonard pocket diary (Sept. 6–9, 13–14 and 24, 1937), JKC; "I think":

Chennault to Leonard (Sept. 24, 1937), GDP; copyright permission Anna C. Chennault; *I Flew:* 145–146; Leonard to Chennault (draft), (Oct. 5, 1937), GDP; Leonard to Jacob (Sept. 26, 1937, with addendum Oct. 2, 1937), MLP; *I Flew:* 132–133.

[56] Samson, *Chennault*: 30–31; "The Presidency," *Time* (Oct. 18, 1937): 17–19; Leonard, pocket diary (Oct. 17–18, 1937), JKC.

[57] Samson, *Chennault:* 33–34; Reminiscences of Sebie Biggs Smith, 109, in the Oral History Collection of Columbia University; Chennault to Leonard (Oct. 24, 1937); Leonard to Capt. Stennes (Nov. 8, 1937); Leonard to Donald (Oct. 13, 1937), GDP; Leonard pocket diary (Oct. 27–28, 1937), JKC; "jacking up" and "In fact": Leonard to Chennault (Oct. 29, 1937); Chennault, Colonel Aviation, to Leonard (Nov. 9, 1937); Chennault telegram to Leonard (Nov. 10, 1937), GDP; Chennault, *Way of a Fighter:* 69–71; Malcolm Rosholt, *Flight in the China Air Space 1910–1950:* 102–106.

[58] Young, *Helping Hand:* 18–22, 54–57; F.F. Liu, *A Military History of Modern China, 1924–1949:* 166–171; Leonard pocket diary (Nov. 24 and 26–30, 1937), JKC.

[59] "Report to MacArthur" is published in *I Flew for China* at 260–283; "This is a most intriguing paper": *I Flew:* 283; "MacArthur, Douglas" 14 *American National Biography:* 195–199; Michael Schaller, *Douglas MacArthur: The Far Eastern General:* 35–39.

Although Royal believed that the Japanese destroyed his report when they occupied the Philippines, it is preserved in the National Archives: "Aerial Warfare in China" dictated to Lt. Col. Henry C. McLean, G-2, Dec. 14, 1938, Headquarters Philippine Department, Office of Assistant Chief of Staff for Military Intelligence, Records of the War Dept. General and Special Staffs, File 439.1051, RG 165 (NARA).

Chapter 8

[60] Young, *Helping Hand*: 26; Chennault, *Way of a Fighter:* 55, 59, 88; "The death" and Leonard and Wong quotes: *I Flew:* 190-191 and 192; ibid 189; F. Tillman Durbin, "Nanking Speeding Strong Defenses," *New York Times* (Nov. 24, 1937); Iris Chang, *The Rape of Nanking*: 6, 69–70, 87–88, 102, 160–161.

[61] Leonard pocket diary (Jan. 11, May 24, June 5, 7, 15 and 17, Aug. 29, Oct. 10 and 28, Nov. 25, and Dec. 11, 1937 and Feb. 12, 1938), JKC; *I Flew:* 162–163, 180; "War In China," *Time* (Dec. 27, 1937): 13; Hamilton Darby Perry, *The Panay Incident: Prelude to Pearl Harbor*: 41–42, 63–113, 224; Robert S. Thompson, *A Time for War: Franklin Delano Roosevelt and the Path to Pearl Harbor*: 49–50; "They did it": Leonard to Bertha Leonard (Dec. 19, 1937), RSLP.

[62] "The slaughter": *I Flew*: 139–140; Leonard pocket diary (Jan. 25, 1938), JKC; Leonard to Alice Evans (Feb. 8, 1938), AEP; "[O]ne big puff": Leonard to Morris Leonard (Feb. 9, 1938), MLP.

[63] "Enemy expected" and "After the Russians": *I Flew:* 158–159; ibid 157; Leonard pocket diary (Mar. 11, 12 and 15, 1938), JKC; Leonard to Alice Evans (Apr. 29, 1938), AEP; *I Flew:* 154–155.

[64] Leonard pocket diary (May 4–7, 15 and June 26–July 11, 1938), JKC; Fred Jacob to Odlums (June 11, 1938), Bx 4, Aviation-General Correspondence January-July 1938 (2) File, JCP; "Royal was": Kasy Sutter telephone interviews by author (July 30 and Nov. 12, 2001); Samson, *Chennault:* 41, 45.

[65] Leonard to Donald (July 24, 1938); W.H. Donald to Leonard (July 29, 1938); Madame Chiang Kai-shek to Leonard (Aug. 4, 1938); Commendation, Headquarters of the Generalissimo, Wuhan, China (Aug. 3, 1938), GDP; Leonard to Alice and Ben Evans (Nov. 28, 1938), AEP.

[66] "Mystery Shrouds Fate of Ex-T.W.A. Flyer, Now in China," *Los Angeles Evening Herald and Express* (Sept. 16, 1937); "a piquant brunette" and "Yes": *I Flew:* 236 and 237; author interview of Maxine Leonard, Studio City, CA (Oct. 25, 1989); American Consular Service, British Crown Colony of Hong Kong, Certificate of Marriage (Sept. 8, 1938), JKC; "Mme Chiang's Pilot Weds American from Paramount Studios," *South China Morning Post* (Sept. 19, 1938).

Royal had previously married Grace Cooper in January 1933; they divorced the same year ["Marriage Announced," *Los Angeles Times* (Jan. 8, 1933); Royal Leonard Application for Passport (June 24, 1938), Royal Leonard Passport File, U.S. State Dept., Washington, DC].

[67] Robert L. Willett, *An Airline At War: The Story of Pan Am's China National Aviation Corporation and Its Men*: 46; H.L. Woods, "Pilot's Report" (Aug. 26, 1938) in China National Aviation Association Foundation (hereafter cited as CNAAF), III *Wings Over Asia*: 45–48; Leary, *Dragon's Wings:* 118–121.

[68] *I Flew*: 195–196; Bond biographical memo, Bx 1, Biographical Folder, W. Langhorne Bond Papers, Hoover Institution Archives, copyright Stanford University (hereafter cited as WLBP); Leary, *Dragon's Wings:* 49; Bond to S.W. Morgan (Sept. 21, 1938), Bx 1, S.W. Morgan 1938 Correspondence Folder (WLBP); Ernest M. "Allie" Allison biographical outline, courtesy of Nancy Allison Wright; "Soong, T.V.," Boorman, 3 *Biographical Dictionary:* 149–152; Royal Leonard, "Summary of the Leonard Case": 2–4 [When Royal returned from India to the U.S. in October 1943, he submitted to the Office of Strategic Services (OSS) in San Francisco a 139-page "Summary of the Leonard Case" presenting his side of the mail-smuggling prosecution described in Chapter 14 of this book (hereafter cited as Leonard Defense)], GDP; Capt. Evelle J. Younger memo to Maj. Roger A. Pfaff (Dec. 28, 1943), File 5038-125, RG 226 (NARA); "Leonard is": Bond to Bixby (Sept. 18, 1938), Bx 1, H. M. Bixby Correspondence 1938 Folder; copyright permission Stanford University (WLBP); Bond handwritten answers on Bixby to Bond (April 7, 1944) [Pan American & World Airways, Inc. copy among documents provided by Pan Am Historical Foundation to author (hereafter cited as PAM)]; Minutes of the 37th Meeting of the Board of Directors of China National Aviation Corp., Chungking (Nov. 17, 1938), Bx 103, CNAC 1938-1940 Chungking Folder, Arthur N. Young Papers, Hoover Institution Archives (hereafter cited as ANYP); measuringworth.com; Baitsell, *Airline Industrial Relations:* 105; "In memoriam – Charles Lamar Sharp, Jr.", CNAAF, III *Wings Over Asia*: 1–2; "He expressed": Leonard to Bixby (Sept. 2, 1943); Leonard to David L. Behncke, Pres., ALPA (Mar. 29, 1945), GDP.

[69] Liu, *Military History:* 201–202; Royal and radioman quotes from *I Flew:* 202-203; ibid 198-201; "Do you think": Leonard to Alice and Ben Evans (Nov. 17, 1938), AEP; "Don't be foolish": W. Langhorne Bond (James E. Ellis, ed.), *Wings for an Embattled China:* 195; Bond to Kitsi [wife] (Oct. 26, 1938), Bx 1, Kitsi Bond Folder (WLBP); Leonard pocket diary (Oct. 22–23, 1938), JKC.

[70] "We soared": *I Flew:* 209; ibid 204-208; Leonard pocket diary (Oct. 24–25, 1938), JKC; Theodore H. White, "China's Last Lifeline," *Fortune:* (May 1943): 146; author interview of Moon Chin, Hillsborough, CA (Mar. 6, 1999); "The men": Bond to S.W. Morgan, Pan American Airways (Oct. 29, 1938), Bx 103, CNAC 1938–1940 Chungking Folder (ANYP); "CNAC men": "Life Line," *New Horizons* (April 1943): 20; Leonard Defense: 4; Leonard to Bixby (Sept. 2, 1943), GDP; Minutes of the 37th Meeting of the Board of Directors of

CNAC, Chungking (Nov. 17, 1938), Bx 103, CNAC 1938-1940 Chungking Folder (ANYP); Leonard pocket diary (Nov. 18, Dec. 14 and 31, 1938), JKC; Leonard to Alice and Ben Evans (Nov. 28, 1938); Leonard to Alice Evans (Dec. 16, 1938), AEP; Leonard to Morris Leonard (Dec. 18, 1938), MLP; Maxine Leonard to Caroline Thayer [her mother] (Dec. 24, 1938 and Jan. 1, 1939), RSLP; "I am beginning": Leonard to Alice and Ben Evans (Nov. 17, 1938), AEP.

Chapter 9

71 "nip-and-tuck": *I Flew:* 220; ibid. 198, 245–246; Leary, *Dragon's Wings:* 126; "Chiang's War," *Time* (June 26, 1939): 29; "War in China," *Time* (Dec. 20, 1937): 15.

72 *I Flew:* 125–126, 198, 210–211; "ceiling" and "Dark": *I Flew:* 212; "his neck": Maxine Leonard to Caroline Thayer (Jan. 24. 1939), RSLP; "Pre-war Shanghai and Hong Kong," CNAAF, IV *Wings Over Asia:* 7; III *Foreign Relations of the United States* (hereafter cited as *FRUS*) (1939): 160; Bond, *Wings*: 219–220.

73 Enzo Angelucci and Paolo Matricardi, 2 *World War II Airplanes*: 126, 128–129, 138–139; "to kill": Carl Crow, "Hell in the Heavenly Kingdom," *Liberty* (Sept. 9, 1939): 46; Smith, *China Pilot:* 1–2; Bond, *Wings:* 218; "The women": Maxine Leonard to Thayer (Jan. 13, 1939); "The boys say": Maxine to Thayer (Feb. 29, 1939); Maxine to Thayer (Mar. 23, 29 and 30, 1939); Maxine memo, Visit to Kunming (Apr. 1–5, 1939), RSLP; Maxine–Claire jibes from author interview of Maxine Leonard, Studio City, CA (Oct. 25, 1989); Daniel Ford, *Flying Tigers: Claire Chennault and the American Volunteer Group*: 36.

74 "War In China," *Time* (May 15, 1939): 26, 29–31; Maxine to Thayer (May 9, 1939), RSLP; www.cnac.org/moonfchin01.htm; *I Flew:* 226–230; Moon Chin telephone interview by author (May 30, 1992) and personal interview, Hillsborough, CA (March 6, 1999); Leonard to Morris Leonard (June 27, 1939), MLP; "These kids": Maxine to Thayer (June 27, 1939); "The boys": Maxine to Thayer (Aug. 3, 1939); "Needless to say": Maxine to Mrs. Mabel Walker Willebrandt (June 9, 1939); Maxine to Thayer (June 20, July 6, 20 and 26, Aug. 2, 3 and 23, 1939), RSLP; *I Flew*: 197; "War in China," *Time* (Aug. 28, 1939): 25; "War in China," *Time* (Sept. 4, 1939): 26; "You know": Maxine to Thayer (Aug. 29, 1939), RSLP.

75 "German-like": *I Flew*: 161–162; Maxine to Thayer (Aug. 2, Sept. 13 and Oct. 4, 1939), RSLP; Bond to Morgan (Apr. 6, 1939), Bx 2, S.W. Morgan 1939–40 Folder (WLBP); *I Flew:* 218–219; "It seems": Maxine to Thayer (Sept. 13, 1939); Maxine to Thayer (Aug. 16 and 23, 1939); "Sounds like": Maxine to Thayer (June 20, 1939), RSLP; Bond to Morgan (Apr. 19, 1939), Bx 2, S.W. Morgan 1939–40 Folder and Bixby to Bond (May 8, 1939), Bx 1, H.M. Bixby Correspondence 1939 Folder (WLBP); "You don't": Theodore H. White, India Notebook (June–Aug. 1942), Theodore H. White Papers, HUM 1.10, Bx 50, Folder 8, courtesy of Harvard University Archives, Cambridge, MA; Johnson to Works (Aug. 17, 1944), PAM; measuringworth.com; "I'd like to": Leonard to Morris Leonard (June 26, 1941), MLP; "crazy": Gellhorn addendum to Leonard to Maxine (June 5, 1942), RSLP; "The throttles": *I Flew:* 216; ibid 215.

76 "WHOOF" and "Then thinking": Leonard to Maxine (Jan. 25, 1940), RSLP.

77 "Kung, H.H.," Boorman, 2 *Biographical Dictionary:* 263–269; *I Flew:* 220.

78 Leonard and Chennault quotes from *I Flew:* 223; ibid 222, 224; Brian Crozier, *The Man Who Lost China*: 6, 8–9; Fenby, *Chiang Kai-shek:* 34; *CNAC Cannon Ball* (May 15, 1994): 14; Arthur N. Young, "Sidelights on Affairs in China" (Sept. 8, 1943), 1–2 (hereafter cited as "Sidelights Memo"), Bx 106, Sidelights on Affairs in China Folder (hereafter cited as "Sidelights Folder") (ANYP); Max T. Chennault to author (Jan. 18, 1992) [confirming death threat and that his father would not have carried it out].

79 Leary, *Dragon's Wings:* 128–129; "Foxy Kent," CNAAF, IV *Wings Over Asia:* 38; "All my life": Capt. Walter C. Kent, "Wings for China," *Atlantic Monthly* (Nov. 1939): 646; http://www.cnac.org/kent01.htm; "Any one" and "[y]ou get": *I Flew:* 137-138 and 117; ibid 139; *Collier's* (May 31, 1941): 86–87; *I Flew*: 221–222; Moon Chin telephone interview by author (May 30, 1992) and personal interview by author, Hillsborough, CA (Mar. 6, 1999).

Chapter 10

80 Martha Gellhorn, *Travels with Myself and Another*: 25; Gellhorn to Charles Colebaugh (Mar. 1, 1941), Caroline Moorehead (ed.), *Selected Letters of Martha Gellhorn*: 108; Peter Moreira, *Hemingway on*

the China Front: 15, 29–30; "Yes": H.L. Woods, "Hemingways to Burma," CNAAF, IV *Wings Over Asia:* 29; Ernest Hemingway, *Islands in the Stream* (1970): 289; "China's life line": Martha Gellhorn, "Flight into Peril," *Collier's* (May 31, 1941): 87.

81 "He became" and "Roy flew": Gellhorn, *Travels*: 25 and 26; ibid 24, 27-29; "I go" and "But he": *Collier's* (May 31, 1941): 85 and 86; ibid 21, 87; Bond, *Wings:* 240–241; Chennault, *Way of a Tiger:* 88; inscribed *For Whom the Bells Toll* in possession of Gerrie Dubé; Leonard to Maxine with Gellhorn addendum (June 5, 1942), GDP; "Roy": Gellhorn to author (April 1995); Leonard to Morris and Elizabeth (Mar. 20, 1940), MLP; *I Flew:* 239–241; Agnes Smedley, *China Correspondent:* 359–360; "Lattimore, Owen," 13 *American National Biography*: 248–250; author interview of Maxine Leonard, Studio City, CA (May 10, 1989); Roger J. Sandilands, *The Life and Political Economy of Lauchlin Currie:* 112; Leonard to Morris Leonard (June 26, 1941), MLP; Leonard to Maxine (Sept. 3, 1941), RSLP; Royal S. Leonard telephone interview by author (May 2010).

82 Martha Gellhorn, "Time Bomb in Hong Kong," *Collier's* (June 7, 1941): 31–32; Maxine Leonard telephone interview by author (June 1989); Moreira, *Hemingway:* 179; *I Flew:* 255.

83 Leary, *Dragon's Wings:* 129–130; Zygmund Soldinski, "My Story of the DC 2 ½," CNAAF, II *Wings Over Asia*: 47–56; Juptner, "Douglas Commercial, DC-2," "Douglas Commercial, DC2-115" and "Douglas DC2-115H," 6 *U.S. Civil Aircraft:* 143, 199 and 251 and "Douglas, DC3-G2," "Douglas, DC3A-3B3G," "Douglas, DC3B-G102" and "Douglas, DC3A-S1CG," 7 *U.S. Civil Aircraft:* 71, 76, 128 and 240 [DC-2 wing span 85 feet and DC-3 wing span 95 feet]; Leonard to Maxine (May 25 and June 6, 1941), RSLP; "Mel": Peter Rand, *China Hands:* 216; *I Flew:* 248.

84 "Typhoon," 19 *World Book:* 540; "The rain," "Hong Kong wind," "British weatherman," "riding in," "That was," "Hey boy!" and "only fool": *I Flew:* 250, 251, 252 and 245; ibid 244, 246-49; http://www.cnac.org/higgs01.htm; Mary Pollman, "Local Hero of a Distant War," *Tri-Village News* (Jan. 15, 1980); "Threat of Typhoon," "Typhoon Threat Passes" and "Typhoon Bus Service," *South China Morning Post* (June 30, July 1 and July 2, 1941); "Edge of Typhoon Hits Hong Kong," *New York Times* (July 1, 1941) [reporting 92 mph winds]; Leonard to Maxine Leonard (July 7, 1941), RSLP; "There's an" quote and Kai Tak landing approach information from Louis Stannard telephone interview by author (Jan. 7, 2007).

[85] Olga and Harry Greenlaw and Royal quotes from Olga S. Greenlaw, *The Lady and the Tigers:* 27–29; Ford, *Flying Tigers:* 66–67, 76; Li, *Madame Chiang Kai-shek:* 91; "The Madame": Leonard to Maxine (Oct. 9, 1941); Leonard to Maxine (Oct. 26, 1941), RSLP; David M. Finkelstein, *Washington's Taiwan Dilemma, 1949–1950: From Abandonment to Salvation*: 10–12.

[86] "Six years" and Royal and copilot quotes: *I Flew:* 253-255; ibid 217; measuringworth.com; Leonard to Maxine (July 25, 1941), RSLP; Pilot Applications for Renewal of License, Jan. 31, 1936 [6295 mi.] and Feb. 23, 1942 [10,118 mi.], Royal Leonard Airman File (FAA); "In all my six years": Leonard to Bond (draft) (March 24, 1942), GDP.

Chapter 11

[87] "The honeybee" and "Oh well": *I Flew:* 141 and 118; ibid 117, 140, 193, 261; "the mission": Leonard to Chennault (draft) (Oct. 5, 1937), GDP; Leonard pocket diary (March 6, 8, and 16, 1938); "Nuts": Leonard pocket diary (May 20, 1938), JKC; Chennault to T.V. Soong, Memo re Preparations for special flight of Douglas transport (Mar. 6, 1938), GDP; Rosholt, *Flight in the China Air Space:* 85–86.

[88] Michael Schaller, *The U.S. Crusade in China, 1938–1945:* 71–79; "Soong, T.V.," Boorman, 3 *Biographical Dictionary*: 149–152; "Pain in the Heart," *Time* (Dec. 28, 1936): 15; "He was": *I Flew:* 219; William M. Leary Jr., "Portrait of a Cold War Warrior: Whiting Willauer and Civil Air Transport," 5 *Modern Asian Studies* (1971): 373; "Whiting W. Willauer, 55, Dies," *New York Times* (Aug. 7, 1962); Ford, *Flying Tigers:* 42–48, 53–54; Samson, *Chennault:* 62–64.

[89] USAF Historical Division, Research Studies Institute, Maxwell AFB, "Biographical Sketch of Brig. Gen. Henry B. Clagett" (Sept. 9, 1955): 4; *I Flew:* 234–235; Leonard to Maxine (June 16, 1941), RSLP; Leonard to Morris Leonard (June 26, 1941), MLP; Brig. Gen. H.B. Clagett, Office of the Commanding General, Philippine Department Air Force, to the Chief of Staff, Washington, DC, "Air Mission to China" (June 12, 1941): 1–11, Adjutant General's File 380.3, RG 407 (NARA); Gordon K. Pickler, "United States Aid to the Chinese Nationalist Air Force, 1931–1949" (PhD diss., Florida State Univ., 1971): 116–122; Samson, *Chennault*: 65–66; Alan Armstrong, *Preemptive Strike: The Secret Plan That Would Have Prevented the Attack on Pearl Harbor:* 74–75, 109, 121; Leonard to Maxine (July 25, 1941), RSLP.

[90] Bomber Command Officer Roster (Aug. 17, 1941); "One of the older": Chennault to T.V. Soong (Sept. 4, 1941) and Madame Chiang Kai-shek cable to Chennault (Nov. 5, 1941), Bx 2, Folder 6 and Bx 6, Folder 6, Claire L. Chennault Papers, Hoover Institution Archives (hereafter cited as CLCP); copyright permission Anna Chennault; Lauchlin Currie to Madame Chiang Kai-shek (Sept. 5, 1941), V *FRUS* (1941): 722.

[91] "Tell them," "Tell'em back" and "The bombing": *I Flew:* 258, 255 and 187; ibid 186; Leonard Defense: 1, GDP; Ford, *Flying Tigers*: 93–94.

[92] Mark Cotta Vaz, *Living Dangerously: The Adventures of Merian C. Cooper, Creator of King Kong*: 283–288; A.M. Archibald, Pan Am Asst. V.P., to Lt. Col. C.H. Woolley (July 28, 1943) and H.M. Bixby memo to Henry Friendly, Pan Am General Counsel (Sept. 13, 1946), PAM; Cooper, Bixby and Leonard quotes from Leonard Defense: 2, 5–10 and Leonard to Bixby (draft) (Sept. 2, 1943), GDP; Thomas M. Coffee, *HAP: The Story of the U.S. Air Force and the Man Who Built It, General Henry H. 'Hap' Arnold*: 280–283; Marilyn Bender and Selig Altschul, *The Chosen Instrument: Pan Am, Juan Trippe, The Rise and Fall of an American Entrepreneur*: 331–333, 351–352, 358–361; author interview of Royal S. Leonard (Sept. 10, 2007); Wayne Biddle, *Barons of the Sky*: 102.

Maxine Leonard described to the author Pan Am management's attempt to hide Royal from army officers while they were staying at the Mayflower Hotel in Washington, DC. She died, however, before the author could interview her in more detail [Interview, Studio City, CA (Oct. 25, 1989)].

Bixby denied trying to hide Royal from Gen. Arnold [Bixby memo to Friendly (Sept. 13, 1946), PAM].

Acting on the advice of Congressmen W.R. Poage (D-TX) and Harry R. Sheppard (D-CA), Royal on Feb. 28, 1944, executed a statement for the FBI about the Pan Am attempt to prevent him from presenting information to the U.S. Army. The FBI commenced an investigation, and the U.S. Attorney General War Frauds section closed the case in March 1948. The author was unable to locate Royal's FBI statement through a Freedom of Information Act (FOIA) Request or in the National Archives or Library of Congress [Leonard Defense: 13; Leonard to W.R. Poage (Feb. 26 and Mar. 24, 1944), GDP; Joseph F. Carroll, Director of Special Investigations, Inspector General Office,

USAF, to T. Vincent Quinn, Asst. AG, Criminal Division, Dept. of Justice (Feb. 11, 1948) and Quinn to Director, FBI (Mar. 3, 1948), Leonard File 62-86593, FBI, Washington, DC; TAI Infms re Report of Investigation re Sworn Statement made by Mr. Royal Leonard, 1751 McCollum St., Los Angeles complaining of Pan Amer Airways interference with his giving him infm concerning activities in CHINA (June 29, 1944), Decimal File 333.9 (431), Reel 42, Hap Arnold Papers, Library of Congress, Washington, DC].

[93] Leonard Defense: 12, GDP; Alfred D. Chandler, Jr. (ed.), 1 *The Papers of Dwight David Eisenhower: The War Years:* xxi, xxxiv; Leonard to Dwight D. Eisenhower (Dec. 13, 1952), GDP; "Notes on Conference" (Jan 19, 1942), War Plans Division File 4389-80, RG 165 (NARA); Barbara Tuchman, *Stilwell and the American Experience in China, 1911–1945:* 254–255; Arthur Zich, *Time-Life Books: The Rising Sun:* 95–97.

[94] "expressed" and "Well your man": Leonard Defense: 12; ibid 13-15, GDP; "Transcript of Notes Taken on Conference with Mr. Roy Leonard," Air Section G-2 (Jan. 20, 1942): 1–9, War Dept. General and Special Staffs Entry 77 (NM-84), Military Intelligence Division, Regional File 1922-44, File China, 9000-9001, Military Aviation and American Volunteer Group, RG 165 (NARA); *I Flew:* 220; Allen Weinstein and Alexander Vassiliev, *The Haunted Wood: Soviet Espionage in America—The Stalin Era:* 159; "on plans": Leonard to Bond (Mar. 24, 1942); Bond to Leonard (Mar. 28, 1942) [approving charge for buying Currie lunch], GDP; "the establishment": Currie Memorandum for the President (Jan. 24, 1942), Bx 5, Pres. F.D. Roosevelt Memoranda, 1942 Folder, Lauchlin B. Currie Papers, Hoover Institution Archives (hereafter cited as LBCP); Robert Daley, *An American Saga: Juan Trippe and His Pan Am Empire:* 239; "Hubler, Richard Gibson," II *Contemporary Authors, New Revision Series* (1981): 339; "a little" and "is the tale": *I Flew:* xii and xx.

[95] Leonard Defense: 15–19, GDP; "should receive": unidentified clipping entitled "Fast Aid for MacArthur and Burma Aces Urged" in Leonard scrapbook (JKC); Frank A. Learman, Gen. Sales Mgr., Consolidated Vultee Aircraft Corp. to Col. Louis Johnson (Dec. 8, 1943), Bx 303, Folder 26, Pan American World Airways, Inc. Records, Special Collections Division, University of Miami Libraries, Coral Gables, FL (hereafter cited as PAC); Duane Schultz, *The Doolittle Raid*: 54–55, 106, 116–117, 179, 183, 215, 217; Transcript of Lowell Thomas interview with Moon Chin (April 23, 1943), Bx 205, Folder 11 (PAC); "We were

losing face": "Yank pilot fears China's downfall," *Los Angeles Daily News* (May 23, 1942); "This is": Doolittle to Leonard (May 23, 1942); copyright permission, Col. John Doolittle, Ret. (GDP).

Chapter 12

[96] Leonard Defense: 4, 16, 21, GDP; handwritten responses on Bixby to Bond (Apr. 7, 1944), PAM; Leonard pocket diary (Oct. 19, 1937), JKC; Bond to Morgan (Apr. 27, 1939), Bx 2, S.W. Morgan Correspondence 1939–40 Folder (WLBP); "CNAC, and myself": Bond to Leonard (Mar. 28, 1942), copyright permission, Langhorne Bond; "continue": T.V. Soong to Leonard (Apr. 11, 1942), GDP; Andre A. Priester, Pan Am V.P. and Chief Engineer, Memorandum re Future Employment of CNAC Captains (Sept. 17, 1941); Leonard to L.C. Reynolds (Feb. 19 and Mar. 7, 1942); Bixby to Leonard (Apr. 2, 1942); Johnson to Leonard (Apr. 6, 1942); S.B. Kauffman Memo to Bixby (May 4, 1944), PAM; "CNAC is" and "You have": "Bondy" to "Royal" (Apr. 22, 1942), copyright permission Langhorne Bond (GDP); Fletcher Hanks, *Saga of CNAC #53:* 182; measuringworth.com; Pan American Airways, Inc. General Accounting Office check numbers 2703-2707 and 2710 (Apr. 30, 1942), PAM; "I had gone": *I Flew:* 258.

[97] "Heroes of Democracy," *Los Angeles Evening Herald & Express* (Apr. 17, 1942); "running away": "Keep Production at Peak, Urges Flyer Back from China," *Los Angeles Examiner* (Dec. 30, 1941); Leonard to Maxine (May 30, June 3 and 4, 1942); "Maybe" and "thought you": Leonard to Maxine (June 18 and 20, 1942), RSLP; Royal Leonard CNAC Statement of Account (Jan. 26, 1944), PAM; Leonard to Maxine (July 8 and 15, 1942), RSLP; Wesley Frank Craven and James Lea Cate (eds.), VII *The Army Air Forces in World War II: Services Around the World:* 114–117.

[98] Oldenburg telephone interview (Jan. 12, 1998) and interview by author, Phoenix, AZ (Mar. 28, 1991); Morris Leonard to author (Mar. 6, 1990); Royal Leonard Colorado National Guard Enlistment Record (July 8, 1928), Colorado State Archives, Denver, CO; Leonard to Maxine (Sept. 17, 1941 and June 20, 1942), RSLP; Charles B. Clayman, M.D. (medical ed.), *The American Medical Association Encyclopedia of Medicine* (1989): 659–660; "Some of the boys": White and Jacoby, *Thunder Out of China:* 154; "a pilot's Hell": J. Gen Genovese, *We Flew Without Guns:* 15–16; "weather": Lt. Gen. William H. Tunner, *Over the Hump:* 73, 75.

[99] George Larson (with CNAC captain Don McBride), "World's Worst Air Bridge," 7 *World War II* (Sept. 1992): 48–49, 53; "black, solid": Theodore H. White, "The Hump," *Life* (Sept. 11, 1944): 86; "the thunderstorms": E.C. Kirkpatrick telephone interview by author (Sept. 28, 1991); "a long dull ache": Bliss K. Thorne, *The Hump*: 134.

[100] Oliver La Farge, *Eagle in the Egg:* 109–110; Hanks, *Saga:* 2, 143, 251; Leonard to Maxine (n.d.); Leonard to Ben Piazza (Nov. 4, 1942); "Strange isn't it": Leonard to David Goodrich (Nov. 4, 1942), RSLP; Bond to Bixby (Oct. 29, 1942), Bx 205, Folder 10 (PAC); "Royal was": Kirkpatrick telephone interview by author (July 20, 1991); Chennault and Bissell quotes from "She Came Without Orders": 12–13, identified by provider as from *Annual Pictorial of the 14th Air Force Association* (1989); Samson, *Chennault*: 9; Lauchlin Currie, Memorandum for the files (Nov. 10, 1942), Bx 3, Chiang Kai-shek Biographical Notes Folder (LBCP); Miles, Travers, and Woods quotes from Milton E. Miles, *A Different Kind of War*: 134–135; Violet Seymour to Capt. Leonard (Apr. 3, May 6 and 28, June 17 and Sept. 17, 1943), RSLP; "Memories of the Past," *CNAC Cannon Ball* (Mar. 15, 1973): 4; "Roy could": author interview of "Doc" Richards, South San Francisco, CA (Oct. 27, 1990); aprocryphical story: "unattributed source(s)," South San Francisco, CA (Oct. 27, 1990); "Royal said": Alice Evans telephone interview by author (Nov. 2, 1990); "new pilot": Hanks, *Saga:* 50–51; http://cnac.org/hanks02.htm; Willett, *Airline At War*: 184.

[101] Leonard Defense: 22–27, GDP; Goutiere to author (Mar. 16, 2000); "during the": Bond to Leonard (Mar. 28, 1942); copyright permission Langhorne Bond, GDP; Willauer Memo, Chungking (Jan. 31, 1943): 7, Bx 2, Whiting Willauer Papers, Public Policy Papers, Dept. of Rare Books and Special Collections, Princeton University Library (hereafter cited as WWP); "Up until": Leonard Defense: 26, GDP; http://www.cnac.org/accident020.htm; Goutiere, *Himalayan Rogue*: 80–81; Leary, *Dragon's Wings:* 233.

[102] Author interview of Peter Goutiere, Burlingame, CA (Sept. 30, 2006); Goutiere to author (Jan. 16, 1996 and Mar. 16, 2000); "One time": Goutiere telephone interview by author (Nov.11, 1997), copyright permission Peter Goutiere.

[103] Bond to Herbert S. Browne (Feb. 21, 1944) ["Every cargo plane that flies over the Hump is overloaded."], PAM; "17,000 feet": Leonard, "Around the Japs, Over the Hump" (probably written in June 1943): 7, AEP.

[104] Leonard Defense: 23–24; *I Flew:* xiii; Leonard, T&WA Northrop Delta Model 1A gas consumption memo (Oct. 19, 1933), GDP; author interviews of Maxine and Royal S. Leonard, Studio City, CA (Sept. 18, 1989); "Royal" quotes from author interviews of Doc Richards and Fletcher Hanks, South San Francisco, CA (Oct. 27, 1990); "was under": Willauer, Memo re Two Speed Blower Installation (n.d.); "being crazy": Willauer Diary, Kunming (Dec. 8, 1942); Willauer, CNAC Memo (Dec. 1942) and Continuation of memorandum summarizing the accomplishments of the trip of TV [Soong] to China (n.d.), 22, Bx 2 (WWP); Bond to Bixby (Oct. 18, 1943), PAM; Sidelights Memo: 3, Bx 106, Sidelights Folder (ANYP); Bond telegram to Young (Aug. 28, 1943), Bx 31, Bond Folder, Stanley K. Hornbeck [Asst. Sec. of State, Far East] Papers, Hoover Institution Archives, Stanford, CA (hereafter cited as SKHP); "jumped right": W.L. Bond to Bixby (July 10, 1942), Bx 205, Folder 10 (PAC); Leonard to "Bondie" (Mar. 24, 1942), GDP; Maxine to Micky and Guy (Feb. 25, 1939); Maxine to Thayer (Feb. 25, 1939); Leonard to Maxine (Oct. 9, 1941), RSLP; "Royal was a single-minded": Ray Allen telephone interview by author (May 1998); "Royal was senior": E.C. Kirkpatrick telephone interview by author (June 20, 1991); "Chuck was": George Robertson, "History of CNAC," *CNAC Cannon Ball* (May 15, 1994): 9; Leonard to Bixby (Sept. 2, 1943), GDP; Soldinski cables to M.X. Quinn Shaughnessy (CDS) (Dec. 18, 1942 and Jan. 4, 1943), Bx 15, Telegrams-CDS Outgoing Folder and Bx 13, Telegrams CDS 1943 Folder, T.V. Soong Papers, Hoover Institution Archives (hereafter cited as TVSP); Rene J. Francillon, *McDonnell Douglas Aircraft since 1920:* 247, 260–261; Armstrong, *Preemptive Strike:* 113; "It was only": Willauer, "Memo of Conference with Bond" (Jan. 5, 1943), Bx 2 (WWP).

[105] Hugh B. Cave, *Wings Across the World: The Story of the Air Transport Command:* 87–88; Coffee, *HAP:* 298–300; Leonard, Report on tests made with S3C4G engines installed in CNAC C-53 No. 48 (Jan. 6–Feb. 3, 1943): 1–8, Bx 303, Folder 26 [hereafter cited as "Report"], PAC; Royal Leonard, "The Toughest Route in the World," XII *Douglas Airview* (Jan. 1945): 14–16, 30; Francillon, *McDonnell Douglas Aircraft:* 245–247, 260–261; *1943–44 Jane's All the World's Aircraft:* 185c–187c; Andrew W. Waters, *All the U.S. Air Force Airplanes, 1907–1983*: 24, 26, 135–136, 144–145; Willauer, "Note: re Two Speed Blower Engines" (Feb. 12, 1962): 4–5, Bx 1; "Finally": Willauer Memo, (Jan. 31 1943): 6, Bx 2 (WWP); "It was like": Leonard, "Around the Japs, Over the Hump": 4, AEP.

[106] Leonard, "Around the Japs": 4–5, AEP.

[107] Report: 8 (PAC); Willauer Memo (Jan. 31, 1943): 7, Bx 2 (WWP); XII *Douglas Airview*: 15.

[108] "It was rough" and "This was": Willauer Memo (Jan. 31 1943): 6–7, Bx 2 (WWP); Leonard to Bond (Jan. 26, 1943), Bx 303, Folder 26 (PAC); Willauer to Shaughnessy and Sinclair (Feb. 7, 1943) and Bond to Bixby (Jan. 18, 1943) cables, Bx 3, Correspondence CDS New Delhi 1942–44 Folder and Bx 12, Telegrams Outgoing Nov. 15, 1942–Oct. 6, 1943 Folder (TVSP); Willauer, "Note re 2 Speed Blower Engines": 5, Bx 1, WWP; "At about": Lance Stalker, "Flying 'The Hump' Was No Job for the Faint-Hearted," *Pacific Flyer* (Sept. 1985): B9; "After flying": Leonard to Willauer (Jan. 17, 1943), Bx 303, Folder 26 (PAC); http://www.cnac.org/accident014htm.

Chapter 13

[109] "Chennault, Claire Lee," 4 *American National Biography:* 778–779; "Stilwell, Joseph Warren," 20 *American National Biography:* 783–785; "After all": Claire to Maxine (Jan. 24, 1943), RSLP.

[110] "They": "Transcript of Notes Taken on Conference with Mr. Roy Leonard," Air Section G-2 (Jan. 20, 1942), Military Intelligence Division, Regional File, 1922-44, File China 9000-9001, Military Aviation and American Volunteer Group, RG 165 (NARA); Chennault, *Way of a Fighter:* 165; Chennault to R. C. Chen (for forwarding to T.V. Soong) (Feb. 27, 1942), Bx 2, Folder 9 (CLCP); "Japan": "Yank pilot fears China's downfall," *Los Angeles Daily News* (May 23, 1942); W.F. Craven and J.L. Cate (eds.), I *The Army Air Forces in World War II: Plans and Early Operations January 1939 to August 1942:* 505; Leonard to Maxine (July 19, 1942), RSLP; Chennault Memorandum to Commanding General, 10th U.S. Air Force (July 29, 1942), Bx 8, Folder 7 (CLCP).

[111] Rafael Steinberg, *Time-Life Books: Island Fighting:* 33–34; Leonard Draft Memo (Sept. 15, 1942): 1–5; "I can not think": Leonard [draft] to Col. C.F. Wang (Sept. 21, 1942): 1–2, GDP; "very good": Leonard to Willauer (Jan. 1, 1943); Leonard to Willauer (Jan. 17, 1943), Bx 303, Folder 26 (PAC); Claire to Maxine (Jan. 24, 1943), RSLP; Leonard Report: 2–8 (PAC); "be, figuratively speaking": Leonard Memo (n.d. - but subsequent to Madame Chiang Kai-shek's February 1943 Congressional speeches): 6; ibid 2, 3, GDP.

[112] Samson, *Chennault*: 175–180; Youngman & Shaughnessy telegram to T. V. Soong, Chungking (Jan. 8, 1943), Bx 14, Office File Telegrams-Chungking, Jan. 1941–March 31, 1943 Folder (TVSP); "advance": Plan for Employment of China Air Task Force in China (Feb. 4, 1943): 2, Bx 8, Folder 14 (CLCP); Soong telegram to Chennault (Mar. 25, 1943), Bx 11,Office File Telegrams Jan. 4, 1943–March 31, 1943 Folder (TVSP).

[113] *World Almanac and Book of Facts for 1943*: 121; "Maupin Memoir," *CNAC Cannon Ball* (July 1993): 5–6, 11–12; song quoted in *CNAC Cannon Ball* (Mar. 15, 1973): 8; "Special flights": Chennault to Leonard (July 24, 1943), GDP; Chennault, *Way of a Fighter:* 247–249.

[114] Samson, *Chennault*: 185, 189–193; Leonard memo (n.d.): 2; "everything had" and "In view": Chennault to Leonard (July 24, 1943); "a friend" and "Since I am not": Chennault to Leonard (Aug. 21, 1943), GDP.

[115] Japanese Minister Tani to Swiss Minister Gorge quoted in Gen. H.H. Arnold to Maj. Gen. Claire Chennault (Apr. 21, 1943), Bx 8, Folder 3 (CLCP); Schultz, *Doolittle Raid:* 265–266, 274–275, 296-297; "fully expected": Leonard to Maxine (Sept. 20, 1943), RSLP.

[116] Samson, *Chennault:* 209–210, 228–229; "Royal": Moon Chin telephone interview by author (May 30, 1992) and interview by author, Hillsborough, CA (Mar. 6, 1999); "was an inventive": Rossi to author (Oct. 27, 1989); author interview of Royal S. Leonard, Glendale, CA (Feb. 27, 1999); "He knew": Jim Bledsoe telephone interview by author (1996).

Chapter 14

[117] Leonard to David Behncke, Pres., ALPA (Mar. 29, 1945); "This all seems": Leonard Defense: 47-48; ibid 30- 46, 81 [British–Indian official W.W. Richardson told Lady Violet Seymour that CNAC personnel set the court "machinery in motion."], GDP; Memorandum of Telephone Conversations re CNAC (Aug. 16, 1943) [Bond: "... possibly ... Sharp has urged the British on because of his personal troubles with Leonard."], PAM; Sidelights Memo: 6–7 [Reports from Chinese secret service confirmed Sharp's interference in the case.], Bx 106, Sidelights Folder (ANYP); Gunther, *Inside Asia* (1942 War Ed.): 222; Leonard to Maxine (Sept. 28, 1943), RSLP; Arthur Young Memo,

"CNAC ACTION RE SMUGGLING" (Aug. 12, 1943): 1, Bx 104, July 1–Dec. 31, 1943 Folder (ANYP).

[118] Leonard Defense: 50–53, GDP; Rules 20 and 21, The Defence of India Rules, 1939, B. Malik, S.C. Manchanda, K.G. Swaminathan and K.K. Singh, I *Encyclopaedia of Statutory Rules Under Central Acts:* 521–522; C.L. Sharp Memo to All Flight Crews (July 4, 1942), Bx 104, July 1–Dec. 31, 1942 Folder (ANYP); "Several weeks": copy of W. L. Bond to Capt. Royal Leonard (May 15, 1943); copyright permission Langhorne Bond; mail prosecution charges from typewritten copy (May 24, 1943), Leonard Defense addendum, (GDP).

[119] Leonard Defense: 53–56, 62, 66, GDP; "in no way" and "petty-truancy": Violet Seymour to Capt. Leonard (Sept. 17 and June 22, 1943), RSLP; CNAC Pilot Roster (Mar. 19, 1943), *CNAC Cannon Ball* (July 4, 1979): (n.p.); Arthur N. Young Biographical Notes, Bx 1 (ANYP); "important CNAC interests": Confidential paraphrase of Young telegram to Bond (July 21, 1943); "stories unfavorable": Ballantine to Bond (July 24, 1943), PAM.

[120] Leonard Defense: 56–59; "under no circumstances": Bissell July 27, 1943 diary entry in Bissell to Bond (Apr. 4, 1945), Bx 303, Folder 11 (PAC); "CAPTAIN ROYAL LEONARD FUGITIVE": CLS to ATC, Dum Dum, July 29, 1943 for forwarding to General Bissell and ATC, Karachi; Registration of Foreigners Form C, July 30, 1943, PAM.

[121] Leonard Defense: 59–65, 70–72, GDP; Sharp to Leonard (Aug. 3 and 4, 1943) and Leonard to Sharp (Aug. 5, 1943), PAM; Sidelights Memo: 5, Bx 106, Sidelights Folder (ANYP); John K. Fairbank, *The United States and China* (4th Ed., Enlarged): 167–171, 337; "Urgent Arthur": Leonard to Maxine (Oct. 9, 1941), RSLP; Confidential paraphrase of Young to Bond telegram (Aug. 15, 1943), PAM.

[122] Leonard Defense: 78–82, GDP; Sidelights Memo: 5–7, Bx 106, Sidelights Folder (ANYP); cf. Secretary of State Cordell Hull telegram to American Embassy, Chungking (Aug. 25, 1943), Bx 58, CNAC Folder (SKHP).

[123] Leonard Defense: 83–97 and appended typed copy of prosecutor's motion to withdraw and of order of acquittal (Sept. 23, 1943), GDP; "vitally important": Confidential paraphrase of Young to Bond telegram (Aug. 11, 1943); Bond cable to Royal Leonard (n.d.) [acknowledging May 15, 1943 letter]; Secretary of State to American Embassy, Chungking (Aug. 25, 1943), Bx 58, CNAC Folder (SKHP);

Young to H.H. Kung (Sept. 21, 1943), Bx 104, July 1–Dec. 31, 1943 Folder (ANYP); Chennault to Leonard (Sept. 26, 1943), GDP; "reasons of state": Leonard typed copy of Petition of Public Prosecutor, Barrackpore Magistrate Court, Sept. 23, 1943, Leonard Defense, GDP; Simpson Memorandum (Nov. 10, 1948), Leonard Passport File, U.S. Dept. of State, Washington, DC; Bond cables to Bixby (Oct. 11 and 20, 1943), PAM; "over-strained": Sidelights Memo: 8, Bx 106, Sidelights Memo Folder (ANYP); "a mental": Bond to Bixby (Oct. 18, 1943); "persecution": Bixby to Herbert S. Browne (Dec. 1, 1943), PAM.

124 Leonard to Chennault (Feb. 17, 1944), GDP; Frank A. Learman, Gen. Sales Manager, to Colonel Louis Johnson (Dec. 8, 1943), Bx 303, Folder 26 (PAC); Rosamonde Kung to Maxine Leonard (July 13, 1944), RSLP.

125 Royal Leonard v. Pan American Airways, Inc. and China National Aviation Corporation, L.A. Co. Sup. Ct. civil action no. 491091 filed Feb. 10, 1944 and Royal Leonard v. Pan American Airways, Inc., Juan T. Trippe, Harold M. Bixby, William L. Bond, and Charles Sharp, L.A. Co. Sup. Ct. civil action no. 491925 filed March 20, 1944, L.A. County Courthouse, L.A., CA; "following the advice": Leonard to Chennault (Feb. 17, 1944); Leonard to Poage (Mar. 24, 1944); Leonard Defense: 90; Leonard to Behncke (Mar. 29, 1945); Leonard to K.R. Ferguson, V.P., Northwest Air Lines (Sept. 13, 1946), GDP; David Thompson, *Consairway, An Airman's Airline:* 96 [copilot roster]; Leonard to Maxine (July 17, 1945, Jan. 11 and 31, 1946), RSLP; Civil Aeronautics Administration, Foreign Flight Authorizations (July 16, 1945 and Jan. 5, 1946), FAA; "The last": Leonard to Maxine (Jan. 11, 1946), RSLP.

Including his Consairway flights, Royal as a pilot or copilot had flown around the world except between Hong Kong and Australia and between Calcutta and Tehran, Iran. He had flown F-32s between northern California and Los Angeles and the *Q.E.D.* from New York to Los Angeles. He had piloted an F-14 from Teterboro, New Jersey, to Miami, Florida, and delivered Jack Sharkey–Phil Scott heavyweight championship fight photos to an Atlanta, Georgia, newspaper. He had taken off from Miami in a B-25, landed at Natal, Brazil, crossed the Atlantic Ocean, and completed the flight at Tehran. As a CNAC pilot, he had flown between Hong Kong, Chungking, and Calcutta. In late 1937, he had been slated to fly an armed Boeing transport from Australia to China, but British authorities, afraid of antagonizing the Japanese, had refused to authorize release of the plane. If he had made this flight or flown from Allahabad to Melbourne in the MacRobertson Race, he would only not have flown the 2,400 miles between Teheran and Allahabad. If he had flown for Pan Am after World War II, he might have closed this gap. [Newspaper clipping from Leonard scrapbook entitled "Plane Fights Storm to Bring Bout Photos Here," *Atlanta Georgian* (n.d.) and Leonard pocket diary (Nov. 30, 1937), JKC; "Sharkey Wins by Knockout When Scott is Disqualified in Third Round," *New York Times* (Feb. 28, 1930); Leonard to Bertha Leonard (Dec. 19, 1937), RSLP; Hollington K. Tong, *dateline: China—The Beginnings of China's Press Relations with the World:* 91–92; Crozier, *Chiang Kai-shek:* 205].

[126] Owen Johnson to Pierce Works (Sept. 14, 1944); Tweedy to Bixby (Sept. 23, 1944), PAM; George. V. Allen, Chief, Division of Middle Eastern Affairs, to W. L. Bond, Oct. 6, 1944 with enclosure American Consulate General, Calcutta, Memorandum, Aug. 24, 1944, Subject: Visit of Captain Royal Leonard ... [redacted sentence], PAM; George V. Allen, Chief, Division of Middle Eastern Affairs, to W.L. Bond, Oct. 6, 1944, Despatch No. 264, M.S. Myers, American Consul General, Calcutta, to Secretary of State with enclosure Memorandum, Aug. 24, 1944, Subject: Visit of Captain Royal Leonard ... [unchanged sentence], State Dept. 1940–44 Decimal File 893.796/8-2444, RG 59 (NARA).

[127] "Back from China, Leonard Sues PAA," *Shanghai Evening Post & Mercury* (n.d.), Bx 4, Printed Materials: Clippings Undated Folder (WLBP); CNAC Pilot Roster, Bx 624, Folder 7 (PAC); "was farmed out": unidentified newspaper clipping entitled "Chiang's ex-pilot awarded back pay" in San Diego Aerospace Museum Archives Collection, San Diego, CA; Bond, *Wings*: 370; Judgment on Verdict in Open Court (Mar. 7, 1947) and Minute Order (May 5, 1947), L.A. Co. Sup. Ct. civil action no. 491091, L.A. County Courthouse, L.A., CA; L. M. Wright (trial attorney) to Joseph Cantwell (Mar. 7, 1947); Bond handwritten responses to questions on Bixby letter to Bond (Apr. 7, 1944) and Cantwell telegram to Wright (Mar. 30, 1948), PAM; Cantwell to Wright (May 9, 1947), Bx 303, Folder 26 (PAC); Dismissals filed Aug. 4, 1948, L.A. Co. Sup. Ct. civil actions no. 491091 and 491925.

Chapter 15

[128] *I Flew*: 36, 52–53; Leonard to Morris Leonard (May 12, 1936), MLP; "I was" and "talked just": *I Flew* mss.: 401-402 and 515, RSLP; Leonard to Alice Evans (Feb. 8, 1938), AEP; Jeffrey S. Abrams, "James Marshall McHugh: An American Encounter with Chiang Kai-shek,

1937–1942" (B.A. Thesis, Cornell Univ., 1972): 26; Jimmy [Elder] to T.V. Soong (Nov. 17, 1941), Bx 3, James C. Elder 1940–43 Folder (TVSP); Israel Epstein, *The Unfinished Revolution in China*: 153–154; "I do not think": *I Flew:* 77; Taylor, *Generalissimo*: 3, 327; "I think": Selle, *Donald:* 366 [Donald interview 1946]; "But I never": Larry I. Bland (ed.), *George C. Marshall Interviews and Reminiscences for Forrest C. Pogue:* 367; ibid 368; Zanchen, *Yang Hucheng*: 212–214, 277.

[129] Crozier, *Chiang Kai-shek:* 276–277, 317, 330; "nonperson": Robert Payne, *Chiang Kai-shek:* 219; Suzanne Pepper, *Civil War in China: The Political Struggle, 1945–1949*: 9–10, 25–26, 175–180, 201–204; Fenby, *Chiang Kai-shek:* 452, 465–467, 474–478; "as an additional step": Consul General at Mukden (Ward) to Ambassador in China (Stuart) (May 23, 1947), VII *FRUS (1947)*: 141–142; Ambassador in China (Stuart) to Secretary of State, Nanking (July 1, 1947), Col. David D. Barrett, Asst. Military Attaché, Memo (Aug. 1947) and Consul General at Mukden (Ward) to Secretary of State (Dec. 16, 1947), VII *FRUS (1947)*: 211–212, 707–709 and 403-404; Liu, *Military History*: 257–260; Boorman, "Li Tsung-jen," 2 *Biographical Dictionary:* 340–341; Finkelstein, *Washington's Taiwan Dilemma:* 45, 63, 114–118, 125–126, 136–145, 175–177; Gary Marvin Davison, *A Short History of Taiwan, The Case for Independence*: 49–51, 75–87; Li, *Madame Chiang Kai-shek:* 283–286, 314; "We think": Pakula, *Last Empress:* 587–588; ibid 589-591; "Sun Li-jen," Boorman, 3 *Biographical Dictionary:* 165–167.

[130] Articles of Incorporation of Royal Leonard, Inc., No. 217699, filed June 9, 1947, California Secretary of State, Sacramento, CA; Lt. Col. Robert F. Layton, USAF, Air Liaison, Memo (Sept. 3, 1950), FOIA Request, U.S. State Dept., Oct. 25, 1994; Leonard to David Goodrich (Nov. 9, 1948), GDP; "Poage, William Robert," *Biographical Dictionary of the American Congress 1774–1996:* 1671–1672; Taylor, *Generalissimo:* 370–371, 403–404, 433–435; Leonard to Poage (Feb. 11, 1949); Leonard to George B. Shaw, Director, Commercial Sales, Glenn L. Martin Co. (Feb. 21, 1949); "The Gimo": Leonard to Shaw (Mar. 26, 1949), GDP.

[131] Leonard to Shaw (May 17, 1949), GDP; Leonard to Poage (March 12, 1949), RSLP; China Handbook Editorial Board (comp.), *China Handbook 1950*: 629–630; Lam to author (July 11, 1991); "still standing by": Leonard to Alice and Ben Evans (June 6, 1949), AEP; Leonard to Glenn L. Martin Co. (May 7, 1949) and Leonard to Poage (July 6, 1949), GDP; Tillman Durbin, "Two Chinese Airlines Join

Reds; 12 Planes Leave Hong Kong Base," *New York Times* (Nov. 10, 1949); "You couldn't": Moon Chin telephone interview by author (May 30, 1992); "Royal had": E.C. Kirkpatrick telephone interview by author (June 20, 1991); "Incidentally": Leonard to Alice and Ben Evans (June 9, 1949), AEP; Juptner, "Martin-Liner, 2-0-2 (202A)," 8 *U.S. Civil Aircraft:* 328–331.

[132] Leonard to Poage (Mar. 3, 1950); Poage to Leonard (July 22, 1950); "The Gimo": Leonard to Poage (Aug. 17, 1950), RSLP; Zanchen, *Yang Hucheng*: 179.

[133] Finkelstein, *Washington's Taiwan Dilemma:* 310–312; Leonard to Poage (Aug. 17, 1950), RSLP; "Royal was kind of": Angela Shrawder telephone interview by author (Mar. 28, 1999); Mike Freeman, "Denizen of China recounts eras," *The Bulletin* (Bend, OR) (Feb. 1, 1987); "Escapes from Hong-Kong," *Times* (London) (Apr. 2, 1942); Virginia (Duff) Black telephone interview by author (Oct. 20, 2001); J. Arthur Duff to Paul Cullen, Sperry Gyro Co. (Dec. 6, 1947), GDP; Leonard to Maxine (Mar. 13, 1949), RSLP.

[134] J. Arthur Duff memos to Dr. Keith Eiler (Sept. 23, 1984): 1–3 and to Maxine Leonard (June 1988): 1–6, Bx 21, J. Arthur Duff Folder, Keith E. Eiler Papers, Hoover Institution Archives; J. Arthur Duff Biographical Note, Bx 1, Folder 1, J. Arthur Duff Papers, Hoover Institution Archives, copyright Stanford University, Stanford, CA.

[135] "It was": Nicholas D. Kristof, "Chiang Kai-shek's Kidnapper Talks," *New York Times* (Feb. 20, 1991); "the Young Marshal": Tao Peng interview by author, Los Altos, CA (Dec. 7, 1991).

[136] "Fletcher Bowron is Dead at 81; Mayor of Los Angeles, '38-'53," *New York Times* (Sept. 12, 1968); Maxine Leonard v. Royal Leonard, L. A. Sup. Ct civil action no. 415160, L.A. Co. Courthouse, L.A., CA; untitled clipping in Gerrie Dubé scrapbook from *Los Angeles Daily News* (Dec. 31, 1952); measuringworth.com; Pilot's copy, The Flying Tiger Line, Inc. C-46 Equipment Check (June 20, 1951), GDP; Royal Leonard Flying Tiger Line, Inc. Term Card (June 20, 1951–April 11, 1952), FedEx, Memphis, TN; Frank Cameron, *Hungry Tiger: The Story of the Flying Tiger Line:* 124–134; "Royal was": Gerrie Dubé telephone interview by author (Apr. 18, 2002); Alice Evans telephone interview by author (Nov. 2, 1990); author interview of Frank Evans, Sacramento, CA (June 20, 2003); U.S. patent number 2,987, 209 (filed Jan. 2, 1957); "Boot*Leggers" advertising handout, GDP; State of California, Dept. of Health Services Certificate of Death no. 11908 (June

22, 1962); "a guy": unidentified clipping from Gerrie Dubé scrapbook entitled "Famed Aviator Visits Oakland" by J.O. Stendal (Apr. 12, 1953), GDP.

Epilogue

[137] Boeing Historical Archives, "Boeing 307 Stratoliner, The World's First High-Altitude Airliner": 9; "Thrills-Suspense-Hardships-Humor Mark Adventurous Sky Trails of the Late Julius Barr over War-torn China," 8 *The Air Line Pilot* (April 1939): 4; "Cochran, Jacqueline," 5 *American National Biography:* 117–118; author interview of Royal S. Leonard, Studio City, CA (Feb. 27, 1999).

[138] "limited": Bond, *Wings:* 15; ibid 13, 194–195, 345, 381; Leonard to Maxine (Dec. 23, 1948), RSLP; Herbert S. Browne to Bixby (Jan. 4, 1944) and Bond to Browne (Feb. 21, 1944), PAM; "William Langhorne Bond," *Washington Post* (Aug. 3, 1985); "In memoriam, Charles Lamar Sharp, Jr.," CNAAF, III *Wings Over Asia:* 1–4; Bill Maher interview by author, Albuquerque, NM (Sept. 27, 2003); "If so": H.L. Woods, "Organizing the Assam Airlift into China," CNAAF, II *Wings Over Asia:* 68.

[139] "But I do": Madame Chiang Kai-shek to Mrs. Geraldine F. Leonard (July 25, 1962), GDP; "Chiang Kai-shek's widow dies at 105," *Sacramento Bee* (Oct. 24, 2003); State of California, Dept. of Health Services, Certificate of Death no. 90-071195 (Apr. 2, 1990); Li, *Madame Chiang Kai-shek:* 454.

[140] "Whiting W. Willauer, 55, Dies; Envoy to Costa Rica, 1958-'60," *New York Times* (Aug. 7, 1962); Stephen Schlesinger and Stephen Kinzer, *Bitter Fruit: The Untold Story of the American Coup in Guatemala*: 93, 116, 140, 145, 156 and 217.

[141] "Chang Hseuh-liang," Boorman, I *Biographical Dictionary*: 67–68; Wu, *Pivotal Point:* 207–208; "With mutual affection": Nicholas D. Kristof, "Chiang Kai-shek's Kidnapper talks," *New York Times* (Feb. 20, 1991); "embarked": Harrison E. Salisbury, "The Kidnapper and His Dream," *New York Times* (June 14, 1991); Payne, *Chiang Kai-shek:* 306; Li, *Madame Chiang Kai-shek:* 419, 437, 444, 446, 459; Nicholas D. Kristof, "Zhang Xueliang, 100, Dies; One-Time Chinese Warlord Who Changed Course of Chinese History," *New York Times* (Oct. 17, 2001); "will be": Tien-wei Wu, "New Materials on the Xian Incident:

A Bibliographic Review," 10 *Modern China* (Jan. 1984):128; Tao Peng telephone interview by author (Feb. 19, 1994); The Reminiscences of Peter H.L. Chang (Young Marshal) in the Oral History Collection of Columbia University, Finding Aid [no mention of Royal Leonard].

BIBLIOGRAPHY

Primary Sources

A. Unpublished Documents

Air Line Pilots Association Collection. Archives of Labor and Urban Affairs, Wayne State University, Detroit, MI.

Allison, Ernest M. Papers, in possession of Nancy Allison Wright, Spokane, WA.

Arnold, Henry H. Papers. Library of Congress, Washington.

Barr, Julius Scrapbook. Museum of Flight, Seattle, WA.

Boeing Historical Archives. Seattle, WA.

Bond, W. Langhorne Papers. Hoover Institution Archives, Palo Alto, CA.

Brooks Air Force Base Archives. San Antonio, TX.

Chennault, Claire M. Papers. Hoover Institution Archives, Palo Alto, CA.

Clagett, Brig. Gen. H.B. to the Chief of Staff. "Report of Air Mission to China" (June 12, 1941). Adjutant General File 380.3, RG 407, Modern Military Records Division, National Archives and Records Administration, Washington.

Cochran, Jacqueline Papers. Dwight D. Eisenhower Library, Abilene, KS.

Currie, Lauchlin B. Papers. Hoover Institution Archives, Palo Alto, CA.

Duff, J. Arthur Papers. Hoover Institution Archives, Palo Alto, CA.

Gatty, Harold Papers. Library of Congress, Washington.

Hornbeck, Stanley K. Papers. Hoover Institution Archives, Palo Alto, CA.

Kelly Air Force Base Archives. San Antonio, TX.

Leonard, Royal Airman File. Airmen Certification Branch, Federal Aviation Agency, Oklahoma City, OK.

Leonard, Royal Files. Pan Am World Airways Collection. Richter Library, Univ. of Miami, FL.

Leonard, Royal Papers, in possession of Geraldine Dubé, northern CA, Elizabeth Leonard, Wichita, KS, Royal S. Leonard, Chatsworth, CA, and John Korampilas, Folsom, CA.

Leonard, Royal Passport File. Office of Passport Services, U.S. State Department, Washington.

Leonard, Royal v. Pan American Airways, Inc., etc. al, Superior Court actions no. 491091 and 491925. County Courthouse, Los Angeles, CA.

Lindbergh, Charles A. Papers. Missouri Historical Society, St. Louis, MO.

McHugh, James M. Papers. Cornell University Library, Ithaca, NY.

Military Records of the State and Territory of Colorado. Colorado Division of State Archives and Public Records, Denver, CO.

Morganthau, Henry M. Papers. Franklin Delano Roosevelt Library, Hyde Park, NY.

Smith, Sebie Reminiscences. Oral History Collection. Columbia University, New York City.

Soong, T.V. Papers. Hoover Institution Archives, Palo Alto, CA.

Texas Collection. Baylor University, Waco, TX.

Turner, Roscoe Papers. American Heritage Center, Laramie, WY.

University of Wisconsin-Madison Archives. Madison, WI.

Western History Department. Denver Public Library, Denver, CO.

White, Theodore H. Papers. Harvard University Archives, Cambridge, MA.

Willauer, Whiting Papers. Seeley G. Mudd Manuscripts Library, Princeton, NJ.

Young, Arthur N. Papers. Hoover Institution Archives, Palo Alto, CA.

B. Published Documents

Chief of the Air Corps. *Handbook of Service Instructions for the Model R-1340-47 Engines and Associated Models*. Dayton, O., 1939.

Malik, B., S.C. Manchanda, K.G. Swaminathan, and K.K. Sing [comp.]. I *Encyclopaedia of Statutory Rules under Central Acts*. Allahabad, India, 1963.

United States Department of Commerce, Aeronautics Branch, Information Division. *Airway Bulletin*. Washington, 1927–30.

United States Department of State, *Foreign Relations of the United States: Diplomatic Papers*. Washington, 1939-41.

——. *Foreign Relations of the United States, the Far East, China, 1946, 1947*. Washington, 1972.

——. *Foreign Relations of the United States, the Far East, China, 1949*. Washington, 1978.

C. Contemporary Publications

Bertram, James M. *First Act in China: The Story of the Sian Mutiny*. New York 1938.

Boothe, Clare. "Chungking's Broadway." *Vogue*, Sept. 11, 1941.

Boudreaux, Ray H. "The Ocker-Myers Method of Blind Flying." 13 *Aero Digest*, July 1928.

Brooks Field. *The Flying Cadet* (Aug. 1927). San Antonio, TX.

Cave, Hugh B. *Wings Across the World: The Story of the Air Transport Command*. New York 1945.

Chiang, General Kai-shek and Madame. *The Account of the Fortnight in Sian When the Fate of China Hung in the Balance*. Garden City, 1937.

China Handbook Editorial Board (comp.). *China Handbook 1950*. New York, 1950.

Chinese Ministry of Information Office (comp.). *China Handbook 1937-1945*. New York, 1947.

Consairway Flight Deck (January 10, 1944 - July 25, 1945).

Crow, Carl. "HELL in the Heavenly Kingdom." *Liberty*, Sept. 9, 1939.

Dallin, Alexander and F.I. Firsov (eds.). *Dimitrov and Stalin 1934-1943: Letters from the Soviet Archives*. New Haven, 2000.

Davies, R. W., et al. (comp. and eds.). *The Stalin-Kaganovich Correspondence 1931-1936*. New Haven, 2003.

Davis, Lt. W. V., Jr. "Where are we?" 4 *Western Flying*, Sept. 1928.

Dyke, A.L. *Dyke's Aircraft Engine Instructor*. Chicago, 1928

Epstein, Israel. *The Unfinished Revolution in China*. Boston, 1947.

Gellhorn, Martha. "Flight into Peril." *Collier's*, May 31, 1941.

——. "Time Bomb in Hong Kong." *Collier's*, June 7, 1941.

Genovese, J. Gen. *We Flew Without Guns*. Philadelphia, 1945.

Greenlaw, Olga. *The Lady and the Tigers*. New York, 1943.

"Guerilla Airline." *Southern Flight*, Dec. 1943.

Gunther, John. *Inside Asia* (1942 War Edition). New York, 1942.

Holland, Harvey H., 1st Lt. "Air Navigation." (Brooks Field, TX c.1928).

Jane's All the World's Aircraft. London, 1943-44.

Kelly Field. *The Flying Cadet* (Feb. 1928). San Antonio, TX.

Kennedy, Frank M. "Keeping in Touch." 8 *Western Flying*, Oct. 1930.

Kent, Capt. Walter C. "Wings for China." *Atlantic Monthly*, Nov. 1937.

Koester, Capt. Hans. "Four Thousand Hours over China." *National Geographic*, May 1938.

"Learning to Use Our Wings." *Scientific American*, June 1930.

Leonard, Royal (with Richard G. Hubler). *I Flew for China*. New York, 1942.

——. "A Modern Marco Polo Flies to Aid China." 11 *Air Line Pilot* (June 1942): 4 and (July 1942): 4.

——. "Check by Sextant - How Celestial Navigation may be used in Checking Dead Reckoning of an Air Liner." 13 *Western Flying*, May 1933.

——. "The Toughest Route in the World." XII *Douglas Airview*, Jan. 1945.

Lindbergh, Charles. *We*. New York, 1927.

Lonnquest, Lt. Theodore C. "Aircraft Instruments." 25 *Aviation*, July 9, 1928.

Luce, Henry. "China to the Mountains." *Life*, June 30, 1941.

Miller, J. Earle. "Mystery of Port of Missing Planes Solved?" *Popular Mechanics*, March 1928.

Moorehead, Caroline (ed.). *Selected Letters of Martha Gellhorn*. New York, 2006.

Moseley, Maj. C.C. "Hitch Your Airport to the Stars." 34 *Aviation*, Nov. 1935.

Ocker, William C. and Carl J. Crane. *Blind Flight in Theory and Practice*. San Antonio, 1932.

Post, Wiley and Harold Gatty. *Around the World in Eight Days: The Flight of the Winnie Mae*. New York, 1931.

Priester, A.A. "For Pilots in the Soup." 13 *Western Flying*, Jan. 1933.

Redpath, Peter H. and James M. Coburn. *Air Transport Navigation for Pilots and Navigators*. New York, 1943.

Smedley, Agnes. "How Chiang Was Captured." 144 *The Nation*, Feb. 13, 1937.

Smith, Henry Ladd. *Airways: The History of Commercial Aviation in the United States*. New York, 1944.

Smith, Wesley L. "How I Fly at Night." 19 *The Journal of the Society of Automotive Engineers*, Sept. 1926.

Stettinius, Edward R., Jr. *Lend-Lease Weapon for Victory*. New York, 1944.

Sues, Ralf. *Shark's Fins and Millet*. Boston, 1944.

Toynbee, Arnold J. *Survey of International Affairs*. London, 1937, 1938, 1941.

Underhill, Capt. E.A. "Pilots under the Hood." 10 *Western Flying*, Sept. 1931.

Utley, Freda. *China at War*. London, 1939.

Weed, F.W., Lt. Commander. "The Fight with Fog." 4 *Western Flying*, March 1928.

Western Air Express. *The Dashboard Record* (1929-30).

"The West Point of the Air." *Popular Mechanics*, April 1930.

White, Theodore H. "China's Last Lifeline." *Fortune*, May 1943.

——. "The Hump: The Historic Airway To China Was Created By U.S. Heroes." *Life*, Sept. 11, 1944.

White, William. *By-Line: Ernest Hemingway, Selected Articles and Dispatches of Four Decades*. New York, 1967.

Who's Who on the Pacific Coast. Chicago, 1949.

Woolley, James C. "Operation of Western Air Express." 25 *Aviation*, Nov. 17, 1928.

Zand, Stephen J. "Douglas – the Silent Transport." 13 *Western Flying*, Sept. 1933.

Secondary Sources

Abrams, Jeffrey S. "James Marshall McHugh: An American Encounter with Chiang Kai-shek, 1937-1942." BA thesis, Cornell University, 1972.

Allen, Oliver E. *The Epic of Flight: The Airline Builders*. Alexandria, VA, 1981.

Allen, Richard Sanders. *Revolution in the Sky: Those Fabulous Lockheeds, The Pilots Who Flew Them*. Brattleboro, 1967.

——. *The Northrop Story, 1929-1939*. New York, 1990.

Ancell, R. Manning with Christine M. Miller. *The Biographical Dictionary of World War II Generals and Flag Officers: The U.S. Armed Forces*. Westport, Conn. 1996.

Angelucci, Enzo and Paolo Matricardi. *2 World War II Airplanes*. Chicago, 1977.

Armstrong, Alan. *Preemptive Strike: The Secret Plan That Would Have Prevented the Attack on Pearl Harbor*. Guilford, CT, 2006.

Arnold, Henry H. *Global Mission*. New York, 1949.

Baitsell, John M. *Airline Industrial Relations: Pilots and Flight Engineers.* Boston, 1966.

Bender, Marilyn and Selig Altschul. *The Chosen Instrument: Pan Am, Juan Trippe, The Rise and Fall of an American Entrepreneur.* New York, 1982.

Biddle, Wayne. *Barons of the Sky.* New York, 1991.

Bilstein, Roger, and Jay Miller. *Aviation in Texas.* San Antonio, 1986.

Bland, Larry I. (ed.). *George C. Marshall Interviews and Reminiscences for Forrest C. Pogue* (rev. ed.). Lexington, VA, 1991.

Boeing Historical Archives. "Boeing 307 Stratoliner, The World's First High-Altitude Airliner." Seattle, 1989.

Bond, W. Langhorne (James E. Ellis, ed.). *Wings for an Embattled China.* Bethlehem, PA, 2001.

Boorman, Howard L. (ed.). *Biographical Dictionary of Republican China.* New York, 1967-1979.

Bowers, Peter M. *Boeing Aircraft since 1916.* London, 1968.

——. *Curtiss Aircraft 1907-1947.* London, 1979.

Braun, Otto. *A Comintern Agent in China, 1932-1939.* Stanford, CA, 1982.

Brown, Bruce. *Gatty: Prince of Navigators.* Sandy Bay, Tasmania, 1997.

Brown, Dorothy M. *Mabel Walker Willebrandt: A Study of Power, Loyalty, and Law.* Knoxville, 1984.

Buck, Bob. *North Star over My Shoulder.* New York, 2002.

Byrd, Martha. *Chennault: Giving Wings to the Tiger.* Tuscaloosa, 1987.

Caidin, Martin. *The Ragged Rugged Warriors.* London, 1966.

Cameron, Frank. *Hungry Tiger: The Story of the Flying Tiger Line.* New York, 1964.

Cearley, George W., Jr. *Fly the finest… FLY TWA.* Dallas, 1988.

Chang, Iris. *The Rape of Nanking: The Forgotten Holocaust of World War II.* New York, 1997.

Chang, Jung and Jon Halliday. *Mao: The Unknown Story.* New York, 2005.

Chapin, John T. "Sky Conqueror." 7 *Wings*, Aug. 1977.

Chennault, Claire L. *Way of a Fighter*. New York, 1949.

Chiang, Kai-shek. *Soviet Russia in China: A Summing-Up at Seventy*. New York, 1957.

China National Aviation Association Foundation. *Cannon Ball* (1973-2009). Loch Arbour and Princeton, NJ.

——. *Wings Over Asia*, 4 vols. NP, 1971-1976.

Cleveland, Reginald M. *Air Transport at War*. New York, 1946.

Cochran, Jacqueline. *The Stars at Noon*. Boston, 1954.

Cochran, Jacqueline, and Maryann Bucknum Brinley. *Jackie Cochran: An Autobiography*. New York, 1987.

Coffey, Thomas M. *HAP: The Story of the U.S. Air Force and the Man Who Built It General Henry H. "Hap" Arnold*. New York, 1982.

Collins, Reba N. *Will Rogers & Wiley Post in Alaska: The Crash Felt 'Round the World'*. Claremore, 1984.

Colorado National Guard. *Colorado Pride: A Commemorative History, 1923-1988*. Dallas, 1989.

Cornelius, Wanda and Thayne Short. *Ding Hao, America's War in China, 1937-1945*. Gretna, LA, 1980.

Courtwright, David T. *Sky as Frontier: Adventure, Aviation, and Empire*. College Station, TX, 2005.

Craven, Wesley Frank and James Lea Cate (eds.). I *The Army Air Forces in World War II: Plans and Early Operation, January 1939 to August 1942*. Chicago, 1948.

——. VI *The Army Air Forces in World War II: Men and Planes*. Chicago, 1955.

——. VII *The Army Air Forces in World War II: Services Around the World*. Chicago, 1958.

Crozier, Brian. *The Man Who Lost China*. New York, 1976.

Daley, Robert. *An American Saga: Juan Trippe and His Pan Am Empire*. New York, 1980.

Damon, Ralph S. *"TWA" Nearly Three Decades in the Air*. New York, 1952.

Davies, R.E.G. *Airlines of the United States since 1914*. London, 1972.

——. *Delta: An Airline and Its Aircraft*. Miami 1990.

——. *Airlines of Asia since 1920*. London 1997.

Davis, Kenneth S. *The Hero: Charles A. Lindbergh and the American Dream*. Garden City, NY, 1959.

Davison, Gary Marvin. *A Short History of Taiwan, The Case for Independence*. Westport, CT, 2003.

Drage, Charles. *The Amiable Prussian*. London, 1958.

Dubofsky, Melvyn and Foster Rhea Dulles. *Labor in America: A History*. Wheeling, IL, 1999.

Dwiggins, Don. *They Flew the Bendix Race*. Philadelphia, 1965.

——. *Hollywood Pilot: The Biography of Paul Mantz*. New York, 1969.

Fairbank, John K. *The Great Chinese Revolution: 1800-1985*. New York, 1987.

——. *China: A New History*. Cambridge, MA, 1992.

——. *The United States and China* (4th ed.). Cambridge, MA, 1979.

Fairbank, John K. and Albert Feuerwerker. *13 The Cambridge History of China*. Cambridge, MA, 1986.

Fenby, Jonathon. *Chiang Kai-shek: China's Generalissimo and the Nation He Lost*. New York, 2003.

Finkelstein, David M. *Washington's Taiwan Dilemma, 1949-1950: From Abandonment to Salvation*. Fairfax, VA, 1993.

Ford, Daniel. *Flying Tigers: Clair Chennault and the American Volunteer Group*. Washington, 1991.

——. *Flying Tigers: Clair Chennault and His American Volunteers, 1941-1942* (updated and revised edition). Washington, 2007.

Francillon, Rene J. *Lockheed Aircraft since 1913*. London, 1987.

——. *McDonnell Douglas Aircraft since 1920*. London, 1979.

Frillman, Paul. *China: The Remembered Life*. Boston, 1968.

Furuja, Keiji. *Chiang Kai-shek: His Life and Times* (Abridged English edition by Chun-Ming Chang). New York, 1981.

Gann, Ernest K. *Fate Is The Hunter*. New York, 1961.

Gellhorn, Martha. *Travels with Myself and Another*. London, 1978.

Gibson, Maj. James G. II. "Blind Flying's Men of Vision." *The MAC Flyer*, Jan. 1980.

Gleason, Gene. *Hong Kong*. New York, 1963.

Glines, Carroll V. *Roscoe Turner: Aviation's Master Showman*. Washington, 1995.

——. *Chennault's Forgotten Warriors: The Saga of the 308th Bomb Group in China*. Altgen, 1995.

——. *The Doolittle Raid*. New York, 1988.

——. *Jimmy Doolittle: Daredevil, Aviator and Scientist*. New York, 1972.

Goutiere, Peter J. *Himalayan Rogue: A Pilot's Odyssey*. Paducah, 1994.

Gwynn-Jones, Terry. *Farther and Faster: Aviation's Adventuring Years, 1909-1939*. Washington, 1991.

——. "'Prince of Navigators' Harold Gatty." 12 *Aviation History*, Sept. 2001.

Hanks, Capt. Fletcher. *Saga of CNAC #53*. Bloomington, IN, 2004.

Haslam, Jonathan. *The Soviet Union and the Threat from the East, 1933-41*. London, 1992.

Hemingway, Ernest. *Islands in the Stream*. New York, 1970.

Hereford, Jack and Penny. *The Flying Years: A History of America's Pioneer Airline*. Los Angeles, 1946.

Holbrook, Francis X. and John Nikol. "Harold Gatty and the Bridging of the Pacific." 29 *Aerospace Historian*, Sept. 1982.

Hopkins, George E. *The Airline Pilots: A Study in Elite Unionization*. Cambridge, MA, 1971.

——. *Flying the Line: The First Half Century of the Air Line Pilots Association*. Washington, 1982.

Jackson, A.J. *DeHavilland Aircraft since 1909*. Annapolis, 1978.

Jacob, Fred E. *Takeoffs and Touchdowns: My Sixty Years of Flying*. San Diego, 1981.

Juptner, Joseph P. *U.S. Civil Aircraft*. Aero Publishers, Inc., 1964.

Kennedy, Arthur with Jo Ann Ridley. *High Times: Keeping'em Flying*. Santa Barbara, 1992.

Kert, Bernice. *The Hemingway Women*. New York, 1983.

Klotz, Alexis. *Three Years off This Earth*. Garden City, 1960.

Koginos, Manny T. *The Panay Incident: Prelude to War*. Lafayette, 1967.

Komons, Nick A. *Bonfires to Beacons: Federal Civil Aviation Policy under the Air Commerce Act 1926-1938*. Washington, 1978.

Kuo-t'ao, Chang. *The Rise of the Chinese Communist Party 1928-1938: Volume Two of the Autobiography of Chang Kuo-t'ao*. Lawrence, KS, 1972.

La Farge, Oliver. *The Eagle in the Egg*. Boston, 1949.

Larkins, William T. "The Aircraft History of Western Air Lines." 21 *American Aviation Historical Society Journal*, Spring 1976.

Larson, George, with Don McBride. "World's Worst Air Bridge." 7 *World War II*, Sept. 1992.

Leary, William M., Jr. *The Dragon's Wings: The CNAC and the Development of Commercial Aviation in China*. Athens, GA, 1976.

——. *Perilous Missions: Civil Air Transport and CIA Covert Operations in Asia.* Tuscaloosa, 1984.

——. "Aircraft and Anti-Communists: CAT in Action, 1949-52." 52 *The China Quarterly*, Oct.-Dec. 1972.

——. *Aerial Pioneers: The U.S. Air Mail Service, 1918-1927*. Washington, 1985.

Levine, Steven I. *Anvil of Victory: The Communist Revolution in Manchuria, 1945-1948*. New York, 1987.

Lewis, W. David. *Delta: The History of an Airline*. Athens, GA, 1979.

Li, Laura Tyson. *Madame Chiang Kai-shek: China's Eternal First Lady*. New York, 2006.

Liu, F.F. *A Military History of Modern China*. Princeton, 1956.

MacKinnon, Janice R. and Stephen R. *Agnes Smedley: The Life and Times of an American Radical*. Berkeley, 1988.

Mandrake, Charles G. *The Gee Bee Story*. Wichita, 1956.

Mendenhall, Charles A. *The Gee Bee Racers*. North Branch, MN, 1979.

Miles, Milton E. *A Different Kind of War*. New York, 1967.

Moorehead, Caroline. *Gellhorn: A Twentieth-Century Life*. New York, 2003.

Moreira, Peter. *Hemingway on the China Front: His WWII Spy Mission with Martha Gellhorn*. Washington, 2006.

Mumey, Nolie. *Epitome of the Semi-Centennial History of Colorado's Airmail*. Denver, 1977.

Munson, Kenneth. *Airliners between the Wars, 1919-1939*. New York, 1972.

Nankwell, Maj. John H. *History of the Military Organization of the State of Colorado*. Denver, 1935.

Neumann, Gerhard. *Herman the German: Enemy Alien, U.S. Army Master Sergeant #10500000*. New York, 1984.

Nielson, Dale (comp. and ed.). *Saga of the U.S. Air Mail Service 1918-1927*. Air Mail Pioneers, Inc., 1962.

Office of History. *A Pictorial History of Kelly Air Force Base, 1917-1980*. San Antonio, 1984.

Osborn, Michael and Joseph Riggs (eds.). *"Mr. Mac": William P. MacCracken, Jr. on Aviation, Law, Optometry*. Memphis, 1970.

Pakula, Hannah. *The Last Empress: Madame Chiang Kai-shek and the Birth of Modern China*. New York, 2009.

Payne, Robert. *Chiang Kai-shek*. New York, 1969.

Pepper, Suzanne. *Civil War in China: The Political Struggle, 1945-1949*. Berkeley, CA, 1978.

Perry, Hamilton Darby. *The Panay Incident: Prelude to Pearl Harbor*. Toronto, 1969.

Pickler, Gordon K. "United States Aid to the Chinese Nationalist Air Force, 1931-1949." PhD dissertation, Florida State University, 1971.

Rand, Peter. *China Hands: The Adventures and Ordeals of the American Journalists Who Joined Forces with the Great Chinese Revolution*. New York, 1995.

Rhodes, Richard. "The Toughest Flying in the World." *1 World War II Chronicles* (American Heritage Collectors Edition).

Robertson, George. "History of CNAC." *CNAC Cannon Ball*, May 15, 1994.

Rollyson, Carl. *Nothing Ever Happens to the Brave: The Story of Martha Gellhorn*. New York, 1990.

Romanus, Charles F. and Riley Sutherland. *US Army in World War II: China-Burma-India Theater; Stilwell's Mission to China*. Washington, 1953.

US Army in World War II: China-Burma-India Theater; Stilwell's Command Problems. Washington, 1956.

Rosholt, Malcolm. *Flight in the China Air Space 1910-1950*. Rosholt, WI, 1984.

Ruiquing, Luo, Zhengcao Lu and Bingnan Wang. *Zhou Enlai and the Xian Incident: An Eyewitness Account*. Beijing, 1983.

St. John Turner, P. *Heinkel: an aircraft album*. New York, 1970.

Samson, Jack. *Chennault*. New York, 1987.

Sandilands, Roger J. *The Life and Political Economy of Lauchlin Currie: New Dealer, Presidential Adviser, and Development Economist*. Durham and London, 1990.

Schaller, Michael. *The U.S. Crusade in China, 1938-1945*. New York, 1979.

——. *Douglas MacArthur, The Far Eastern General*. New York, 1989.

Schecter, Jerrold and Leona Schecter. *Sacred Secrets: How Soviet Intelligence Operations Changed American History*. Washington, 2002.

Schoneberger, William. *California Wings: A History of Aviation in the Golden State*. Woodland Hills, 1984.

Seagrave, Sterling. *Soong Dynasty*. New York, 1985.

Selle, Earl Albert. *Donald of China*. New York, 1948.

Serling, Robert. *The Only Way to Fly: The Story of Western Airlines, America's Senior Air Carrier*. New York, 1976.

——. *Howard Hughes' Airline: An Informal History of TWA*. New York, 1983.

Shamburger, Page. *Tracks across the Sky: The Story of the Pioneers of the U.S. Air Mail*. Philadelphia, 1964.

Sheng, Michael. *Battling Western Imperialism: Mao, Stalin, and the United States*. Princeton, 1997.

——. "Mao, Stalin, and the Formation of the Anti-Japanese United Front." 129 *China Quarterly*, March 1992.

Smedley, Agnes. *China Correspondent.* London, 1943.

Smith, Dean C. *By the Seat of My Pants.* Boston, 1961.

Smith, Felix. *China Pilot: Flying for Chiang and Chennault.* Washington, 1995.

Snow, Edgar. *Random Notes on China (1936-1945).* Cambridge, MA, 1957.

Solberg, Carl. *Conquest of the Skies: A History of Commercial Aviation in America.* Boston, 1979.

Spence, Jonathan D. *The Search for Modern China.* New York, 1990.

Spencer, Otha G. *Flying the Hump: Memories of an Air War.* College Station, TX, 1992.

Stalker, Lance. "Flying 'The Hump' Was No Job for the Faint-Hearted." *Pacific Flyer*, Sept. 1985.

Steinberg, Rafael. *Time-Life Books: Island Fighting.* Chicago, 1978.

Sterling, Bryan B. and Frances N. Sterling. *Will Rogers & Wiley Post: Death at Barrow.* New York, 1993.

Swanborough, Gordon and Peter M. Bowers. *United States Military Aircraft since 1909.* Washington, 1989.

Tao-Ming, Madame Wei. *My Revolutionary Years: The Autobiography of Madame Wei Tao Ming.* New York, 1943.

Taylor, Jay. *The Generalissimo: Chiang Kai-shek and the Struggle for Modern China.* Cambridge, MA, 2009.

Thompson, David. *Consairway: An Airman's Airline.* San Diego, 1984.

Thompson, Robert S. *A Time for War: Franklin Delano Roosevelt and the Path to Pearl Harbor.* New York, 1991.

Thorne, Bliss K. *The Hump.* Philadelphia, 1965.

Tong, Hollington K. *dateline: CHINA: The Beginning of China's Press Relations with the World.* New York, 1950.

Tong, Te-kong and Li Tsung-jen. *The Memoirs of Li Tsung-jen.* Boulder, CO, 1979.

Tuchman, Barbara W. *Stilwell and the American Experience in China, 1911-1945.* New York, 1970.

Turner, William H., Lt. Gen. *Over the Hump.* Washington, 1985.

Underwood, John. *Madcaps, Millionaires, and "Mose": The chronicle of an exciting era when the airways led to Glendale*. Glendale, 1984.

Van der Linden, F. Robert. *The Boeing 247: The First Modern Airliner*. Seattle, 1991.

——. *Airlines and Air Mail: The Post Office and the Birth of the Commercial Aviation Industry*. Lexington, KY, 2002.

Vaz, Mark Cotta. *Living Dangerously: The Adventures of Merian C. Cooper, Creator of King Kong*. New York, 2005.

Vorderman, Don. *The Great Air Races*. Garden City, 1969.

Waters, Andrew W. *All the U.S. Air Force Airplanes, 1907-1983*. New York, 1983.

Weinstein, Allen and Alexander Vassiliev. *The Haunted Wood: Soviet Espionage in America - the Stalin Era*. New York, 1999.

Wheeler, Keith. *Bombs over Tokyo*. Alexandria, VA, 1982.

White, Theodore and Annalee Jacoby. *Thunder Out of China*. New York, 1946.

Whitnah, Donald R. *Safer Skyways: Federal Control of Aviation, 1926-1966*. Ames, IA, 1966.

Willett, Robert E. "Forgotten Heroes of the CNAC." 16 *Aviation History*, Nov. 2005.

——. *An Airline At War: The Story of Pan Am's China National Aviation Corporation and Its Men*. NP, 2008.

Wright, Nancy Allison. "Over the Hump: Pioneering China's Air Routes." 9 *Aviation History*, Nov. 1998.

——. "Claire Chennault and China's 'Airline Affair'." *41 American Aviation Historical Society Journal*, Winter 1996.

Wu, Tien-wei. *The Sian Incident: A Pivotal Point in Modern Chinese History*. Ann Arbor, 1976.

——. "New Materials on the Xian Incident: A Bibliographic Review." 10 *Modern China*, Jan. 1984.

Yagoda, Ben. *Will Rogers: A Biography*. New York, 1993.

Young, Arthur N. *China and the Helping Hand, 1937-1945*. Cambridge, MA, 1963.

Youwei, Xu and Philip Billingsley. "Behind the Scenes of the Xi'an Incident: The Case of the *Lixingshe*." 154 *China Quarterly*, June 1998.

Zanchen, Mi. *The Life of General Yang Hucheng*. Hong Kong, 1981.

Zich, Arthur. *Time-Life Books: The Rising Sun*. Alexandria, 1977.

INDEX

P

Q

R

S

CPSIA information can be obtained at www.ICGtesting.com
Printed in the USA
LVOW090214111111

254495LV00001B/47/P